AF538947

LORD WELLESLEY AND POLICY OF EXPANSION

Encyclopaedic History of Indian Freedom Movement Series

LORD WELLESLEY AND POLICY OF EXPANSION

Edited by
OM PRAKASH

ANMOL PUBLICATIONS PVT. LTD.
NEW DELHI - 110 002 (INDIA)

ANMOL PUBLICATIONS PVT. LTD.
4374/4B, Ansari Road, Daryaganj
New Delhi - 110 002
Ph.: 23261597, 23278000
Visit us at: www.anmolpublications.com

Lord Wellesley and Policy of Expansion
© Reserved
First Edition, 2004

ISBN 81-261-1509-2

[Responsibility for the facts stated, opinions expressed, conclusions reached and plagiarism, if any, in this book is entirely that of the Editor. The Publisher bears no responsibility for them, whatsoever.]

PRINTED IN INDIA

Published by J.L. Kumar for Anmol Publications Pvt. Ltd., New Delhi - 110 002 and Printed at Mehra Offset Press, Delhi.

Contents

Contents

Preface

'Golden bird' as India was known in yore days, rich in natural resources and well-developed cottage industries it was considered an affluent country. Indian spices, fabrics and other handicrafts were in great demand the world over. In the lure of having these goods and riches, many European powers made adventurous voyages to locate India.

The story of European expansions in Asia forms one of the great epics of modern times. India was the cornerstone of European imperialism in Asia. It was the lure of the lucrative 'Indian trade' which incited European adventurers to seek a new route to India, thus inaugurating a new era of contact between these two distant lands. Among the European empires in Asia, the British empire was the most enduring and prosperous one. And India was the finest jewel of the British dominion. It is worthwhile to remember that European exploration and adventure in the east were encouraged by the great demand in Europe for the products from Malabar like spices and calicoe cloth. Symbolically, the European age in Indian and indeed Asian history began with the landing of Vasco-de-Gama at Calicut on the 27th of May 1498. During this period, there was a continuous struggle between European traders and their native rivals and among the Europeans themselves. By the end of the eighteenth century this struggle for supremacy had been resolved in favour of the English.

The European traders were originally in the position of supplicants before the native rulers in India. For example, when William Hawkins arrived at the court of Jehangir with a letter from King James I asking for trade facilities, he had brought with him, a gift of 25,000 Gold pieces. As Lane Poole observes,

"There was nothing to suggest the most distant dream that in two centuries and a half the slight introduction Hawkins was then effecting between England and India would culminate in the sovereignty of a British Queen over the whole empire."

But unlike their European rivals like the Portuguese and the Dutch, the English made their bid for power in India only when the powerful Mughal empire had begun to decline. In any case the Portuguese and the Dutch had only small coastal settlements in India even at the height of their power and influence in this country.

By the end of the seventh Century, the Portuguese had been displaced by their Dutch rivals in Malabar and in the islands, of the East Indies. As for the Dutch, they were compelled by force of circumstances to regard the factories "which they established on the main land merely as marketing points for the products of an Empire which had its capital at Batavia in the East Indies."

Moreover, the Dutch power in India was largely jeopardised on European battle fields.

The wars with England and France drained the resources of this nation. Thus, it was left to the French to provide real opposition to the English in India.

The same pattern can be detected in the story of European activity in Malabar. Here the intensity of their rivalry was greater because of three main reasons. Malabar with its many fine harbours and backwaters was more accessible from the sea, increasing the scope for European interference.

Thus, European powers who came to India with the intention of trade snatched the political power and sovereignty from the local states, principalities and feudal lords. And established complete control over India. After over hundred years colonial rule, the feeling of national integration and freedom from the clutches of foreign power developed among the Indians. Thus, began the saga of freedom movement.

This encyclopaedic study is phased into two most significant and historic diversions having deep bearing on varied kinds of events which moulded the destiny of millions of people of Indian sub-continent. These events having complete political overtones, became a glaring phenomenon with the downfall of the Mughal Empire almost with the commencement of the 18th century. The ambitious piercing eyes of four European powers — the British, the French, the Portuguese and the Dutch—did cast upon several gainful economic successes in India.

Of these powers, the East India Company's government, with well organised force, bureaucracy and diplomats achieved phenomenal successes against their adversaries. The first phase,—therefore has been marked from Plassey to the Mutiny of 1857 (The First War of Independence) when the Company's role came to an end.

The second phase, naturally, came very much in the hands of the British Government functioning under the Whitehall and ended with the dawn of Swaraj on 15 August 1947.

This multi-volumes study would take up several themes, viz. political, socio-economic, religious, constitutional, educational, press, revolutionaries, local pioneers, legislation, revenues and judicial policy, on-going process of reaction — violent and non-violent, moderates and extremists, local and all India movements, reaction of the British Raj, efforts for conciliation, significant Acts passed by the Central Legislature, the impact of two global wars, 1914-1919 and 1939-1945; Congress, Muslim League, Hindu Mahasabha and the British Policy, a significant change in Britain soon after 1945, the Labour Government of Clement Attlee and Partition of India in August 1947.

In the first lot eleven volumes have appeared while in the present second lot ten volumes are being brought out namely the Marathas and their administration; Lord William Bentinck and Metcalf era of reforms; Raja Rammohun Roy: the reformer; Mutiny and its aftermath; History of Anglo-Sikh wars;

Emergence of Maharaja Ranjit Singh; Lord Hastings and his administrative measures; Ranjit Singh administration and British policy; British policy of intervention and expansion; and Lord Wellesley and policy of expansion.

This prestigious project is arranged, managed and looked after by a team of most dedicated and long experienced scholars of modern Indian history.

In gathering the authentic information, we have taken liberty to draw the material from the learned works of many great scholars in the field. We are deeply beholden to all those whose works are partially cited or substantially made use of in the project. I am indebted to Mr. J.L. Kumar, Managing Director, Anmol Publications Pvt. Ltd., New Delhi for his constant inspiration and moral support and finally to bring out this work. Last but not the least I am thankful to all those who have assisted me one way or other while preparing the manuscript.

—Om Prakash

1

Historical Background

Sir Thomas Munro, 1761-1827

Thomas Munro was the son of Alexander Munro, a Glasgow merchant, trading with Virginia. He was sent to a grammar school at a very early age, and was only a boy of thirteen when he proceeded to the University, where he remained till he was sixteen. It was at the University that he developed the taste for history and literature that he retained throughout his career in India. His favourite reading consisted of voyages, Plutarch's *Lives,* Shakespeare, political economy, and history. A boy's reading does undoubtedly have an influence on his after career as a man, and so it was with Munro. One illustration of his industry and perseverance may be given: he learnt Spanish with the help of a dictionary and grammar, in order that he might have the pleasure of reading the immortal work of Cervantes, *Don Quixote,* in the original. It is acknowledged by all who take the trouble to learn a new language, and more especially a language that has great literature, that one of the most interesting results of so doing is the new world that is opened up to the imagination, a result that translations do not achieve to the same extent. The author of this sketch has few more interesting reminiscences than that of reading in the original one of the plays of the great Sanskrit dramatist, Kalidasa, amidst the pine forests of Kashmir, amidst much of the scenery, indeed, in which the action of the play is laid. Munro's athletic tastes in his early youth were a good preparation for his after career in India both as a soldier and an administrator. Nature, it has been said, had given him a personal appearance which inspired confidence, his own training and work supplied the rest. He was tall and robust in appearance, and excelled in all games and sports, was possessed of great agility, presence of mind, and a high courage; these qualities were combined with great self-denial, which amounted almost to austerity, and great powers of endurance, the natural outcome, no doubt, of his extremely simple habits.

His tastes were all in the direction of a life of adventure, such as a military career offered in the times he was living in; his ambition, however, was not to be gratified till after he had spent some time as a clerk in his father's business firm. He had been offered a commission in the Army, but, out of deference to his father's wishes, he had declined it, though not without a feeling of very deep disappoinment. On the failure of his father's business, when he was nineteen years of age, the opportunity came again, and he did not neglect it. He was offered and accepted a military cadetship in the service of the East India Company. He could not afford to pay for a passage out to India, so he worked his way out, as an ordinary seaman, on board ship, thus showing early the stuff he was made of.

He arrived in India in the year 1780. One of his early experiences soon after he had landed was an unpleasant one enough in its consequences. He had engaged a venerable looking Madrasi as a body-servant; this individual calmly walked off one day with all his wardrobe of European clothes, and with nearly all his available supply of money: he professed to be going to exchange the clothes for something better adapted to the climate. Munro gave a more or less humorous account of the incident in a letter to his mother: "It is customary with gentlemen," said the old man to me, "to make a present of all their European articles to their servants, but I will endeavour to dispose of yours to advantage." Trusting the old man, whose venerable countenance inspired confidence in his sincerity, I handed them over, and he departed with them. Some unfortunate accident must, however, have happened to him, for he never turned up again'. It is only fair to the Indian servant to say that as a class they are scrupulously honest where things have been specially entrusted to their care: Munro's experience must therefore have been exceptional. Considering that his pay at that time was only about fifty rupees a month, he must have been put to a great deal of inconvenience by his loss, and he pathetically remarked that it was six months before he could buy fresh linen; but, amidst all his misgivings his sense of humour never deserted him.

Munro had not been long in India before the second war with Haidar Ali, of Mysore, broke out. The disunion in the English Council at Madras had given an opening to the enemies of England, and, though an alliance which Haidar Ali had contemplated making, between himself, the Nizam of Haidarabad, and the Marathas, had been frustrated by the foresight and sagacity of Warren Hastings. Haidar Ali was confident of a successful issue to the struggle for supremacy between himself and the English, and he had some reason for his confidence, for had he not, some years before, himself dictated terms of peace to the British outside the walls of Madras? Munro was actively employed, but only in a subordinate capacity, throughout the war. His letters and journals throw considerable light on the chief incidents of the war, and contain some masterly criticisms on the conduct of the operations by some of the general officers employed. The strategy opposed to them in the earlier part of the war, by which the enemy succeeded for long in keeping the different units of the British force divided, was a masterly one; one body of troops was completely cut up. However, the English retrieved the disasters of the early part of the war by the brilliant victory of Porto Nuovo. Haidar Ali had given orders before the battle that no prisoners were to be taken, but he was so decisively beaten that he had no chance of taking any. His death in 1782 did not interrupt the war: his son Tipu Sultan carried it on till 1784, when the Treaty of

Mangalore brought it to a not altogether successful issue, so far as the English were concerned. Munro's criticism of the last battle of the war, which was fought between an English and a French force, was very severe: 'There seemed no connexion,' he wrote, 'in our movements; every one was at a loss what to do, not nothing saved our army from a total defeat, but the French being, like ourselves without a general.'

A period of peace ensued, and Munro made excellent use of the enforced leisure which this period gave him. He made a series of walking tours of the country, and thus gained an extensive acquaintance with the Madras presidency; he also studied Hindustani and Persian. He is said, in the course of his Oriental studies, to have discovered the story of Shylock, the Jew, or at any rate a story very similar, in a Persian manuscript; in its Persian dress it was the story of a Jew and Muhammadan. It must not be forgotten that Europe is indebted to the East for many of its most familiar and popular fables and tales. To take the story of Gelert, the gallant Welsh hound and the wolf, as one instance, there is a similar story, if it is not, as has been said, the actual original, in Sanskrit story; in its Oriental dress, it is the story of a mungoose and a cobra. In each case the gallant protector of an infant child is slain by the owner under a misapprehension.

During this period of comparative calm the important event took place of the cession to the Company, by the Nizam, of the Guntur Circar, which gave the Company the possession of the East Coast from Jagannath Puri practically down to Cape Comorin: as they had already annexed the Northern Circars, this fresh acquisition of territory gave them the command of an extensive portion of the East Coast. As a matter of fact, it was a restitution rather than a cession, as this region had at one period belonged to the Company. Munro took an important part in this business as an intelligence officer, for which position his acquaintance with the languages of the country well qualified him. It is curious to note that, in some of his letters written at this time, Munro expressed his anticipation of the restoration of French ascendancy in Southern India, anticipations which were fortunately not destined to be realized. France was never able to get that command of the sea on which alone her chances of gaining that ascendancy could have depended. Munro never lost his interest in the history of the world around him, both European and Asiatic, as this correspondence abundantly shows. It is, indeed, very essential for the healthy life of the Englishman in the East that he should maintain this interest, if he is not to fall behind his contemporaries in the West, and if he is to avoid becoming what has been styled 'a Sultanized Englishman'.

The interest of this portion of Munro's life lies mainly in his descriptions of the life of a subaltern: it was life of hardships and poverty. The contrast between what people in England dreamt of and the actual reality was a very marked one. The romance of the gorgeous East had doubtless appealed to his youthful imagination, as it does to many a youth in England, till he has found by experience how unromantic life in the East can really be. In Munro's case the contrast between what he had dreamt of and the actual reality had wrought a complete disenchantment. He had, moreover, to endure, what few young men in these days have to suffer from, the difficulty of inadequate means arising from poor pay; 'Poverty,' he complained, 'was his constant companion.' It speaks well for his grit that, notwithstanding, he and his brother between them managed to contribute from their small pay a sum of £100 a year, to enable their father to end his days in comparative comfort. His words written to his father on this subject were characteristic of a man one of whose distinguishing traits was filial piety: 'The loss of fortune is but a passing evil; you are in no danger of experiencing the much heavier one of having unthankful children'. It also speaks well for his character that he did not suffer has disenchantment to extinguish his enthusiasm in his work. This is one of the apparent anomalies of an Eastern career: disenchantment may come earlier or later; it is bound to come some time; but enthusiasm may still remain, and when one has finally left the scene of one's labour, the call of the East still occasionally stirs the imagination. Hence the very appropriate name applied to India by Sir Alfred Lyall, the Land of Regrets'. Munro kept up his deep interest in his surroundings and some of the special interest of his correspondence at this time lies in the glimpses it gives of his walks and talks with the people of the country; he could always adapt himself to his environment, and the main secret of this was his intimate acquaintance with the colloquial vernacular.

Not many years after the conclusion of peace with the Ruler of Mysore, Tipu Sultan, the English again found themselves at war with him. The cause of this, the Third Mysore War, was Tipu Sultan's invasion of the territory of the Raja of Travancore who was an ally of the English. Munro was actively engaged in this war, but again in the capacity of a subaltern only. The unpreparedness of the English was as conspicuous on this occasion as it has been on the outbreak of the previous war, and again they narrowly escaped defeat in the earlier part of the campaign. The faulty strategy of the English commanders placed Tipu in a superior position on more occasions than one, and it was fortunate for the English that he failed to take advantage of it. Munro noted this fact, and commented on it thus: 'There seems to be a fatality sometimes attending even the greatest geniuses, which deadens the energy of their minds, and reduces them to the level of common men just when their best concerted schemes are about to be crowned with success'. A certain incident happened during this period of Munro's career which brings out conspicuously his dislike of anything approaching self-advertisement, even when there was a good prospect of its advancing his interests. His relatives at home had published in *The times* a graphic description of the war, which he had sent them; this led him to destroy a very interesting manuscript, in the shape of a long treatise on the war. He remarked, as he did venture to send it to those for whose amusement it was intended. This war with Tipu Sultan was brought to a close with the Treaty of Seringapatam, in 1792.

Munro would have liked to see the war carried to a final issue, of which there seemed every prospect at the time that peace was concluded. It was known that Tipu considered affairs so critical, the British army lying all round his capital, that he was preparing for instantaneous flight, remaining outside the fort in a tent among his horsemen. The Treaty caused great disappointment also in the army generally: Its terms were thought to be far to easy. Lord Cornwallis is reported to have been unwilling to capture the capital, and to have remarked, 'Good God, what shall I do with the place'. Be this as it may, Munro thought that the policy of conciliation was unsuited to the times, and to the man whom Lord Cornwallis was attempting to conciliate, and he by no means stood along in holding this opinion. He somewhat caustically remarked: 'Everything is now done by moderation and conciliation; at this rate we shall all the Quakers twenty years hence'. The policy in favour at the time was the maintenance of a balance of power, whereas Munro thought that conquest was the policy best suited to the times, and the only policy likely to secure permanent security. The soundness of these views was proved by after events: within the short period of seven years the Fourth Mysore War had to be undertaken by the Marquis Wellesley. Tipu Sultan during this interval was busy concerting measures for the over throw of the English power in India. He sent a mission to Constantinople, another to Zaman Shah, in Afghanistan, and another to Napoleon Buonaparte. In order to win over the Sultan of Turkey to his side, he had pronounced himself as 'the Champion of Islam against the Kafirs'.

By the terms of the Treaty that brought the Third Mysore War to a close, Tipu lost half his dominion; they were divided between the British, the Nizam of Haidarabad, and the Marathas. The British share consisted of the regions known as Malabar, Dindigul, part of the present district of Madurai, and the Bara-Mahal, part of the present district of Salem. The assistant-superintendentship of the latter was given to Munro, and his service lasted for some seven years. The natural beauties of this district, which have been noted by all travellers, appealed to Munro's love of natural scenery, and he was able to give full scope to his taste for gardening. A short time back attempts were made to locate the garden that Munro made for himself near Dharmapuri, in which he used to spend at least an hour every day. Unfortunately, these attempts were unsuccessful. When his time to leave the district came, he said that to quit it gave him as much regret as forsaking an old friend. He left memorials of himself all over the district in the shape of tanks, rest-houses, and avenues of roadside trees. The literatures of the East attribute great merit to rulers who provide for their people things so necessary for the comfort of travellers in the East, as water, shelter, and shade. Had Munro been a Hindu, he would have been storing up merit for the next world; as it was, he left behind him a kindly place in the hearts of the people of the district, and to this day his memory is handed down as that of Tom Munro Bahadur, 'the Ryots' Friend'.

His chief work was in the direction of revenue reforms: the old oppressive system whereby the revenue was collected by the Zamindars, who farmed out the land, was abolished in favour of what is known as the Ryotwari system, a system which was afterwards extended over the Madras presidency. Under this system, the Ryot is considered as practically a peasant-proprietor, paying revenue direct to Government. Munro always carried into practice, during this period of what he has described as a time of plain hard labour, his own theory of what constitutes the duty of an administrator, of seeing things with his own eyes; he was always personally most active in the matter of touring, and he utilized to the full his practical knowledge of colloquial vernacular, a knowledge which he always regarded as a very important tool for officers of the Government. In some of his correspondence in this period, he touched on one important matter, a matter which afterwards did receive the closest attention from the Government, the necessity of giving Government officers good pay for the work to be done. 'Even men of education and character,' he wrote, 'when placed in situations where they cannot become independent by their regular pay, if it is small, are tempted to hasten the period of their independence by dishonest means, where ever they can without danger of being discovered. It is only ignorance of human nature for Government to ignore that fact.' In the present day that temptation no longer exists: the pay is in most cases commensurate with the work. The efforts of successive Rulers of India to secure the purity of the administration have been rewarded; so that now, in the present day, the encoming passed on the services, civil and military, by the late Viceroy of India, Lord Curzon, that they are 'the highest-minded services in the world', is recognized by all who know India best, as no more than the bare truth. All Indian administrators recognize the expediency of giving free access to their presence to all visitors, of keeping, as it is styled in Oriental parlance, 'Char darwaze khole,' 'four doors open;' but all at the same time recognize it as a great tax upon their time. Munro has some amusing remarks in his correspondence on this practice, which at the same time he always recognized as part of the day's work: 'I wonder we waste so much time in praying against battle, and murder, and sudden death, which seldom happens, instead of calling upon heaven to deliver us from the calamity we are daily exposed to, of troublesome visitors; they have frequently given me a headache, and I would rather walk all day in a hot sun than sit listening to a dull fellow. I wish they would all come and see me in the mass and not singly.'

This period of Munro's civil administration was interrupted for a time by the Fourth Mysore War, already alluded to, in which he was called upon to take part, this time as captain of a transport and commissariat corps. At the close of the war, which ended in the final conquest of Mysore, Munro was appointed secretary to the commission that was nominated to arrange the disposal of the country. One of the districts that came at this time under British administration, under the terms of the new Partition Treaty made between the British, the Nizam, and the Marathas, was the district of Canara. Munro was placed in administrative charge of it, and remained so for about a year. The world in which he expressed his regret at leaving the scene of his old labours, the district of Salem, mark the enthusiast: 'I have now turned may back on the Bara-Mahal and the Karnatic, with a deeper sense of regret than I felt on leaving home. I see nothing in the future to compensate me for what I have lost, a country and friends that have endeared to me fore the last twenty years'. His sense of public duty and the nearer prospects of leaving home were his principal reasons for accepting the post offered to him by the Governor-General. At the same time he found the new life and work in Canara exceedingly irksome, and he made an attempt to get a transfer. This called forth from his superior officer a striking tribute to the unique character of his work: 'I regret,' wrote Mr. Cockburn, the senior member of the Board of Revenue, 'that your situation should be so irksome, more so as any attempt to procure your removal would be considered treason to the State, your services are so esteemed, and there is no one equal to the performance of the difficult task you are engaged in'.

His chief work in this district lay in settlement operations and in the suppression of crime. He was in the habit of keeping a journal, and the entries in this give an insight into the heavy nature of the task he was engaged in. One entry will suffice to show this: 'In one year, I have gone through more work than in almost all the seven years I was in the Bara-Mahal'. His life was spent almost entirely in tents. The crowds that used to throng his tent, not leaving him very often till near midnight, gave him a good insight into the character of the people. Grumbling is an ineradicable attribute of the agricultural classes all the world over, whatever the seasons may bring, and the cultivators of Canara were no exception to the rule. Silence on their part was by no means regarded as golden, on the contrary it would imply an acknowledgement on their part that they could well afford to pay enhanced rents: hence their vociferous clamours, whenever Munro appeared amongst them, of hard times and poverty. This, with the Indian cultivator, Munro in his journal notes, was by no means lying, but only an Oriental evasion of the truth, a habit formed as the result of many centuries of oppression under hard task-masters, and one not to be easily eradicated even under a milder régime. 'The old system,' noted Munro, 'of always prying into their affairs in order to lay ever new burdens upon them, forced them to deny what they had in order to save their property at all, and, after all, concealment of the real facts, and exaggeration of losses are characteristic of the class.' He gives an amusing instance of this tendency to exaggeration which he observed even in the younger generation of cultivators: he one day asked the youthful son of a cultivator who had been set to frighten birds off the crops with the primitive sling and stones, still to be seen in the fields of the East, 'How many bushels of grain do you expect?' The boy simply replied: 'There is nothing in our house now to eat: the birds will eat all this, and we shall be starved.' It has been sometimes argued that Government measures of relief have in these latter days, in times of famine, had the effect of demoralizing the agricultural classes, but this is not really so: their characteristics have not altered materially for centuries, and they remain much the same under the benevolent despotism of British rulers as they were under the harsher rule of despotic task-masters: and the old Sanskrit Proverb that runs: 'Speech benefits a Brahman more than silence', is as applicable now to the Indian cultivator when he thinks that speech will help him to get his rents lowered, or altogether remitted, as ever it was. As usual with him, Munro availed himself of the opportunities the settlement operations gave him to walk and talk with the people of the district: he also indulged in his love of Nature, humorously remarking: 'Notwithstanding the want of music and damsels, I love to rise before the sun, and prick my steed through the woods and wilds under a serene sky.'

Munro's good work in Canara at last met with its reward in a more important appointment being conferred upon him. There were certain districts which had been originally granted to the Nizam after the Third and Fourth Mysore Wars, which had at a later period been ceded by him to the British as a guarantee for the payment of the cost of subsidiary troops. Munro was placed in charge of these districts. The Governor of Madras, Lord Clive, offered the appointment to Munro in most complimentary terms: Munro had in the first instance asked for it, and Lord Clive wrote: 'The wishes of so excellent a fellow and collector ought to be cheerfully complied with'.

The first step in the settlement of the new districts, of which Bellary and Cuddapah were the chief, was the subjection of the petty chiefs of those parts, who were known as Naiks, or Polygars, and their armed followers, whose numbers amounted to some 30,000, and who all subsisted by violence and plunder. In describing his work as collector, Munro thus wrote: 'My annual circuit is near a thousand miles, and the hours I spend on horseback are almost the only hours I spend alone'. He never travelled with a guard even in disturbed districts, for, as he remarked, nothing short of a company would give protection. He trusted entirely to the prestige of his office as collector, recognizing that this prestige with the people of India, with all their respect for authority, is really very great. 'The natives of India,' he remarked on one occasion, 'have a good deal of respect for public authority: collectors, they consider, only act by orders from superior powers: they ought not, therefore, become objects of resentment.' Times have changed a good deal since these words were penned, but one has only to associate freely with all classes of Indians to realize that, even in these days, the prestige of the higher Government officials, and especially of the District Officer, is as great as it ever was, with the great body of the people. Munro's first land settlement was a village one: under this system each village was treated as a separate community, and assessed as a whole; the cultivators as a body were made responsible for the payment of the amount due. His next settlement was a step towards the Ryotwari system already referred to: under this system a settlement was made with the cultivators individually; the head-men of the villages were at the same time made responsible for defaulters, or absconders. Munro's Survey Settlement was a very thorough piece of work; so much so, indeed, that to this day it is said to be a safe guide in most village disputes. The Board of Revenue used to insist on their officers keeping a diary, which they were called upon to submit periodically; Munro's comment upon this was somewhat caustic: 'I cannot see what purpose it would answer here except to hinder me from looking after more important matters.'

Englishmen in India in those days enjoyed much greater opportunities of relaxation than Englishmen of Munro's days, and Munro during this period of hard work complained deeply about it: he recognized that work can only be carried on vigorously, and without a jaded feeling, where relaxation was possible. One of the most curious anomalies of the present day is the harsh criticism that is so often passed upon their countrymen in India, who are engaged in doing their country's work, by men who have themselves held official position in India, and who may be supposed to know something of the conditions under which that work is done, whereas much of their criticism goes to show their actual ignorance. The possible explanation may be found to be in the different points of view from which men of this class have viewed things while in India. Men belonging to one class of these critics have gone about with a veil of visionary idealism over their eyes which has prevented their seeing things as they actually are: men of another class have moved chiefly in great cities, and men living in cities know nothing of the life of the country at large: they have no real idea of the conditions under which Englishmen carry on their work in the Mufasal, as the country districts of Indian are styled. All this goes to show the danger of dogmatizing in matters concerned with the conduct of Englishmen or the feelings of Indians. A recent critic has alleged against the relaxations of the modern Englishman in India that they are frivolous, and that this frivolity is causing loss of prestige which amounts to more serious-minded Indian fellow subjects. Now, 'coelum non animum mutant qui trans mare current': an Englishman does not lose his characteristics even when his work does lie East of Suez, and the only difference between him and his countrymen at home, who has besides many more interests to absorb his attention, is perhaps the extra zest with which he throws himself into his amusements. No one who realizes the actual conditions under which the average official carries on his duties in the Mufasal, devoting his best hours and his best thoughts, during his long working hours, to the interests of the people entrusted to his charge, will grudge him his well won play-hours, or be surprised if he enjoys them with all the zest and enthusiasm almost of a schoolboy. In all that concerns the real business of life the Englishman in India can be serious enough, but relaxation is his very life: it is, indeed, the only thing that helps to preserve the balance of his moral and physical well-being, and saves him from becoming that degenerate and Orientalized hybrid immortalized by Thackeray. Without his relaxation and the renewed energy that it gives him for work, he would indeed be in danger of losing his prestige. He is ever ready, moreover, to welcome at his out-door sports and pastimes his Indian friends who may show sufficient skill to join him. As a matter of fact the Indian whose opinion is most worth having, if he thinks at all about the matter, which is exceedingly doubtful, certainly does not think the less of him for enjoying his hours of relaxation in a manner characteristic of his race. After all, 'East is East, and West is West.' Relaxation so necessary for the Englishman, may not be so necessary for the Indian: each has the traditions of his race: the Englishman has his, and the Indian has his, and both cannot help being themselves.

During this period of his career, Munro was able to render valuable assistance to Arthur Wellesley, his life-long friendship with whom had dated from the time when he had been secretary to the commission for disposing of Mysore territory after the death of Tipu. He supplied the transport that was needed during the Maratha campaign of 1802. Arthur Wellesley fully recognized Munro's military skill and sagacity, and was always glad to have his opinion on military matters, regarding him as a good judge of a military operation.

The Sepoy Mutiny of Vellore, which occurred towards the end of this portion of Munro's career, produced some correspondence between him and Lord William Bentinck, who at the time was Governor of Madras. Bentinck had attributed the mutiny to intrigues among Tipu's sons: Munro, on the other hand, conceived that the proximate cause was religious disquietude, induced by certain vexatious military regulations. This will generally be found to be at the bottom of every disturbance of the masses in India, who are so intensely credulous, and whose minds are very easily worked upon by the cry that those who wish to incite rebellion generally raise first: 'Your religion is in danger.' Such a cry once set in motion will affect even the more intelligent natives of India. In no country in the world does rumour, and especially false rumour, run more swiftly. A recent Governor of Madras, Lord Ampthill, once appositely said, 'A slander runs twice round the world while Truth is putting on her boots.' A report once started is universally believed. It was not an ignorant native, but a high-caste and loyal native officer, who, at the time of the great Mutiny, speaking of the general belief that the Government wished to take away the caste of the people, remarked in perfect sincerity: 'What everybody is saying must be true.; Munro wrote to his father an account of the affair at Vellore, and quoted some of the regulations that had caused such offence: 'Caste marks and earrings on parade were forbidden; shaving was ordered; the shape of the hair on the upper lip was to be regulated, and a specially-shaped turban was ordered to be worn'. These orders to an Englishman would appear trifling enough, and perhaps even a subject for ridicule, but, to an orthodox Hindu, they would be disturbing in the highest degree to his religious prejudices.

An interval of rest for Munro was now to follow: he had been absent from home for twenty-seven years, and was now forty-six years of age. His decision to take furlough called forth a well-deserved eulogy of his work in the ceded districts from the Madras Government. The despatch that went to the Court of Directors referred to Munro's 'exertions in the advancement of the public service under circumstances of success unparalleled in the records of this, or probably of any other Government'. Munro's correspondence at this time expresses his mixed feelings: pleasure at the idea of going home was mingled with regret at leaving India. He anticipated, however, a speedy return to India, and , naturally, after his successful career he was ambitious to obtain a higher sphere of action. In one of his letters he wrote: 'I am not satisfied with the subordinate line in which I have moved, and with my having been kept from holding any distinguished military command by way of rank; I shall never be able to sit down quietly to enjoy private life, and I shall probably return to India, in quest of what I may never obtain.'

As a matter of fact, he remained in England for a period of seven years, much longer than he had ever anticipated, but he was not idle during this enforced period of leisure from official duties; for one thing, he took up the study of chemistry. The study of science has often beguiled the leisure hours of great statesmen; the late Marquis of Salisbury, one of England's most distinguished premiers, spent many of his leisure hours in his laboratory. Munro was also consulted by the Court of Directors in connexion with the subject of the renewal of the Company's Charter in 1813; his services on the occasion have been thus recorded: 'Among all those whose opinions were sought on that occasion, Colonel Munro made the deepest impression upon the House by the comprehensiveness of his views, by the promptitude and intelligibility of his answers, and by the judgement and sound discretion which characterized every sentiment to which he gave utterance'. The Court of Directors recognized his services by giving him the appointment of President of a special Commission to inquire into and reform the judicial system in the Presidencies of Bengal and Madras.

Munro returned to India again in the year 1814: it seems strange in these days of quick locomotion to read his description of his voyage out as 'a quick voyage of sixteen weeks'. He had married just before returning to India, and not unnaturally, after his long period of bachelorhood, he found the etiquette of paying and returning visits that his marriage involved somewhat uncongenial and irksome, but he accepted the position as one of the necessary responsibilities of his new state. He found it hard to work with the Madras Government at first, owing to the divided counsels that prevailed, a not unusual characteristic apparently of the Madras Government in these early days of British rule. In his usual shrewd and masterful way he wrote to the India Board suggesting that they should write out 'we order' or 'we direct', in place of the usual formula 'we wish', or 'we propose'.

Notwithstanding the opposition he had to encounter in the course of his work on the Judicial Commission, the new regulations framed by that Commission were eventually passed into law; Munro's share of the task has been thus recorded: 'They are a monument not only of Munro's force of character in accomplishing his object against the most powerful opposition, but of his high administrative ability and statesman like views'. The changes made were all in the direction of a more efficient, and at the same time, a simpler system of administration. Thus the superintendents of the police, and the functions of the district magistrate were transferred from the judge to the collector. Hereditary village officials were to be employed mainly as policy. A system of Village and district Panchayats, as the simple village Tribunals, or Courts of Arbitration are styled, was legalized, and power was even given to selected head-men of villages to hear suits. Munro attached great importance to the Panchayats, as being adapted to native habits and usages.

On the completion of this work, Munro expressed his keen desire for military employment: he was essentially a soldier first, and a statesman afterwards. Operations had commenced against the Mahratts and the Pindaris, and Munro had asked for the command of the subsidiary forces of Haidarabad and Nagpur. His wish, however, was not to be at once gratified, and the only reply he received was his appointment to the commissionership of the Southern

Maratha country, which had been recently ceded by the Peshwa. This was a purely civil appointment, and Munro could not refrain from expressing his annoyance in these terms: 'I regret deeply to feel for the first time the army in advance shut against me'. At the same time he accepted the situation loyally.

His patience was at last rewarded, and he was given a command as brigadier of the division of the army detailed to reduce the Southern Maratha country. The confidence and goodwill of the people which he had won during the short period of his civil administration was now to stand him in good stead. He had already, in correspondence with the Marquis of Hastings, given his theory as to the best way of dealing with predatory hordes, such as the Pindaris, which was, 'to carry the war into the enemy's country' : he now proceeded to put this theory into practice by occupying the districts these hordes were to assemble in. His plan of procedure was, while reducing their strongholds, to simultaneously issue conciliatory proclamations to the people: he thus kept the enemy fully employed in the defence of their own possessions. The people of the territories he thus invaded had such confidence in him that they actually assisted in driving out their own masters, and in collecting the revenue for the British. The strongholds of the enemy were all taken possession of by his irregulars in the name of 'Thomas Munro, Bahadur'. Sir John Malcolm, writing of the modus operandi of Munro, summed up his qualities in the telling phrase, 'a master-workman'. As usual his correspondence was full of humorous descriptions of men and things: in one of his letters he drew a contrast between the Maratha freebooter and the Highland cateran, Rob Roy. 'The difference between the two', he wrote, 'is that the one does from choice what the other did from choice what the other did from necessity: for a Maratha would rather get ten pounds by plunder than one hundred pounds by an honest calling.'

Munro was not again compelled to take furlough to England: his incessant labours had injured his eyesight. He remained at home for about a year. He found honours awaiting him this time, as his fame had preceded him. Mr. George Canning, in proposing a vote of thanks to the Army, after the termination of the Maratha War, thus alluded to his services: 'Than Colonel Thomas Munro, Europe never produced a more accomplished statesman, and India, so fertile in heroes, a more skilful soldier.' He was promoted to the rank of Major-General; and, on receiving the appointment of the Governorship of Madras, was created a Knight Commander of the Bath. Mr. canning, in mentioning his name to the Court of Directors, spoke of the usual practice of appointing men of eminence in England to the Indian Governorships, but he added that three men had so distinguished themselves in India that he was determined to offer them these high posts: the three were Malcolm, Elphinstone, and Munro. At the banquet given in Munro's honour, before he left England and at which, among other distinguished men, his old friend, the Duke of Wellington, was present, Mr. Canning again paid a remarkable tribute to him: 'We bewilder ourselves,' he said, 'in this part of the world with opinions respecting the sources from which power is derived; some suppose it to arise with the people themselves, while others entertain a different view; all, however, are agreed that it should be exercised for the people; if ever an appointment took place to which this might be ascribed as the distinguishing motive, it is that which we have now come together to celebrate'. Munro, writing to a friend, said of the speech, 'It is worth while to be a Governor to be spoken of in such a manner by such a man'.

The leading principles of Munro's administration as Governor are given in a letter he wrote to Mr. Canning: 'The relief of the people from novel and oppressive modes of judicial process, the improvement of internal administration by the employment of Europeans and Indians in those duties for which they are respectively best suited, and the strengthening of the attachment of Indians to our Government by maintaining their ancient institutions and usages.' He continually urged the wider employment of Indians in the higher administrative charges, as the one necessary condition of an improvement in their moral character: he thus prepared the way for the reforms which were afterwards inaugurated by Lord William Bentinck in this direction. He saw the benefits that would accrue from the introduction of a general system of education amongst the people, and he wrote thus on the subject: 'Whatever expense Government may incur in the education of the people will be amply repaid by the improvement of the country, for the general diffusion of knowledge is inseparably followed by more orderly habits, by increasing industry, by a taste for the comforts of life, by exertions to acquire them, and by the growing prosperity of the people'. His views, moreover, of the lines on which the higher education of the people should proceed, were very sound: 'A knowledge of their own literature,' he held, 'should be extended among them side by side with the language and literature of England.' It was, indeed, on these lines that the Government at a later period, as seen in the despatch of Sir Charles Wood in 1854, contemplated that higher education in India should proceed; it is unfortunate, but perhaps inevitable, that, as time went on, this view was lost sight of, and the Indian vernaculars were practically ignored. It was left to the late Viceroy of India, Lord Curzon, to endeavour to bring education in India back on to the right track again, by insisting on greater prominence being given to the languages and literatures of India. Munro always upheld the sound policy of religious neutrality for officers of Government; this is shown by the rebuke he gave to a sub-collector of one of the districts of his Province, who had been displaying an excess of religious zeal, which had led him to transgress the rules of religious neutrality: 'The best way for a collector,' he wrote to this man, 'to instruct the natives is to set them an example in his own conduct: to try to settle their disputes with each other, and to prevent their going to law: to bear patiently all their complaints against himself and his servants, and bad seasons, and to afford them all the relief in his power, and, if he can do nothing more, to give them at least good words.'

The first Burmese War occurred during Munro's tenure of office, and he was able to be of material assistance to the Governor-General, Lord Amherst, chiefly in facilitating the despatch of troops and material. His long experience, moreover, of Indian warfare, and knowledge of Asiatic character, enabled him to be a wise counsellor. He received a very handsome acknowledgement from the Governor-General in Council for his services, as well as the thanks of the Court of Directors; Lord Goderich, in the House of Lords, declared that 'it was impossible for any one to form an adequate idea of the efforts made by Sir Thomas Munro, at the head of the Madras government, to further the successful issue of the campaign.'

Munro kept up his old habit of living in tents whenever he went on the district tours he was so fond of, and which he valued as the best means of obtaining that intimate acquaintance with the people so essential for an administrator. The difficulties of touring in his days were far greater than they are in these days of better communications; but, in some of the more backward Provinces, many of these difficulties still remain. In this way, he managed to renew his old acquaintance with the districts of the Bara-Mahal, and the ceded districts. Writing of one of these districts, Cuddapah, he said: 'I still like this country, notwithstanding its heat; it is full of industrious cultivators, and I like to recognize among them a great number of my old acquaintances, who, I hope, are as glad to see me, as I am glad to see them.' In 1826, Munro had applied to be relieved of his office, but as some delay occurred in the appointment of his successor, he set out for a farewell tour in the ceded districts. There is a legend still surviving in connexion with this last tour of his. He was marching among the hills in the Cuddapah district, when he suddenly looked up at the steep cliffs above him, and remarked: 'What a beautiful garland of flowers they have stretched across the valley!' His companions all looked up, but could see nothing; 'Why, there it is,' he again remarked, 'all made of gold'. Again they looked up and saw nothing: thereupon one of his old servants exclaimed: 'Alas, master! A great and good man will soon die.' Very shortly after this, Munro was attacked with cholera, and though it was at first hoped that he would recover, it was not to be: he died the same evening. His sweetness of temper was never more conspicuously displayed than during his last illness: during one of the rallies, he exclaimed, in a tone of peculiar sweetness, 'It is almost worth while to be ill to be so kindly nursed.' Among those near him at the time of his death was the future famous missionary and Tamil scholar, Henry Bower, then a boy. Munro passed away calmly on the night of July 6, 1827, at the age of sixty-six.

In the *Gazette Extraordinary* issued by the Government of India, this tribute was paid to his memory: 'His sound and vigorous understanding, his transcendent talents, his indefatigable application, his varied stores of knowledge, his attainments as an Oriental scholar, his intimate acquaintance with the habits and feelings of the native soldiers and inhabitants generally, his patience, temper, facility of access, and kindness of manner, would have ensured him distinction in any line of employment. These qualities were admirably adapted to the duties which he had to perform in organizing the resources, and establishing the tranquillity of those Provinces, where his latest breath has been drawn, and where he had long been known by the appellation of "The Father of the People"'.

At a public meeting held in Madras to concert measures to perpetuate his memory, his death was spoken of as a public calamity; one of the speakers at the meeting said: 'His justice, benevolence, frankness, and hospitality were no less conspicuous than the extraordinary faculties of his mind'. Various memorials in his memory were erected throughout his territory: a groove of trees was planted, and a well dug, near the place where he died; a similar well and a rest-house were constructed at Gooty, where for several years food was distributed gratuitously in his honour; but his best memorial lay in the affections of his people.

Munro was pre-eminently the soldier-statesman: his military qualities were recognized by so great a master of the art of war as the Duke of Wellington, his administrative qualities were even greater. His most distinguishing characteristic, perhaps, was his modesty and unassuming nature. For nearly twenty-eight years without a break, during his first spell of service, he had worked in silence, adopting as his motto the noble lines of the blind patriot bard of England, John Milton:—

To know

That which before us lies in daily life
Is the prime wisdom: what is more is fume,
Or emptiness, or fond impertinence:
And renders us in things that most concern,
Unpractised, unprepared, and still to seek.

Mr. George Canning, in the course of that magnificent eulogy on Munro already referred to, thus noted this great characteristic: 'Apart from the public eye, and without the opportunities of early special notice, was employed a man whose name I should be sorry to pass over in silence.' The greater portion of his work was done in silence, but history has provided that his memory shall not be held in silence, and Lord Dalhousie, in some correspondence he once had with Sir Henry Lawrence, was able to say in proof of this assertion: 'All the world unites in acknowledging the talents and merits of Sir Thomas Munro'.

The legend, still current in his old Presidency, of an incident that occurred on his last tour has been referred to, and how his old retainer had interpreted the sign to mean that a great and good man was about to die: this was a true forecast: a great and good man passed away in the person of Sir Thomas Munro.

2

Lord Wellesley's Career

"Some men are born great, some achieve greatness, some have greatness thrust upon them." The two brothers Wellesley, the great Marquess, as he was called in India, and his illustrious brother, whose name is inseparably connected with the final defeat of the greatest warrior the world has ever seen, combined in their own persons two out of the three categories mentioned by Shakespeare. They were born great, and they achieved greatness. Writing of such men it becomes possible to dispense with a pedigree stretching back, though that pedigree may, stretch into the earlier age of English history. It will be sufficient to state that the family of the Wellesleys can be traced back to the year 1239; that it is of Saxon origin, deriving it's name from the manor of Wellesley, anciently Welles-leigh, in the country of Somerset; that, in 1339, the representative of a branch of the family, Sir William de Wellesley, was summoned to Parliament as a Baron of the realm, and received from King Edward II. A grant by patent of the custody of the castle of Kildare; that, on transferring that castle to the Earls of Kildare, he was granted by Edward III., in 1342, the custody of the manor of Demor; that thenceforward, for services rendered to the Crown, the successive representatives of this branch of the family increased their possessions and influence until the year 1745, when Garret Wellesley, or Wesley, as the name was then often spelt, dying without issue, bequeathed all his possessions to his cousin, Richard Colley or Cowley. The Cowleys, an old Staffordshire family, had settled in Ireland in the reign of Henry VIII., and had prospered. The Richard Cowley, who succeeded, in 1745, to the Wellesley property, had inherited his father's estate of Castle Carbery in 1700. He was cousin once removed of Garret Wellesley, and in his veins there flowed the blood of the Wellesleys and the Cusakes, descendants from Dermot Macmorough, Kind of Leinster. On his accession to the Wellesley estates, Richard Cowley assumed, as required by the testator, the family name, then spelt Wesley. He was shortly afterwards raised to the peerage by the title of Baron Mornington. His son, Garret, who succeeded him, was further advanced to the dignities of Viscount Wellesley of Dengan Castle, and Earl of Mornington, of Country Meath. This nobleman had, by Anne, eldest daughter of Arthur Hill Trevor, first Viscount Dungannon, six sons and two daughters. Of these sons the subject of this memoir was the eldest.

Richard Cowley Wellesley—it will be convenient to give the names as they were subsequently spelt—was born on June 20th, 1760. His father, who had a passion for music, and who attained some eminence as a composer, placed him at an early age at Eton. There the young Irishman speedily developed abilities of no common order. His contributions to the three volumes of *Musæ Etonenses* give evidence of very considerable classical attainments, and he had achieved a great reputation as a scholar when he went up to Oxford. He matriculated as a nobleman at Christ Church, on December 24th, 1778. There, likewise, he was much distinguished for his proficiency in classical literature, and for the capacity he displayed to deal with large questions. His father dying in May, 1781, Wellesley, called away to important duties in his own country, could not stay to take his degree. He returned to Ireland, and, having attained his majority, entered at once upon the duties of his position. "His first act," writes the author of the *Wellesley Memories,* Mr. R. R. Pearce, "on becoming of age, was characteristic of the generosity and integrity of his manly nature. He voluntarily took upon himself the numerous pecuniary obligations of his deceased father, and exhibited his filial affection towards his surviving parents by placing the estates, to which he had succeeded, under the management of his mother. His Lordship also directed his attention to the intellectual training of his brothers, who were all greatly indebted to him for his watchful and prudent care in early life." His brother Arthur was then twelve years old.

That same year the young Earl of Mornington took his seat in the House of Peers, in College Green, Dublin. The Irish Parliament had passed, the year preceding, the memorable resolution: "that the King's most excellent Majesty, and the Lords and Commons of Ireland, are the only power competent to make laws to bind Ireland." Following this resolution, a body of volunteers, 50,000 strong, demanded from England the recognition of the legislative independence of the island. Lord Mornington, though imbued with a sterling love for his native country, could not tolerate proceedings which appeared to him to strike at the very root of orderly and constitutional government. The fact that an armed assembly should hold regular sittings in the vicinity of the Houses of Parliament, with the object of dictating to, or overawing, the members of those Houses, was in his eyes a monstrous proceeding, not to be endured. He took, then, a leading part in the debate on the Address of both Houses to the Crown, declaring "the perfect satisfaction which we feel in the many blessings we enjoy under His Majesty's most auspicious Government, and our present happy Constitution; and to acquaint His Majesty that at this time we think it peculiarly incumbent upon us to express our determined resolution to support the same inviolate with our lives and fortunes." The resolution was carried. The support accorded to it by Lord Mornington must not be interpreted to imply that he was perfectly satisfied with the social or political condition of Ireland. On the contrary, he was, even at that early period, a strong advocate for the removal of the disabilities which weighed on the Roman Catholics, and for the extension of the liberties of the Press. In his eyes, too, the position of the Irish Parliament, powerful for discussion, but powerless for action, was eminently unsatisfactory. His support of the resolution, then, was prompted solely by his desire to place on record his disapproval of the practice of intimidation sanctioned by the volunteers.

It was impossible that a man with his original and daring mind, a man born for action, should for long be content with the limited sphere within which the duties of the Irish Parliament were confined. At the General Election of 1984, then, Lord Mornington stood, and was returned for the borough of Beeralston, in Devonshire. It is strange that his first speech should have been on an Indian subject. He attacked Lord North for his support of Warren Hastings, in the face of his declaration that the Court of Directors had condemned every one of his actions; and he called upon that Lord to explain how, with that opinion before him, he had arrived at the conclusion that it would be wrong to recall the Indian Governor. This speech, and the speeches which followed, were delivered with so finished an elocution, and were marked by so much spirit and point, the Lord Mornington was speedily recognised as a speaker who had to be reckoned with. His promotion, was unusually rapid. In 1785 he was sworn a Privy Councillor for Ireland. In September of the following year he was nominated a Lord of the Treasury. In the February following, then member for Saltash in Cornwall, he supported, in a most able speech, the measures proposed by Mr. Pitt for a commercial treaty with France; and, in 1788, as member for Windsor, he supported, alike in the English House of Commons and the Irish House of Lords, the measure regulating the Regency proposed by Mr. Pitt. Four years later he earnestly supported Wilberforce in his efforts to extinguish the slave-trade. He opposed, the year following, Mr. Grey's motion for a reform of the English House of Commons. He showed how, notwithstanding the admitted imperfections of the then existing system, the nation had, under its auspices, made a man vellously quick recovery from the humiliation and misfortunes caused by the result of the war with the

American colonists; and contacted the state of France, emerging red-handed from a drastic revolution, with that of prosperous and contented England. Grey's motion was defeated by 232 to 41, and shortly afterwards (June 21st, 1793) Lord Mornington was sworn a member of the English Privy Council, and nominated a Commissioner for the Affairs of India, that is, a member of the Board of Control. This was the first step, and a most important step, to the important post which he was to fill in India.

On February the 11th, 1793, England, Spain, and Holland had joined Austria and Prussia in the first coalition against France. A resolution brought forward early in the session in the House of Commons condemning the war was lost by 270 to 44 votes, and there can be no doubt that vote truly represented the feeling of the majority of the nation. On the reassembling of Parliament of January of the following year, another important debate took place, during the discussion of the Address, on the policy and progress of the war. In this debate there was assigned to Lord Mornington a leading part. Speaking early, he argued that, if the original necessity for the war had ceased, he would be the first to recommend a return "to the secure and uninterrupted enjoyment of a flourishing commerce, of tranquil liberty at home, and of respect and honour abroad," but that, in fact, the necessity not having ceased, there was no alternative before Parliament. The choice lay between the vigorous prosecution of hostilities, and an ambiguous state neither of open hostility nor of real repose—a state in which the nation would suffer most of the inconveniences of war, and enjoy none of the solid advantages of peace. He pointed out that the aggressive action of the French Republic had roused not England only, but all Europe; that, in the decree of November 19th, 1792, she had made to the subjects of the several sovereigns of the European States offers of universal fraternity and assistance, and had ordered her generals everywhere to aid and abet those citizens of foreign countries who had suffered, or might hereafter suffer, in the cause of what she called liberty. "Her sense of liberty," continued the speaker, "as applied to

England, was shown by the reception of seditious and treasonable addresses, and by the speeches of the President of the National Convention, expressing his wish for the suspicious institution of a British Convention." After quoting several instances of the infraction by France of international law in the case of Belgium, of the United States, and of Constantinople—the declaration of Brissot that his object in freeing and arming the negroes of the French West India Islands was to accomplish the destruction of the British colonies in that part of the globe—Lord Mornington urged that at the time when war was declared the men who governed France had hatched an extensive conspiracy against the order of society and the peace of mankind. Invoking in support of this charge the words and acts of the accused, proving that the plan was not peculiar to one faction, but had been accepted by all, the speaker proceeded to show how such language had been understood in Europe; the dangers which were threatening the British Empire, and which could only be averted by timely recourse to defensive measures; and the absolute necessity of a policy which should be open and undisguised. It is very remarkable, looking at his subsequent career, that he should have illustrated this part of his argument by a reference to India and to the Sultan of Maisur. He said:—

"In India the French: have been expelled from all their possessions except Pondichery, the capture of which could not (according to the latest advises) be long delayed. The acquisition of the port of Mahé, on the coast of Malabar, is of the greatest advantage to our new territories on that coast, both with a view to the commerce and good government of those countries; in a political view it is obviously of considerable importance that the French should not continue to hold a possession which afforded them the means so direct and says an intercourse with Típu Sultán."

Lord Mornington then entered into a long enumeration of the acts of the French Government, both at home and abroad, and concluded with the following appeal, a speech which for more than two hours had captivated the attention of a full House:—

"All the circumstances of the case are now before you. You are now to make your option. You are not to decide whether it best becomes the dignity, the wisdom, and the spirit of a great nation to rely for existence on the arbitrary will of a restless and implacable enemy, or on her own sword. You are now to decide whether you will entrust to the valour and skill of British fleets and British armies, to the approved faith and united strength of your powerful and numerous allies, the defence of the limited Monarchy of these realms, of the constitution of Parliament, of all the established ranks and orders of society among us, of the sacred rights of property, and of the whole frame of our laws, our liberty, and our religion; or whether you will deliver over the guardianship of ali these blessings to the justice of Cambon, the plunderer of the Netherlands, who, to sustain the baseless fabric of the depreciated assignats, defrauds whole nations of their rights of property, and mortgages the aggregated wealth of Europe;— to the moderation of Danton, who first promulgated that unknown law of nature which ordains that the Alps, the Pyrenees, the ocean, and the Rhine should be the only boundaries of the French dominion; —to the religion of Robespierre, whose practice of piety is to murder his own Sovereign, who exhorts all mankind to embrace the sam faith, and to assassinate their Kings for the honour of God;—to the friendship of Barrère, who avows, in the face of all Europe, that the fundamental article of the Revolutionary Government of France is the ruin and annihilation of the British Empire;—or, finally, to whatever may be the accidental caprice of any new band of malefactors, who, in the last convulsions of their exhausted country, may be destined to drag the present tyrants to their own scaffolds, to seize their lawless power, to emulate the depravity of their example, and to rival the enormity of their crimes."

The House was attracted not so much by the graceful elocution, the sonorous yet manly voice, the high-bred manner, and the self-reliant attitude of the speaker, as by the strength and cogency of his arguments. It is almost supererogation to say that those arguments would not, in the presence of accomplished facts, influence the existing generation. To accomplish facts, influence the existing generation. To understand their effect in the past, we must carry our minds back to the state of affairs when they were spoken. The French Revolution was just beginning its career of aggression. It was certain that the nearest neighbours of France, the most ancient and most reliable allies of Great Britain in her wars with the princes of the House of Bourbon, would be the first victims of the new crusade. Danton, then a ruling power in France, and supposed by many to be the man of the future, had openly claimed for France boundaries, which England had refused, which Germany and Holland had refused, to Louis XIV., in the days of his greatest power. Brissot, the mouthpiece of a more thoughtful school of Frenchmen, had placed the annihilation of England as the first article of his programme. The fever was not confined to individuals; it had roused to superhuman action the whole nation. That the speech of Lord Mornington only interpreted in elegant language the thoughts which were burning in the minds of the great majority of the members of the House, was proved by the fact that although the Opposition put up their most eloquent orator, the brilliant Sheridan, to reply, he failed to make an impression on the House. Even Mr. Fox, who spoke later, could only say that, if the principle of the speech were accepted, it would mean that "while the present or any other Jacobin government exists in France, no propositions for peace can be made or received by us." The division was decisive. Two hundred and seventeen members voted for the vigorous prosecution of the war; only fifty-seven for the amendment, moved by Mr. Fox.

On November the 29th following, Lord Mornington was married, at St. George's, Hanover Square, to Mademoiselle Hyacinthe Gabrielle Roland, a native of France, only daughter of Pierre Roland and of Hyacinthe Gabrielle Daris, of the city of Paris, who had for nine years lived with him and borne him children. Notwithstanding the beauty of the lady, her wit, her wonderful fascination, the marriage was not a happy one. I may state, in anticipation, that when Lord Mornington proceeded to India, he felt that under the circumstances he could not take her. Nor did she live long with him after his return. For reasons which have never been given to the public they agreed to live separately. The lady died in 1816.

It is not necessary to quote from other speeches which Lord Mornington delivered in the course of this session, or of the sessions that followed. His reputation as an orator was dready made, and in addition, he was establishing himself as a man of excellence in business. To this end he attended with industry to his duties at the India Board; thoroughly mastered the peculiar details which distinguish the affairs of our Indian Empire; and gave evidence on more than one public occasion of the interest with which he watched the dangers threatening it from the ambition of France. The public were not surprised, then, when the announcement was made that Lord Mornington had been selected by Mr. Pitt to succeed Sir John Shore as Governor-General of India.

The selection was not made without some uncertainty on the part of the Prime Minister. The retiring Governor-General had succeeded Lord Cornwallis in 1792. The selection of a civil servant of the Company to fill so lofty a post had been a bitter disappointment to Lord Habart, Governor of Madras, who had given proofs of capacity, and who, it was understood, had accepted the lesser appointment on the understanding that he was to have the reversion of the greater. Upon the retirement of Sir John Shore, Lord Hobart had then regarded his succession as certain. But Mr. Pitt, as soon as he heard of the vacancy recommended to his sovereign the reappointment of Lord Cornwallis to the joint posts of Governor General and Commander-in-Chief. Lord Conrwallis actually accepted the two posts, and then, after a brief interval, that is, the interval of two or three weeks, resigned from them. The announcement of Lord Cornwallis's resignation was accompanied by the statement that, "under the circumstances and for reasons of a peculiar nature," the Earl of Mornington had been appointed Governor-General. Naturally the public were mystified, and the mystification was not at the time cleared up. But the author of the Wellesley Memoirs, Mr. R. R. Pearce, gives the following explanation of the transaction:—"The turn" he writes, "appears to be this. Lord Teignmouth [Sir John Shore] was desirous of enjoying his newly-acquired honours at home; Lord Hobart, who had been involved in some unpleasant altercations with the Supreme Government and the Court of Directors, was not an acceptable person to the Company; and Mr. Pitt and Mr. Dundas nearly saw that the exigencies of the times required to garner all energies for Lord Cornwallis who was the only one capable of bringing to bear on the government of India."

This explanation affords honourable testimony to the reputation which Lord Mornington had acquired. He was then in his thirty-eighth year, the period of life to which the late Lord Beaconsfield referred "as the prime, if not the perdition, of manhood;" had served upwards of thirteen years during a troubled period, in the House of Commons; had acquired, at the Board of Control, a thorough knowledge of all the details of Indian Government, of the policy pursued by his predecessor, and of the dangers which might threaten the stability of British interests from the independent action of native princes in the very centre of the peninsula, at a time when Great Britain was engaged in a war conducted with more than ordinary bitterness with a revolutionary power. He had many qualities which made him suitable for the post. He was gifted with a strong will; possessed the faculty of quick decision; an intelligence which enabled him to arrive, almost by intuition, at the point of question, however involved, or however hidden by oriental phrases; a capacity, unmarred by the faintest tint of jealousy, which enabled him to distinguish merit in others, and to select for particular employments the men who were most capable of bringing the allotted task to a successful issue. When I add that Lord Mornington had a gracious presence, and was gifted with a charm capable of impressing, I might indeed add, of almost always winning, those with whom he came in contact, I should have said enough to prove the deep insight into character displayed by Mr. Pitt in selecting such a man, in such a crisis, to proceed to India as virtual representative of the Crown. The appointment bore date October the 4th, 1797.

3

Lands at Madras

Lord Mornington quit England November the 7th, 1797. He landed at Madras April the 26th, 1798. It is well, whilst he is making that long sea voyage, that the reader should examine the state of affairs in the country, which would demand the earnest attention of the new Governor-General on his landing. I propose to take him in the fist instance to India south of the Vindhya range, generally known as Southern India.

There, not very many years had elapsed since Haidar Alí, the Muhammadan Ruler of Maisur, had dictated terms of peace to the English shut up in Madras; and, although during the struggle which followed at a somewhat later period, the fortune of England had prevailed, yet to the last hour of his life Haidar, a man of innate genius, had been a very formidable enemy. His son and successor, known as Típu Sultán, not only did not posses even a bit of his father's genius, but was saturated with prejudices from which his father had been free. The war, which was still waging on is accession, languished with varying fortunes for fifteen months; and it is a proof of the extremity to which our countrymen were reduced, that at the end of that period they were glad to conclude a treaty—the Treaty of Mangalore (March 11th, 1784)—by which the contracting parties agreed to restore all places, and all prisoners, taken during the war.

The interval of peace which followed gave abundant and repeated evidence that genius no longer directed the affairs of the only State in India which had waged war not unequally with the English. Haidar would have both husbanded his resources, paved the way for new alliances against the Foreign Power, which he had felt during his lifetime would otherwise swallow the estates of the native princes in detail. Típu, swayed by prejudice and bigotry, listened only to his passions. Instead of conciliating, he molested his neighbours. At last, he was rash enough and foolish enough to attack a protected ally of the English, the Rájah of Travankúr. War followed. In that war Típu was worsted. Bangalore fell into the hands of the English. Seringapatam was invested; and within two years Tipu obtained peace by the sacrifice of one-half of his dominion, and the payment of an indemnity of upwards of three millions sterling.

Only six years had elapsed between the signature of this peace (March 19th, 1792) and the landing of Lord Mornington at Madras (April 26th, 1798), and six years do not count much in the memory of a prince, the main aim of whose life was to recover all that he had lost. Such was the aim, the constant, unwavering aim, of Típu Sultán. Scarcely was the ink dry with which the peace of 1792 had been signed than he began to strengthen the fortifications of Seringapatam. He provided for the accruing to his soldiers of advantages in the shape of pension or in bestowing upon them of grants of land. Then, in 1793, he opened negotiations for a general alliance of the native princes against the English with Madhaji Scindhiá, the ablest of all the Maráthás, whose death, the year following, was a fatal blow to their cause. To aid in bringing about the same result, he found means to correspond with Zamán Sháh, ruler of Kábul; and a little later he played the card which brought matters between himself and the English to extremes—he reopened negotiations with France. As one consequence of these negotiations was exactly contemporaneous with the arrival of Lord Mornington at Madras, I propose to deal with it somewhat in detail.

Before the war, which terminated so disastrously for the Maisur ruler in 1792, Típu had, in 1788, despatched by the hands of a Frenchman, whose name is entered in the Maisur Manuscripts as Monsieur Macnamara, a letter to Louis XVI., in which he stated his apprehensions of immediate war with the English, and his confidence that in that event the French King would assist him. To this letter he received in due course a reply to the effect, that whilst the King wished him well, and was desirous in every legitimate way to promote his views, should opportunity offer, there were reasons, which the letter set forth, why it was impossible that France should, at the moment, declare war against England. After the French Revolution had broken out, and the French armies had begun planning victory for which it required the combination of all the Powers of Europe to stop, Típu was persuaded to renew his offers to form a league for the expulsion of the English. It would seem that the first overtures direct to Paris were made through the intervention of a Frenchman named Pierre Moneron, an adventurer long resident of Maisur, in 1795 or 1796; but it is certain that indirect communications were opened at an earlier period, for the same purpose, with General Cossigny, Governor of the Isle of France, and by him transmitted to Paris. The fact that England and France were in 1795 actually at war, had imparted to the Sultán a confident belief that the alliance, so long hoped for, might at last be consummated.

His mind was in this buoyant condition when, early in 1797, a French privateer from the Isle of France put in, dismasted, into the port of Mangalore, and solicited the means of repair. It happened that the Lord of the Admiralty at that port was one Ghulám Álí, one of the men who had accompanied Macnamara to France in 1788, and had acquired some proficiency in speaking of the French language. He at once gave the required permission to repair damages. Then—after much conversation with the master of the vessel, a man named Ripaud,—he reported to his sovereign that the arrival was most opportune, for the Ripaud represented himself to be the officer second in authority at the Isle of France, and that he had been specially instructed to touch at Mangalore, for the purpose of ascertaining the Sultán's wishes regarding the co-operation of a French force with the troops of His Highness for the expulsion from India of their common enemy. Ghulám Áli was promptly instructed to bring Ripaud to Seringapatam.

It can easily be conceived that Ripaud was nothing more than a common impostor, and as such he was recognised by the officers of Típu's Court. They even proceeded so far as to write a memorandum on the subject to their master, and to represent it as quite possible that Ripaud might be an English spy. But it was one of the weaknesses of Típu to believe that to be true which he wished to be true, and he answered his councillors with the platitude, of which he was in the habit of making daily use: "Whatever is the will of God, that will be accomplished." Ripaud's vessel was purchased, and the purchase-money was made over to one of his companions, to be taken to the Isle of France. Ripaud himself was directed to stay at Típu's Court in the unofficial capacity of an ambassador, and four envoys from the Sultán, posing as merchants, were directed to proceed to the island, to solicit from its Governor the despatch to Mangalore of a fleet and army. With that fleet and army one of them was to return, whilst the other three were to continue their journey to Paris, to execute the functions of ambassadors. An event of a ludicrous character disconcerted these proceedings. The four native ambassadors were on the eve of starting from Mangalore, accompanied by the Frenchman who had been deputed by Ripaud to convey to the Isle of France the purchase-money of the disabled privateer, when the Frenchman and three of his compatriots absconded in a boat, taking with them the money. Nothing more was heard of them, and it was supposed that they had been captured by the English. Of this, however, there is no record, and the probabilities are that they perished with their ill-gotten gains.

Such an occurrence ought to have opened the eyes of Típu to the true character of the class of foreigners with whom he was dealing. This state existed only due to him and he stated that at the moment he felt heartily ashamed of himself and of Ripaud. Charging the latter with collusion with his absconding countrymen, with the view to obtain double payment, he placed him under restraint. But reflecting, a little later, that if the vessel should arrive in the Isle of France without the purchase-money he had paid for her she was liable to be confiscated by her owners, he determined to release Ripaud, and to send him to the island with the ambassadors, now reduced to two, taking from him a bond for the money he had received, and for which the vessel was declared to be a collateral security. These questions and considerations caused delay, and the privateer, which was to have sailed in April, did not quit Mangalore until October.

She had scarcely lost sight of the coast when the two ambassadors of the Maisur Sultán had a fresh experience of the style of Frenchman whom their sovereign had delighted to honour. No sooner was he sure that he was beyond the control of Maisur than Ripaud collected his European crew, numbering five or six, and, addressing the ambassadors, reproached them for the treatment he had received from their master, and insisted that they should place in his hands the letters they were carrying to the island, threatening that unless they should comply he would proceed on a privateering cruise. After much demur and protestations the ambassadors complied. Ripaud at once opened the letters, read their contents, and finding that these did not confirm the apprehensions he had formed, continued his course for the island, and cast anchor in Port Louis, January 19th, 1798.

The Governor of the Isle of France was General Malartic, a very distinguished officer of ancient lineage and high reputation. His power in the two islands was absolute; for, when the Directory, jealous of his popularity, had despatched to commissaries from France to watch him, and restrict his authority, it was only with difficulty that Malartic saved them from the fury of the populace. His Council refused to recognise them, and they were sent back to France as soon as possible. Never again was the authority of Malartic interfered with or controlled from France. His power remained absolute till his death, in July, 1800.

Learning from Ripaud the real quality of the two Maisurians who had arrived, Malartic sent some gentlemen to wait upon them, and to arrange the time of their landing. When they did land they were received with full honours, conducted to Government House through a double line of troops, received there with ceremonious distinction, and assigned a public dwelling. Malartic found that the despatches contained the project of a treaty between the Sultán of Maisur and the Isle of France, the main point of which was the co-operation on Indian soil of a corps of from five to ten thousand French troops, backed by from twenty to thirty thousand Africans. The Sultán engaged that these, on landing, should be joined by sixty thousand Maisurians; the object of the joint operation being, according to the proposal of Típu, to take Goa from the Portuguese, and Bombay from the English, on the western coast; to reduce and raze Madras on the eastern; then to subdue the Maráthás and the Nizam; and, finally, to expel the English from Bengal. Malartic could not object that the scheme was not comprehensive. But he was without the necessary means of complying even in part with the requisition. He could spare no troops from the already too small garrison of the islands. The best he could do was to forward the proposals of the Sultán to France. This he did promptly, despatching the Sultán's letters in duplicate in two frigates, and meanwhile comforting the ambassadors with the assurance that the Mother Country would most certainly comply with the requisition. Meanwhile, despite the protests of the ambassadors, who told him that they required an army, and not a few recruits only, he issued a proclamation in which he invited the people of the islands to enlist to serve under the banners of Típu. Ultimately, the ambassadors re-embarked for Mangalore, on March 7th, 1798, on board the

Preneusc frigate, taking with them ninety-nine men, including civil and military officers, for the service of the Sultán . The capture of two English Indiamen, in the Tellicheri Roads, detained them a few days, and they reached Mangalore on April 26th, 1798, the very day that Lord Mornington landed at Madras.

I have been somewhat minute in recording the proceedings of Típu and his allies, in order to show that the things which he did were not done in a corner: that not only was he contemplating the waging of war with the English in India, but the waging of it on a scale which should place the result beyond a doubt, in concert with, and largely aided by, the hereditary enemy of England, then at war with England, and whose troops at the moment, though Típu knew it not, were preparing to embark to make a raid on Egypt, as the first step to India. It is true that he would have been glad had his negotiations been conducted with greater secrecy and discretion. But, secret or published, they were still negotiations; and, in point of fact, the proclamations of General Malartic, the language openly held by him in the presence of the ambassadors, and repeated and confirmed by them, were sufficient to publish to the world the hopes, the designs, the hostile manœuvres of the Sultán of Maisur. He gave a further proof of his intentions by according to the ninety-nine volunteers a brilliant reception, and by giving them quarters in his fortress of Seringapatam.

Whilst, thus, the condition of the still powerful kingdom of Maisur was of a nature to demand the earnest attention of a Governor-General fresh from Europe, the state of the dominions of the Nizam, the second great native power in Southern India, was but little more assuring. Up to the year 1759, the country known under the term Haidarábád, comprising then an area of 95,337 square miles, had been for many years completely under French influence. But when, in that year, Colonel Forde, acting under the inspiration of Clive, expelled the French from the country known as the Northern Sirkars, he forced upon the Nizam of the day, then called the Subahdar, who had marched to the assistance of the French, a treaty whereby he renounced the French alliance, agreed never to allow a French contingent within its dominions, and ceded a large territory to the English.

Had the conditions of that treaty been always insisted upon the Haidarábád difficulty would never have arisen, or, at least, it would never have assumed an aggravated form. But, in course of time, the position of the English in Southern India became often very precarious. It is true that occasionally they were able to make their authority felt. Thus, in 1768, they made a new treaty with the Nizam, whereby, in return for certain important considerations, they agreed to furnish him, upon requisition, with two battalions of sipáhis and guns, on condition of his paying their expenses. Eleven years later, in 1779, the brother of the Nizam, Basálat Jang by name, who despite the Treaty of 1759, had taken French levies into his service, pressed by Haidar Álí, had implored the aid of the English, and to obtain it has agreed to substitute for his French levies a detachment of English troops, and to yield to the English the district of Guntur. In spite of the protests of the Nizam, the Governor of Madras had assented to his arrangement. But the Home Government had disapproved the act, and had recalled the Governor. The Nizam, however, had been so outraged, that in the interval he had negotiated with Scindhiá and Haidar Álí for a common alliance against the English; and, what is more germane to the present subject, he had taken into his germane to the present subject, he had taken into his employment French officers to drill his troops. This was in direct contravention of the Treaty of 1759. But the English were then threatened by Haidar, and they had no power at the moment to notice the infraction; and it remained unnoticed. It is a proof of their waning influence at this period, that although, on the death of Basálat Jang, in 1782, the district of Guntur lapsed by treaty to the British, they allowed the Nizam to seize it, and to hold it for six years.

When, in 1789, the first war broke out between the English and Típu Sultán, the Nizam was forced to take a side. He distrusted Típu, and the English promised much. He declared, therefore, for the English; and, when victory crowned their efforts, he received as a reward territories bearing, then, an annual revenue of 52,64,000 Rs., besides a third of the amount in cash, amounting to three millions sterling, levied from Típu. To that war the Maráthás had likewise been a consenting party, and they, too, had their share of the plunder. With the division of the spoil with them came danger to the Nizam, and in spite of the proffered mediation of the then Governor-General, Sir John Shore, which the Peshwá refused, war ensued between the rival claimants. The campaign was short but decisive. Rejecting the bold advice of the Commander of his French contingent, Monsieur Raymond, the ablest of the adventurers in the service of the native princes the Nizam, after fighting not unequally a pitched battle, retreated during the night that followed, was pursued, and forced to accept a treaty which cost him three millions sterling in money, and territories yielding an annual revenue of £350,000.

During that short war, the Governor-General, at peace with both parties, had, whilst refusing active aid to the Nizam, carried his compliance beyond the bounds of true propriety, by allowing British sipáhis to guard the Nizam's dominions, whilst that prince should take the field with his own troops. Notwithstanding this compliance, the refusal of the Governor-General to lend him active assistance rankled in the mind of the Nizam, and his first step, after he had signed peace with the Maráthás, was to dismiss the British battalions at the same time that he increased the number of French sipáhis and of their officers. Suddenly, however, there occurred one of those outbreaks to which the native States of India were prone in those days. The British battalions had actually started on their return journey when the eldest son of the Nizam, Álí Jáh, broke out in rebellion. The French contingent was despatched against him, and succeeded in bringing him back a prisoner. But, meanwhile, the British battalions, hearing of the crisis, had returned, and the Nizam, terrified and unnerved, determined then to retain them.

Still the French force was there, and what is more, its numbers had been increased to 14,000 men. The sipáhis composing it were well drilled and efficient, and they were commanded in chief by a man of great ability, animated by a national hatred to the English. Raymond was born at Sérignac, in Gascony, in 1755, and at the age of twenty had engaged as a sub-lieutenant in a French corps, commanded by the Chevalier de Lasse, in the service of Haidar Álí. His distinguished conduct on several occasions had attracted the notice of the commanders of the army, and he obtained the rank of captain in the regular service of France. When Bussy came out to India in 1783 to co-operate with Haidar against the English, he made Raymond his aide-de-camp. On Bussy's death, the then Governor of Pondichery recommended, Raymond to the Nizam as an officer upon whom he could entirely rely. Raymond soon justified the recommendation. Commissioned to form one regiment, he soon produced a body of men, the equal of whom, in efficiency and drill, the Nizam had never seen. Gradually the number was increased to fourteen, and it had just arrived at that strength, when, on March the 6th, 1798, he died, not without suspicion of having been poisoned. Seven weeks later, April the 26th—a day of many striking coincidences—Lord Mornington arrived at Madras.

But if, on that date, there was an accumulation of evidence that Maisur was conspiring with an European Power with which Great Britain was at war; that the Nizam, secretly unfriendly, was acting in contravention of the terms of a treaty which still existed; there was little in Northern, North-Western, Central, or Western India to reassure the mind of the incoming Proconsul. In those parts the Maráthá influence was everywhere preponderant. The chief cities of the west and of the northwest, cities and centres such as Puna, Bárodah, Ásirgarh, Nagpur, Burhanpur, Indur, Ujjen, Gwaliar, Ágra, Dehlí, and Aligarh were firmly held by one member or another of the powerful confederacy. The armies of Scindhiá and Holkar were to a large extent trained and commanded by Frenchmen. Dáolat Ráo Scindhiá, the most powerful of the Maráthá chiefs, was known to entertain no friendly feeling towards the British. He was still very young, and it was still possible that he might yet take up the threads of that secret negotiation for union against the foreigner, which had been the dream of his immediate predecessor.

The chance that he would not take up that thread constituted, at this period the one hope for the English. Madajhí Scindhiá had died but four years earlier, just as he had succeeded in the difficult, the almost impossible, task of giving one direction to the foreign policy of the five Powers who formed the Maráthá Confederacy, the Peshwá, the Bhonslá, the Gaikwár, Holkar, and Scindhiá. His adopted son and successor, Dáolat Ráo, had, up to the moment of which I am writing, displayed neither the ability nor the will to follow in his track; whilst Jaswant Ráo Holkar, who had but just succeeded the wise and prudent Tukají, seemed animated chiefly by a desire to wreak his vengeance for past insults on his powerful neighbour, Scindhiá.

Nor, if a glance were directed at the provinces outside the range of Maráthá influence, was the prospect of a nature to reassure. The recognition by Sir John Shore of the claims of Saadat Álí to the vacated *masnad* of Oudh, though strictly in accordance with justice, had left a strong party in that province which viewed with great disfavour the interference of the British; whilst in the adjoining province of Rohilkhand, inhabited by a brave and war-like race, who had suffered from the same interference, there prevailed a strong hope that the ruler of Kábul, Zamán Sháh, would repeat, and even surpass, the achievements of Nádir Sháh and Ahmad Sháh.

Such was the condition of India, and such were the feelings of the princes, and, to a great extent, of the people, of India, when, on April the 26th, Lord Mornington landed at Madras to assume the office of Governor-General of India. The reader would, however, fail to grasp the nature of his position to its fullest extent, unless he had some knowledge of the character of his predecessor; some distinct idea of the kind of policy which that predecessor had attempted to pursue.

Sir John Shore, created on his retirement Lord Teignmouth, was a man possessing great amiability of character, and was actuated in all his dealings by a determination to pursue the course which to him was the right course. But he was an idealist, a philosopher, who shaped his policy, not from the standpoint of things as they were, but from the standpoint of things as, in his opinion, they ought to be. Believing that the British dominion in India had reached its limit, no hostile combination of native princes would have induced him to extend it. He wished that all the native States of India should be maintained in their integrity. Consequently, throughout his tenure of office, he had not only proclaimed, but had maintained, a policy of non-interference. The more ambitious Princes of India, Tipu, Madajhí Scindhiá, and, to a certain extent, the Nizam, had derived from this policy enormous consolation, for they had found it only necessary to protest to be believed. Indeed, it is a very curious fact that the very day Lord Mornington landed at Madras, a letter from Tipu, who had openly allied himself with the French Republic for the expulsion of the English from India, reached the Governor-General, containing the Sultan's assurance of his desire to strengthen the "foundations of harmony and concord established between the two States". Sir John Shore never realised the fact that although, throughout his incumbency of office, he had maintained peace, yet that very peace had been largely instrument in bringing about a revolution of thought in the minds of the native princes; that generally they had substituted, for jealousy of one another, a desire to combine against the foreigner. This policy had, it is true, been temporarily interrupted by the death of Madhají Scindhiá (February the 12th, 1794) just as it was about to mature, and by the character of the Madhají successor. But it was certain to revive. It had become a principle never to be forgotten, though, in consequence of the impetuous passions incident to youth, often to be neglected.

Such was the state of India at the time of the arrival of the new Governor-General . Such were the subjects which drew his attention.

4

Tipu, Nizam, and Peshwa

In the course of his voyage from England, Lord Mornington touched at the Cape (February, 1798). There he not only received despatches, giving him the latest Indian news, and dealing especially with Típu Sultán and the Nizam, but he met Major Kirkpatrick, an officer who had filled the office of a British Resident at Haidarábád, and who was well acquainted with the political position of the several native princes of India. Assisted by this competent adviser, Lord Mornington set diligently to work to master the situation, and it is a proof of the clear head, the comprehensiveness, the quickness of his intellect, that in his despatches from the Cape to the President of the Board of Control he laid down the policy for dealing with the Nizam and with Típu on the precise lines on which he subsequently carried it out. Thus, writing on February 23rd, he enclosed a copy of the questions he had put to Major Kirkpatrick, and the written answers he had received from that officer, on the position at Haidarábád; and, drawing his own conclusions, stated that as the existence and the augmentation of the French contingent might easily be made the basis for establishing a French party in the very heart of Southern India, means ought to be taken to check its influence. Glancing rapidly at the result of the last war between the Nizam and the Maráthás, and the consequent decline of the *prestige* of the former, Lord Mornington, believing that a loyal Nizam would constitute a powerful mainstay of British power in Southern India, expressed his conviction that it would be a wise policy to check by timely aid the rapid decline of the Nizam's weight among the Powers of Hindustan. This, he thought, could be done in no manner so effectual or unobjectionable as by furnishing him with a large increase of the British force the pay of the augmented force to be secured in the manner best calculated to prevent future discussion and embarrassment. "In granting this force to the Nizam, we ought," he said, "not only to stipulate for the disbanding of Raymond's corps, but we ought to take care that the officers should be immediately sent out of India."

One other point is mentioned by Lord Mornington in the same letter, as a point of much difficulty and danger, expressed by that Prince to obtain a British guarantee of his possessions against the Maráthás and against Típu. That it should be necessary to consider such a point, and to regard it as one of great difficulty and danger, indicates most clearly the vital difference between India of the present day and the India which Lord Mornington went to govern. In that India, Great Britain was only one Power amongst many others, all equally jealous of their independence. Far from being supreme, she was not admitted even to be preponderant. Haidar Álí had within twenty years waged with her a not unequal war, and the son of Haidar Álí was an independent prince, allying himself with the enemies of England. Equally independent, and possessing a predominating influence in Western, North-Western and Central India, were the five Maráthá Princes already enumerated, one out of the five, at least, considering himself predestined to be the successor to the Mughul, and already occupying both his capitals. The Nizam was not so independent, for his treaty obligations fettered his action; but, as had been shown in that very decade, he was free to wage war with the other native prices. In fact, he was but just emerging from that disastrous war with the Maráthás which had followed the defeat of Típu in 1792. And now he, as a condition of dismissing his French sipáhis, that is, as a condition of placing himself and his territory more absolutely under British control, was demanding a guarantee of his possessions against the independent native prices of India, and, in addition, the right previously denied to him, of employing against those native princes the sipáhis, drilled by British officers, furnished to him by the British government. No wonder that Lord Mornington, writing from the Cape of Good Hope, should regard this proposal as involving much delicacy and danger. Yet even then he grasped the position, and he grasped it in the same decided and statesmanlike manner which at a later period characterised all his dealings with native princes on the spot. A one-sided guarantee he at once rejected as impracticable, unless Great Britain were to have absolute control over the foreign relations of the Nizam. Típu's hostility had even then been too clearly manifested to permit Lord Mornington to entertain the ideal of any engagement with him. But, writing from the Cape, before he had set foot on Indian soil, he thought it might be expedient to induce the Maráthá powers to enter into such a joint guarantee; that he might prove to them that it was in their interest to agree to respect the actual dominions of the Nizam, provided the British should guarantee them against any attack from that prince. Even then he discerned that Típu was the first enemy he would have to encounter. In fact, in this conception regarding a mutual guarantee, we can discern the earnest desire, that in the contest which seemed to loom in a very near future, Típu should stand alone, unaided by either of the two powers, the Nizam and the Maráthás, his rivals then, but possibly under other circumstances his allies.

Details, such as he could gather from Major Kirkpatrick, regarding the Maráthá princes, followed in this remarkable letter. It was followed by another, of an equally statesmanlike character, giving a comprehensive review of the occurrences in India during that decade; showing how the policy of abstention from all interference with native powers, adopted by his immediate predecessor, had changed the relative positions of England and the independent native states, and had made it all but impossible to assure such a combination against Típu as had been conducted with such marked success in 1788. He pointed out, further, how the declension of the influence of the Peshwá among the Maráthás, and the consequent rise of that of Scindhiá, had not tended to improve the relations between the people and the English. Arguing then, the possible effects of an invasion of India by Zamán Sháh, and an alliance of that prince with Típu, he arrived at the following conclusion—a conclusion thoroughly warranted by the circumstances of the period—"that the balance of power in India no longer exists upon the same footing on which it was placed by the peace of Seringapatam. The question, therefore, must arise, how it may best be brought back again to that state, in which you have directed me to maintain it." He then proceeded to discuss that question.

I have dwelt at some length upon these interesting letters, because they go far to prove how thoroughly Lord Mornington had examined the position of affairs in India, in their various and varying details, before he set foot in the country; how he had mastered the principles of action which had animated Típu on the one side, and the Nizam on the other; and how he had arrived at the conclusion that at the present time, in the face of new difficulties arising in consequence of the war with France, it would no longer be possible to pursue the non-intervention policy of his predecessor. With respect to the Maráthás, he could only write vaguely; but even with respect to these his acute mind had arrived at a right conclusion. He had already recognised that the death of Madhají Scindhiá had weakened that formidable branch of the Confederacy, and had deprived the five powers of a man who could have bent their united strength in one direction. He had not heard of the death of Tukaji Holkar, which occurred only in that year, nor could he presage the advent to power of so formidable a successor as Jaswant Ráo. He saw, however, that with the Maráthás there would be, in all probability, no immediate difficulty, and that he would be at liberty, on landing, to concentrate all his attention on the Nizam and Típu Sultán.

The information, then, which reached Lord Mornington when, on April 26th, he landed at Madras, was not of a nature to surprise him. He arrived fully armed, and fully resolved to solve the difficulties in accordance with the principles he had laid down in his letters to Mr. Dunads from the Cape, viz., to restore to England the relative position she had occupied in 1792. For the moment he did not go further. The reader will watch with interest the circumstances which compelled him to assure to his country a position, not of equality merely, not even of preponderance, but of predominance.

April 26th, 1798, was, I have already intimated, a day of coincidences. On that day, Lord Mornington arrived at Madras; the ninety-nine French auxiliaries for the service of Típu landed at Mangalore; and the Calcutta Government received from that potentate a letter full of professions of friendship for the East India Company. At Madras Lord Mornington stayed but a few days. He had been requested by the Court of Directors to endeavour, whilst there, to prevail on the Nawáb of Arkát to agree to a modification of the Treaty of 1792. The result of the negotiation proved how greatly the non-interference system of the preceding six years had lessened the influence of England. The Nawáb of Arkát owed all he possessed in the world to English influence. The efforts of Lawrence and Clive had made valid the somewhat shadowy claims of his father against the pretensions of the candidate supported by the French. He and his family had since been regarded as the special *protégés* of the English, and though they had paid somewhat extravagantly for the protection, it had saved them alike from the raids of the Maráthás and the hatred of Haidar Álí and his son. Under the circumstances of ten years previously the modification required by Lord Mornington would have been granted at once; but, although the nobleman conducted the negotiation in a manner such as to inspire General Harris, the

Commander-in Chief of the Madras army and Acting-Governor of Madras, who was present, with the greatest respect for his abilities, the Nawáb refused to give way; nay, more, when Lord Mornington drew attention to the fact that his debt to the Company, of long standing, still remained unliquidated, the Nawáb declined to make any provision for its repayment. It became evident to the new Governor-General that if a petty prince could thus refuse to attend to the wishes of the power which had made him, the prestige of England must have fallen very considerably indeed.

Lord Mornington stayed at Madras but thirteen days. On May 9th, he continued his journey to Calcutta, and arrived there the 17th of the same month.

There he found, or rather he brought with him for settlement from Madras, one or two matters of some importance which required immediate settlement. The first of these related to the succession to Tanjúr, a province in Southern India, the capital of which, also called Tanjúr, was situated some forty miles from Trichinápalli. Fourteen days after his arrival he had settled this question by the nomination of the candidate whose claim was, really, beyond question, though interested parties had chosen to question it. He was then on the point of turning his attention to the position of the Nizam, when, on June 8th, he was startled by reading, in a Calcutta newspaper, copies of the proclamation issued by Governor Malartic, in the Isle of France, relative to the envoys of Típu, promising material aid from France, and inviting enlistment for that purpose. At first, Lord Mornington was disposed to think that the extracts might be forgeries, but further reflection, leading to the belief that they might be true, he wrote to General Harris the day following, requesting him to adopt the precautionary measure of turning his "attention to the means of collecting a force, if necessity should unfortunately require it, but it is not my desire that you should proceed to take any public steps towards the assembling of the army before you receive some further intimation from me".

Ten days later, Lord Mornington received proof of the authenticity of Governor Malartic's proclamation. I was established, further, to the satisfaction of the Governor-General, that Típu had despatched two envoys to the Isle of France; that the proclamation had been issued subsequently to their arrival, and during their residence in the island. He also learned that succours, small in number indeed, but composed of Frenchmen or French subjects, had actually landed in Maisur territory; and that Típu Sultán, aided by Malartic, had made offers of alliance to the Directory at Paris, and that he was hoping that his request might be responded to by a further and a larger despatch of troops. It was even quite possible that such a force might have been already despatched.

To Lord Mornington, to his Commander-in-Chief, Sir Alured Clarke, and to all the other members of his Council, the situation seemed threatening, requiring prompt and energetic action. There was no electric telegraph in those days to bring instant information. The communication between the Malabar coast and Calcutta was even long and difficult. It had been only by extraordinary efforts that, on June the 18th, Lord Mornington had heard to the arrival of the levies from the isle of France on April the 26th. For ought he knew further levies might have landed, and an army might be on its way from France. Lord Mornington then, backed by all his Councillors, resolved to take precautionary measures—measures which would not precipitate a catastrophe, but would meet it when it should arise. Bookworms have balanced him for taking even such a precaution. Had he not taken it, he would have imperilled the Empire.

Accordingly, on June the 20th, two days after he and his Council had satisfied themselves that the proclamation was authentic, Lord Mornington wrote thus to General Harris:—

"I now take the earliest opportunity of acquainting you with my final determination. I mean to call upon the allies without delay, and to assemble the army upon the coast with all possible expedition. You will receive my public instructions in the course of a few days. Until you have received them, it will not be proper to take any public steps for the assembly of an army; but whatever can be done without a disclosure of the ultimate object, I authorise you to do immediately, intending to apprise you by this letter that it is my positive resolution to assemble the army upon the coast. I wish to receive from you, by express, a statement of the force you can put in motion immediately, and within what time you can make large additions to it."

It may be added, that the allies referred to in this letter were the Nizam and the Maráthás.

As, in all probability, some weeks or even months must elapse before General Harris could complete the preparations necessary for a long campaign, Lord Mornington resolved to lose no time in dealing with the Nizam. The information of the action of Típu had, indeed, brought his case into greater prominence, because madness itself could only have excused the entering upon a war with Típu, supported by French troops, and leaving to the disposal of the Nizam 14,000 sipáhis, drilled and partly officered by Frenchmen.

In a preceding page I have shown how the Nizam, angry with the English on account of their refusal to render him active support in the war which he waged in 1794 with the Maráthás, had actually dismissed the two battalions of English sipáhis, stipulated by the Treaty of 1790, when the rebellion of his son, Álí Jáh, had induced the English commander of those battalions to stay his march; and how the Nizam, suspicious of everybody, but less suspicious of the English than of others, had retained them. The French contingent, counting 14,000 men, besides a numerous artillery, also remained, strong in its numbers, and especially strong in the affection of the French party at the Court of the Nizam. Desirous to render the Nizam relatively stronger, to assure him a force upon which he could rely under all circumstances, and which yet should be exclusively an English force; equally resolved to remove from the flank of a British army, on the eve of engaging with an enemy who might be backed by French troops, a powerful corps of trained sipáhis commanded by Frenchmen; Lord Mornington, in July, directed the Residents at Haidarábád to negotiate with the Nizam a new Treaty, the main provision of which should be the augmentation of the English subsidiary force to six battalions of infantry with a powerful artillery, and the dismissal of the corps commanded by French officers in His Highness's service. It is probable that if such a demand had been made seven months before, whilst Raymond was yet alive, it would have been treated by the Nizam in a manner not dissimilar to that in which the Nawáb of Arkát had replied to Lord Mornington in the preceding April. But the experience of three months of the firm and resolute government of the new Proconsul had convinced the native princes that the supine methods of Sir John Shore had been departed from; that there was a man at the helm who saw for himself, who judged for himself, and who was as resolute in action as he was clear and decided in the expression of his views. The sound of an approaching contest with the ruler of Maisur had gone over Southern India. Under the circumstances, the Nizam felt that he had but one alternative. He must absolutely refuse, or he must absolutely accept. Absolute refusal meant alliance with Típu, whom he detested, and the certainty of having to sustain the first attack of the English—possibly, even, to be abandoned by his ally. He could not hesitate.

The Treaty which the Nizam signed on September the 1st, and which was ratified at Calcutta on the 18th of the same month, declared in its preamble that the augmentation of the British force to the extent above indicated was conceded at the express desire of the Nizam himself; that it was a necessary complement to the Treaty of 1790, which required the allies to take immediate measures for the defence of their respective dominions. It contained, likewise, a stipulation for a Treaty of a triple guarantee of the said possessions between the English, the Nizam, and the Peshwá. Should the latter refuse his assent, then authority was conceded to the English to mediate between the Nizam and the Peshwá—such mediation to be, in its terms, binding on the Nizam. Finally, the Treaty confirmed all existing Treaties between the English, the Peshwa, and the Nizam, and declared the free assent of the latter to similar subsidiary engagements between the English and the Peshwá, in case the latter should express a desire for such an arrangement. The reader will observe that this Treaty was drawn up on the lines of the recommendations made by Lord Mornington in his letters from the Cape to Mr. Dundas.

The first question which presented itself to the Governor-General, after he had ratified the Treaty (September the 18th), was how to carry out its main provision, the disbanding of the French contingent, with promptitude and success. Here there was no hesitation. In anticipation of the agreement of the Nizam to the proffered conditions, Lord Mornington had directed the march of the four additional battalions and the artillery to a point on the border of the territories of the Nizam, whence, at a given signal, they might march on Haidrábád. The commander of those battalions, Lieutenant-Colonel Roberts, received the order to march the moment the information should reach him that the Treaty had been ratified. He obeyed those orders to the letter, marched instantly on Haidarábád, and joined the two battalions stationed there on October the 10th. Then began the hesitations of the Nizam. He was a timid man, and, on the eve of a possible contest between the numerically inferior force of British sipáhis, whom he had brought in, and the superior number of the French contingent, he began to reckon how he might fare in the event of the victory of the latter. But Captain Kirkpatrick, still Resident at his Court, insisted upon the immediate execution of the Article of the Treaty relating to the French contingent, and a movement made by Colonel Roberts having convinced the Nizam that the disbandment would under any circumstances be attempted, he gave the necessary orders. On the evening of October the 21st, a proclamation was issued and distributed in the lines of the French contingent, informing the sipáhis that the Nizam had dismissed the French officers from his service;

that they were relieved from obedience to those officers; and that all who should support them would be punished as traitors. This proclamation created the greatest commotion in the lines. The sipáhis, to whom considerable arrears of pay were due, turned upon their officers, imprisoned them, and threatened them with the forfeiture of their lives, unless those arrears were met. Information of these proceedings having reached Colonel Roberts, the officer proceeded to act with judgement and promptitude. At daylight the following morning, with his own battalions and the Nizam's cavalry, he surrounded the French lines; then, addressing the revolted sipáhis, he offered them full payment of all arrears, and future service under other officers, on condition of laying down their arms. After some discussion, the sipáhis assented to these conditions. "Thus," wrote Sir John Malcolm, who was present in his capacity of assistant to the Resident, "in a few hours, a corps, whose numbers were nearly fourteen thousand men, and who had in their possession a train of artillery and an arsenal filled with every description of military stores, was completely disarmed without one life having been lost." The French officers quietly surrendered. They were not treated as prisoners of war, but were sent, by way of England, to France.

Thus successfully was carried out the first great operation of Lord Mornington's administration. It's importance can scarcely be over-estimated. It was not only that on the eve of a war with a prince, whose influence on the western coast was preponderant, it secured for the English on the eastern coast the absolute security of their right flank. It accomplished, much more. It compelled the Nizam to be not only our ally, but our submissive ally. It virtually deprived him of the right which he had exercised but four years before, of making war on other princes of India, except as an ally of the British. The Treaty brought him in fact within, just within, but still within, the category of protected princes, in which his successors have since remained. It was the thin end of the wedge, inserted at precisely the right moment by a master hand. From that hour the Nizam, in his difficulties, could appeal to none to save the English. From that hour the control of the English over his external relations was absolute.

Nor was Lord Mornington less successful in his negotiations with the Peshwá. At the Court of that prince Dáolat Ráo Scindhiá—young, passionate, and inexperienced—had been unable to maintain the influence acquired by his immediate predecessor, Madhají. He had one rival in Náná Farnávís, supposed to be friendly to an alliance with the English; another in Bálájí Ráo, a secret agent of the Peshwá, who intrigued in the manner best calculated to advance the personal interests of the latter. For the moment, then, it was not difficult to persuade the Court of Puná to express a guarded approval of the arrangements entered into between the Nizam and the British, so far as it affected the interests of the Peshwa. The neutrality of the Maráthás was thus secured for the coming war with Maisur, and although the Peshwa personally wished well to Típu, and even despatched negotiators to communicate with him towards the close of 1798, the intrigue was discovered and frustrated by Náná Farnávís before it had time to bear fruit.

In this manner Lord Mornington, within seven months of his arrival in India, had restored the prestige of the British name. Finding amongst the three independent princes but one who was a determined, an irreconcilable, and a dangerous enemy, he had made of one of the others a protected ally, bound to follow the fortunes and obey the orders of the Governor-General, and had for the moment neutralised the opposition of the third. In the next chapter I shall show how he dealt with the prince whose irreconcilable hostility, and whose alliance with France, made him at that moment supremely dangerous.

5

Administrative Measures Fall of Seringapatam

June, 1798—January, 1799

As stated earlier how, on June the 8th, Lord Mornington, deeply impressed by the revelation of the negotiations of Típu Sultán with the Governor of the Isle of France, and prescient of the danger which might arise to British interests from a serious alliance between that prince and revolutionary France, had requested General Harris to adopt the precautionary measure "of turning his attention to the means of collecting a force, if necessity should unfortunately require it; but," he had added, "it is not my desire that you should proceed to take any public steps towards the assembling of an army before you receive further intimation from me." I propose now to accompany Lord Mornington's despatch to Madras, and to record the effect it produced in the Council Chamber of that Presidency.

Historically, the record of the result produced is of the greatest importance. It affords the clearest proof of the state of abject terror which had been produced in the minds of official Englishmen by the memory of the wars with Haídar Álí, notwithstanding that, in the interval they had forced his son, Típu, to sue for a peace which had cost him half his dominions. The recollection of the earlier miseries remained, whilst the memory of the subsequent triumph had been obliterated. It was not the least of the many services rendered by Lord Mornington to British India that he knew how, by his courageous initiative, to rouse his countrymen from a torpor which, if permitted to rule the counsels of Madras, might have caused the loss of India.

On the arrival, about June the 20th, of Lord Mornington's despatch to the Madras Government, the Acting Governor's Secretary, Mr. Lushington, carried it to Mr. Webbe, the principal Secretary to the Government, with a view to its being considered in Council. In his 'Life of Lord Harris', Mr. Lushington records how Mr. Webbe, on reading the letter, gave expression to his disapprobation in the strongest terms:

> Our unprepared state for war, he adds, in the absence of a large portion of our troops in the Eastern Islands: our empty and bankrupt treasury at Madras:—all the horros of Haídar's merciless invasion of the Karnátik,—of Típu's sanguinary destruction of Colonel Baillie's detachments,—Sir Hector Munro's disgraceful retreat to Madras, and the first failure of Lord Cornwallis against Seringapatam, rushed at once into Mr. Webbe's mind, and he exclaimed with bitterness and grief: 'I can anticipate nothing but shocking disasters from a premature attack upon Típu in our present disabled condition, and the impeachment of Lord Mornington for his temerity.'

In India, appointments to responsible situations, such as that of Secretary to the Government, are almost invariably given on merit. At Madras, the Secretary is, in fact, the most important personage, next to the Governor, in the Government; and, even of the Governor, he is the eye, the ear, and often the guiding mind. In using the language I have quoted, Mr. Webbe was probably then but expressing the general opinion of the official class in Madras. Even the Acting Governor, General Harris, a man not given to panic, thinking clearly, and acting always with decision, was startled by Lord Mornington's letter. Replying to the Governor-

General, on June 23rd, he stated, that although he was satisfied that Típu's inveteracy against us would end only with his life, and that he would certainly seize any opportunity to annoy us, he still thought it worthy of serious consideration whether "it would not be better that he should be allowed to make the *amende honorable,* if he be so inclined, than that we should avail ourselves of the error he has run into, and endeavour to punish him for his insolence." The reader will not fail to gather from this remark of the member of Council, the most favourable to Lord Mornington, that the entire Council had misunderstood the real meaning of Lord Mornington's letter. That letter spoke merely of preparation. It requested General Harris to turn his attention to the means of collecting a force, if necessity should unfortunately require it. Nor did the letter of June 30th, which followed at an interval of three weeks from that of the 8th, though more explicit, pass the boundary of preparation. It simply called upon the Governor to state the number of men he could place immediately in the field, and the time he would require to increase that number. This letter was before the Madras Council when they adopted a memorandum drawn up by Mr. Webbe, earnestly protesting against the orders of the Supreme Government.

Few things show more clearly, the difficulties Lord Mornington had to overcome than this opposition, coming from the men to whom would be entrusted the carrying out of his instructions. General Harris, indeed, belonged to that order of men who, whatever their opinions, are ready to carry out implicitly the lawful orders of their superiors. "On my part", he had written to Lord Mornington, "your Lordship may depend on my following your instructions implicitly". But, in forwarding Mr. Webb's memorandum, approved by his Council, even General Harris showed that he dissented from the opinions of his chief. In that memorandum, the writer, reviewing the history of the past, came to the conclusion that, under existing circumstances, an attack upon Típu Sultán "is more likely to end in discomfiture than in victory." He added his conviction that any hostile preparations on the part of the British Government would produce immediate invasion by Típu Sultán. He concluded thus: "If war is inevitable, and the present are judged the most advantageous circumstances under which it can commence, I fear our situation is bad, beyond the hope of remedy." The other members of the Madras Council adopted the views of Mr. Webbe.

The expostulations of the members of a Government, without one dissentient voice, against the policy he had not only warmly espoused, but directed to be executed, would have been sufficient to induce an ordinary man, stranger than any of the remonstrants to the country and to the ancient method of dealing with native princes, to pause and reflect. But Lord Mornington was no ordinary man, and the times were troublous beyond comparison. He saw that the dangers which threatened Southern India were caused by that very policy, the continuance of which, was advocated by Mr. Webbe in his memorandum. The Treaty of 1792 with Típu Sultán, though it had deprived him of one-half of his dominions, had yet left him that portion which he could use most adversely to the interests of Great Britain. The possession of the seaboard on the Malabar coast had enabled him, at a moment when all Europe was threatened by the ambitious designs of one great power, to open negotiations with that power, and to offer to it the means of landing in his dominions, unmolested, any amount of auxiliaries. The intrigues of Típu with France, with Zamán Sháh, his attempts to negotiate with the Peshwá, were well known to the English world in India; were well known to the native princes of India. The danger arose from the possibility of any one of these alliances taking effect in an untoward moment, when the English were totally unprepared; when the Madras army, which would have to meet the first attack, should still be in that state of unreadiness which was urged by Mr. Webbe as a reason for absolute inaction. Such a sudden combination was possible. It would have been worked before that moment, had there been a sufficiently large body of French troops in the Isle of France, or had the French Directory responded immediately to the invitation of Típu. Had Lord Mornington known that the French Directory had actually responded to that invitation; that, at the very moment he was ordering that the Madras army should be placed in a state of preparation, a French fleet and army, commanded by the brilliant chief who had made the immortal compaign of 1796, had taken Malta, and were progressing towards the other stepping-stone to India, the land of the Pharaohs, he could not have felt more strongly than he did feel the critical nature of the situation. That was then happening which he foresaw, might in some form or other, happen at any moment, and his mind was made up, that whenever that unknown danger should arrive, he would be, ready to meet it, as far as it lay within his power.

The arguments of Mr. Webbe and the Madras Council produced, then, on his mind, an effect which was the opposite of what they were intended to convey. Mr. Webbe had urged the unprepared condition of the Madras army, and, therefore, the danger of provoking Típu, lest he, hearing, as he would be sure to hear, of the prepartions of the English, should invade Madras, and repeat the horrors perpetrated by his father. To Lord Mornington's mind no other argument could have appealed with stronger force in favour of his own views. The case of the supporters of the non-interference policy, the civilians who had been bred in the school of Cornwallis and Shore, had been clearly put by Mr. Webbe. But what did it amount to? Simply that British India, which had been won by the sword, was to be maintained solely by appealing to the good feeling and forbearance of the native powers; that the Governor-General was to respect their susceptibilities to the extent of leaving his coast-army weak and unarmed, even when he possessed the certain knowledge that the most powerful native prince in its vicinity was moving heaven and earth to form a hostile alliance against him—an alliance on the one side with a foe England was actually combating, and on the other with the son of the northern chief who had sacked Dehlí. Lord Mornington's reply to the Madras Government pointed out the extreme danger of such a policy.

Reminding the Government, in a few dignified words, that he had not invited a discussion of his orders, he added, writing for himself and his Council:—

"If we thought it proper to enter with you into any discussion of the policy of our late orders, we might refer you to the records of your own Government, which furnish mor than one example of the fatal consequences of neglecting to keep pace with the forwardness of the enemy's equipments, and of resting the defence of the Karnátik, in such a crisis as the present, on any other security than a stage of early and active preparation for war. But being resolved to exclude all such discussions from the correspondence of the two Governments, we shall only repeat our confidence in your zealous and speedy execution of those parts of the public service which fall within the direct line of your peculiar duty".

He therefore reiterated his orders for bringing the coast army into a state of efficiency.

Had that army been ready, he would have struck at that instant. He had in his hands ample proof of Típu's negotiations for the formation of a hostile league against the British. The negotiations could be accomplished any moment. To strike, then, before that consummation should arrive, whilst Típu was still unsupported save by his ninety-nine Frenchmen, was, he felt, the truest policy. He could not pursue it, because the weapon in his hand was not yet, by the admission of those who forged it, strong enough even for defence. He had, therefore, to temporise, to wait, endeavouring, till that weapon should be ready, to strengthen his position by other means.

How he found those means, first, by the disbandment of the French sipáhi corps at Haidarábád; secondly, by the neutralisation of the powerful Maráthás, I gave in the last chapter. Meanwhile, he did not communicate to Típu the knowledge he had obtained of his intrigues, but continued, without a word of reproach, to receive from that prince letters expressive of the warmest regard and admiration for the

English. This action he justified in an enlightened minute, dated August 12th—a minute so declaratory of the reason which prompted his policy, that I feel compelled to extract largely from it:—

"If the conduct of Típu Sultán," wrote Lord Mornington on that date, "had been of a nature which could be termed ambiguous or suspicious; if he had merely increased his force beyond his ordinary establishment, or had stationed it in some position on our confines, or on those of our allies, which might justify jealousy or alarm; if he had renewed those secret intrigues at the courts of Haidrábád, Puná, and Kábul; or even if he had entered into any negotiation with France, or which the object was at all obscure, it might be our duty to resort in the first instance to his construction of proceedings, which being of a doubtful character, might admit of a satisfactory explanation. But where there was no doubt there could be no matter for explanation. The act of Típu's ambassadors, ratified by himself, and accompanied by the landing of a French force in this country, is a public, unqualified, and unambiguous, declaration of war, aggravated by an avowal, that the object of the war is neither explanation, reparation, nor security, but the total destruction of the British Government in India.

The affect of misunderstanding an injury or insult of such an incident, would either be of weakness or fear. No state in India can misconstrue the conduct of Típu; the correspondence of our residents at Haidarábád and Puná sufficiently manifests the construction which it bears at both those courts; and in so clear and plain a case, our demand of explanation would be justly attributed either to a defeat of spirit or of power. The result of such a demand would therefore be the disgrace of our character, and the diminution of our influence and consideration in the eyes of our allies, and of every other power in India. If the moment should appear favourable to the execution of Típu's declared design, he would answer such a demand by an immediate attack; if on the other hand, his preparations should not be sufficiently advanced, he would deny the existence of his engagements with France, would persist in his denial until he had reaped their full benefit and finally, after having completed the improvement of his own army, and receiving the accession of an additional French force, he would turn the combined strength of both against our possessions, with an alacrity and confidence inspired by our inaction, and with advantages redoubled by our delay. In the present case the idea, therefore, of demanding explanation must be rejected, as being disgraceful in its principle and frivolous in it's object.

In the same minute, Lord Mornington thus defined the grounds of complaint of the Government of India against the Sovereign of Maisure:—

"We complain, that, professing the most amicable disposition, bound by subsisting treaties of peace and friendship and unprovoked by any offence on our part, he has manifested a design to effect our total destruct on; he has prepared the means and instruments of a war of extermination against us; he has solicited and received the aid of our inveterate enemy for the declared purpose of annihilating our empire; and he only awaits the arrival of a more effectual succour to strike a blow at our existence."

In conclusion, the Governor-General thus defined the effect which the action, thus set forth, of Típu Sultán, was bound to produce on the administrators of the British authority in India:—

"Neither the measure of his hostility, nor of our right to restrain it, nor of our danger from it, are to be estimated by the amount of the force which he had actually obtained (from France), for we know that his demands of military assistance were unlimited; we know that they were addressed, not merely to the government of the Mauritius, but to that of France, and we cannot ascertain how soon they may be satisfied to the full amount of his acknowledged expectations. This, therefore, is not merely the case of an injury to be repaired, but of the public safety to be secure against the present and future designs of an irreconcilable, desperate, and treacherous enemy. Against an enemy of this description no effectual security can be obtained, otherwise then by such a reduction of his power, as shall not only defeat his actual preparations, but establish a permanent restraint upon his future means of offence."

The last sentence expresses in clear and forcible language the actual intentions of Lord Mornington with respect to the ruler of Maisur. He desired, by depriving him of the Malabar coast line, to render it impossible for him to communicate with the foreign nations of Europe. The action of Típu had proved most clearly that the maintenance of that line by a native prince was fraught with ever-continuous danger to British interests—a danger who have only known the British India of the present day, with all its native princes acknowledging the supermacy of the British, can hardly realise. To remain passive under the action of Típu was, in the opinion of Lord Mornington, to court destruction. There was no knowing when the French might land, as in the days of Lally and Bussy they had landed, in considerable numbers. There was no certainty that the neutrality of the five Maráthá powers would be long continued. Above all, there was the imminent danger that Típu, learning, as assuredly his father would have taken care to learn, the unpreparedness of the British, might make a dash at their weakest points, and appear before Madras before the news even that he had moved could reach Calcutta. Haidar had done the very thing, and it was not known then how great Típu was, in all the essentials of a daring leader, inferior to his father. In directing, then, the Madras Government to place the coast army on a war footing, to be ready to defend, or, if necessary, to strike, Lord Mornington was taking a precaution which, it would have been thought, should have recommended itself even to the most timid. We have seen that, on the contrary, it alarmed even the boldest, in Madras. We have witnessed the same kind of timidity in our own time—the timidity which may be expressed in the words that a nation must not take defensive precautions lest it should alarm its neighbour and provoke invasion; but it has always brought about the humiliation of the nation that was influenced by it. Happily for the British India of 1798-9, the prescient and courageous mind of Lord Mornington adopted, unhesitatingly, the straight course dictated by common sense.

To clear the British position, to deprive the prince, whose territories would flank an army operating against Típu Sultán, of the power to impede the movements of that army, Lord Mornington carried out in October the measure of disarming the auxiliary corps of sipáhis, officered by Frenchmen, described in the last chapter. This bold action produced an immense effect throughout India. It had a potent influence in securing the neutrality of the Maráthás, and it carried the conviction to every native prince in India, great and small, that the principles of the Shore Administration had been cast to the winds. The effect upon Típu I shall presently relate.

Four days before the disbandment at Haidarábád of the French contingent, that is, on October the 18th, Lord Mornington had received a despatch from the Secret Committee of the India House, informing him that a French fleet and army had sailed from Toulon on the 19th of May. The time of the departure of that fleet and army corresponded so very closely with the date, upon which an answer in force might be given by the French Directory to the urgent requests of Típu, that Lord Mornington recognised the necessity of further pressing the preparations of the Madras Government. A fortnight later, a despatch from England brought him information of the landing of the French in Egypt, and of the destruction of their fleet by Lord Nelson in Aboukir Bay. Up to that time the correspondence of Lord Mornington with the Sultán of Maisur had been a character which might be termed conciliatory. Some claims made by Típu to lands in the Wainád district had, after examination by two commissioners on the spot, been courteously admitted. Lord Mornington had made no remonstrance regarding the negotiations of the Sultán with France, because remonstrance might provoke hostilities, and, whilst the English at Madras were not ready, he had to take into consideration the existence of the French contingent of the Nizam. But the news of the destruction of the French fleet at Aboukir strengthened his position enormously; and as at that time the preparations at Madras were progressing, and orders had been issued for the disbandment of the French contingent at Haidarábád, he found himself in a position to speak very plainly. Yet, even then, Lord Mornington did not depart from the courteous and friendly tone of his previous communications. On November the 4th, he addressed to Típu a letter, in which he informed him of the unprovoked attack made by the French on the dominions of the Sultán of the Turkish Empire and the destruction of the French fleet. Whatever may have been the thoughts of Típu when he read this letter, he showed no evidence of concern or annoyance to appear in his reply. Four days later, November the 8th, the Governor-General, having in the meantime received information of the perfect success of the measures he had taken with respect to the French contingent at Haidarábád, wrote again to Típu, and on this occasion, for the first time, in a tone of remonstrance. Beginning by expressing the pleasure with which he had deputed two officers to examine on the spot into the validity of the claims made by the Sultán to some lands in the Wainád, Lord Mornington proceeded to state that he was well informed of the negotiations which had taken place between the Sultán and the French. Then, after mildly expostulating with him for entering upon friendly relations with people who had shown themselves to be the inveterate foes of public order and the enemies of the British; assuring him that his own views on this point were shared by the Peshwá and the Nizam; and that his and their one desire was the permanent security and tranquillity of their own dominions and subjects; he informed him that to ensure this end he proposed to depute to him an officer, Major Doveton, well known to him, who would explain to him more fully his views, "and particularly the sole means which appear to myself and the allies of the Company to be effectual for the salutary purpose of removing all existing distrust and suspicion, and of establishing peace and good understanding on the most durable foundations".

It is curious that the two Powers who distrusted each other should have expressed their alarm just about the same time. Lord Mornington's letter, of November the 8th, had not reached Típu when, on the 18th, that Prince wrote to the Governor-General to ask him whether the reports which had reached him that he was making warlike preparations were true. The tone of the letter was most friendly, indeed almost affectionate. The delays caused by the defective means of transit in those days may be gathered from the fact that this letter, dated November the 18th, reached Calcutta only on December the 15th following.

Típu was a bigot and a fatalist. The news of the destruction of the French fleet at Aboukir had not in the least impressed him. What concerned him most was that the French were in Egypt, and that Egypt was well on the road to India. The news that the English were arming disturbed him a little, for early action on their part might interfere somewhat with his plans. Still, he thought the balance between good and evil was in his favour. He wrote, then, in reply to Lord Mornington's letter of the 18th, to say that he did not care to see Major Doveton, as existing treaties were a sufficient security for him, and that he could imagine no other means more binding. Then, having a presentiment that the object of the Governor-General was to deprive him of his coast-line, so as to cut off his direct communication with France, he sent envoys to Puná, to Kábul, to the Isle of France, even to Constantinople, to solicit prompt co-operation. He had resolved to use the opportunity which seemed to him to occur by the proximity of the French to strike a blow for his lost dominions. Lord Mornington's letter, of November 8th, produced then but little effect upon him. "If the evil must arrive tomorrow," he said, "let it rather arrive to-day."

He was more disturbed by a second letter from the Governor-General, dated December 10th. In that letter Lord Mornington, who had not then received Típu's reply to his letter of November the 8th, earnestly pressed for an answer to that letter, and stated that he was about to proceed to

Madras to be at hand for the purpose of negotiating. Típu still trusted so much to his power to deceive that, though startled by this information, he believed that a fabulous story of his negotiations with France would impose upon the Governor-General. But when he heard that Lord Mornington had reached Madras, December the 31st, for the purpose of dealing with him in person, his courage somewhat gave way. It receded still further when, a few days later, he received from that lord a letter, dated January 9th, remonstrating with him for his rejection of the proposed envoy; reciting in full detail the whole of his hostile proceedings at the Isle of France; enclosing a Persian translation of General Malartic's proclamation; explaining the necessity imposed upon himself and his allies of seeking relief from this ambiguous state of supposed peace, which was in reality no peace; adding his serious and solemn admonition to assent to the reception of the envoy he was sending; urging him not to postpone an answer for more than one day; and concluding by warning him that "dangerous consequences result from the delay of arduous affairs".

This despatch was, in very deed, a revelation to Típu. Up to that moment he really believed that his impudent fables had imposed upon the credulous Frank. It seemed to arouse him, as it were, from a dream. Engrossed by the sense of additional importance occurring to himself from having as an ally a Power which had defined combined Europe, he had never allowed his imagination to dwell in the consequences which might follow a premature disclosure of his negotiations with that Power, before receiving from her any substantial assistance. And now those consequences were, he realised as he read Lord Mornington's letter, at his very door. A true despot of the oriental type, he sought in the first moments of his anger to wreak his vengeance on the instruments he had employed, through whose imprudence, he persuaded himself, the secret had transpired. Finding, however, but little relief in such action from the necessities imposed upon him by the still unanswered letter; recognising that the practical result of all his intrigues was absolutely fruitless; he was sorely tempted, and had almost resolved, to throw himself upon Lord Mornington's mercy, and to receive the envoy. But, with the indecision of a fatalist—who believes that the next throw of the dice may be in his favour—daily receiving from the French agents at his Court assurances that the French force intended to assist him must by that time have sailed from Suez, and might arrive at any moment, he hesitated and hesitated. Day followed day, and he had despatched no reply. It was to no purpose that, five days later, he received from Lord Mornington a copy of a letter from the Sublime Porte to his address, a letter in which the French were denounced as enemies of all true Muhammadans, and which enclosed a copy of the declaration of war on the part of Turkey against the aggressive Republic. Lord Mornington, in despatching these documents to Típu, had added an earnest appeal to his better nature.

> "May the admonition of the head of your faith," he wrote, "dispose your mind to the pacific propositions which I have repeatedly, but in vain, submitted to your wisdom. And may you at length receive the ambassador who will be empowered to conclude the definite arrangement of all differences between you and the allies, and to secure the tranquillity of India against the disturbers of the world."

Still, Típu could not bring his mind to the point of coming to a decision. All January, Lord Mornington's letters remained unanswered. And when, early in February, the necessity of acknowledging the receipt of the letter from the Sublime Porte could no longer be postponed, the ruler of Maisur attempted to evade a direct reply to Lord Mornington's earnest appeal by the announcement—under the circumstances, the insolent announcement—that he was about to start on a shooting expedition. The announcement ran thus: "Being frequently disposed to make excursions and hunt, I am accordingly proceeding on a shooting expedition; you will be pleased to despatch Major Doveton (about whose coming your friendly pen has repeatedly written), slightly attended (or unattended)."

But, before that letter reached its destination, Lord Mornington had been forced by Típu's long silence to reschedule his departure. The Governor-General had come to Madras so that he could be at hand to confer with Típu. His letter earnestly requesting an immediate reply had been despatched on January 9th, from Madras. The distance thence to Seringapatam was but three hundred miles, a distance which might be traversed by the means at the Governor-General's disposal in six days. Yet January had passed, and no reply had been received to that letter, or to that despatched a week later, covering the missive from the Ottoman Porte. It was evident to Lord Mornington that he was being played with. Believing that Típu's object was to cause delay till the rainy season should set in, and learning that the Maisur sovereign had despatched another envoy to the French, he determined to be fooled no longer. Accordingly, on February 3rd, he issued instructions to the Commander-in-Chief of the Madras army, General Harris, to enter the Maisur territory with the army assembled at Vellur; and to General Stuart, commanding in Bombay, to operate from Malabar. General Harris had actually begun his forward movement (February 11th), when, on the 13th, Lord Mornington received from Típu the reply which I have quoted. With his natural shrewdness he detected at once the motive which had prompted it.

> "The design," he wrote, "is evidently to gain time until a change of circumstance and of season shall enable him to avail himself of the assistance of France. I shall endeavour to frustrate this design; and although I shall not decline even this tardy and insiduous acceptance of my repeated propositions for opening a negotiation, I shall accompany the negotiation by the movement of the army, for the purpose of enforcing such terms of peace as shall give effectual security to the Company's possessions against any hostile consequences of the Sultán's alliance with the French."

Acting upon this principle, Lord Mornington, in his reply to Típu, dated February 22nd, expressed his sincere regret that his urgent representation of the danger of delay had produced no effect, and that the Sultán had postponed all notice of his admonitions until the late on setting of the season rendered the advance of the army necessary for the safety of the allies; that the mission of Major Doveton was therefore no longer expedient; but that General Harris would receive any embassy the Sultán might despatch. He was further informed that General Harris had been directed to despatch this letter to him on the day the British army crosses the Maisur border; and to issue on the same day the Governor-General's proclamation, a copy of which was sent to Típu by the same means.

The proclamation of Lord Mornington, dated February 22nd, bears the impression of the strong, decisive, and vigorous intellect which conceived it. Beginning by enumerating the various proofs he had given of his earnest desire to cultivate friendly relations with Típu Sultán, of the decisions in his favour on the question of boundary disputes, and of the absence of all complaints on the part of the Maisur ruler, Lord Mornington proceeded to express "the astonishment and indignation" which he and his allies had experienced, when, at the very moment the British Government had confirmed his claim to the lands in the Wainád, they had learned of the engagements he had contracted with the French nation, "in direct violation of the Treaty of Seringapatam, as well as of his own most solemn and recent protestations of friendship towards the allies".

Enumerating, then, in full detail all the efforts the Government of British India had made to induce the Sultán to enter into the paths of loyal friendship, Lord Mornington came to the famous reply to his earnest warnings and remonstrances of January 9th and 14th, the reply in which the Sultán announced his intention of proceeding on a shooting expedition:

> "The allies," continued the proclamation, "will not dwell on the peculiar phrases of this letter: but it must be

evident to all the States of India that the answer of the Sultán has been deferred to this late period of the season with no reason other than to preclude the allies, by insidious delays, from the benefit of those advantages which their combined military operations would enable them to secure." Announcing, then, that "the allies cannot suffer Típu Sultán to profit by his own studied and systematic delay;" recounting how, during three months, he had "obstinately rejected every pacific overture in the hourly expectation of receiving the succour which he has eagerly solicited for the prosecution of his favourite purposes of ambition and revenge;" Lord Mornington concluded by declaring that the allies, equally prepared to repel the violence and to counteract the artifices and delay of the Sultán, "are therefore resolved to place their army in such a position as shall afford adequate protection against any artifice or insincerity, and shall preclude the return of that danger which has lately so menaced their possessions."

He added, however that as they were animated by an anxious desire to effect an adjustment with Típu Sultán, the Commander of the British Army, General Harris, "is authorised to receive any ambassador which Típu Sultán may despatch to the head-quarters of the British army, and to conclude a treaty on such conditions as may appear to the allies to be indispendably necessary for the establishment of a secure and durable peace".

Típu was thus afforded the time and the opportunity to save himself. Had he obeyed the first promptings of his heart when he received Lord Mornington's letter of January 9th, and, confessing his misdeeds, had promised reform, he would still undoubtedly have had to consent to being shorn of that part of his dominions which secured to him a seaport on the Malabar coast, but he would have been allowed to retain the still considerable remainder. As it was, he completely outwitted himself. When he despatched the insolent reply to Lord Mornington, intimating that he was about to proceed on a shooting expedition, he actually started to see how best he could surprise the English troops commanded by General Stuart before they should be ready. He did actually attack a portion of that general's army on March 6th, the very day after General Harris had crossed the frontier at another point. War thus became inevitable.

Into the details of that war it is no part of this book to enter. Begun, in the manner related, on March 6th, admirably conducted by General Harris, who personally directed all the details to the movements of the army he commanded, it was brought to a close on May 4th, by the storming of Seringapatam and the death of Típu Sultán. Then it was that it devolved upon the Governor-General to determine in what manner the territories which Haidar Álí had robbed from the Hindu dynasty, of which he had been originally the servant, should be treated.

The task was one which called forth the display of the qualities of a statesman. Lord Mornington had not only to satisfy the just claims which his own Government might prefer—claims which, even before the war had begun, pointed to the secession of the Maisur principality from the sea—but he had to think of those who, under the name of allies, had contributed more or less to the success of the compaign. Those allies were the Nizam and the Peshwá. The former, became, by Lord Mornington's own bold policy, a protected ally; the latter still as independent as were the English. But, whereas the Maráthás had borne no part whatsoever in the war, whilst the Nizam had contributed to it all the resources of his territories, it seemed to the Governor-General to be highly unfair that they should benefit equally from the success which had been achieved. And yet it was necessary to take care so as to act to avoid giving just umbrage to a power which was preponderant in Western and predominant in Central and North-Western India. How Lord Mornington felt on this delicate point was expressed by him in his despatch on the subject to the Court of Directors:

"To have divided the whole territory," he wrote, "between the Company and the Nizam, to the exclusion of any other State, would have afforded strong ground of jealousy to the Maráthás, and aggrandized the Nizam's power beyond all bounds of discretion. Under whatever form such a partition could have been made, it must have placed in the hands of the Nizam many strong fortresses in the northern frontier of Maisur, and exposed our frontier in that quarter to every predatory incursion. Such a partition would have laid the foundation of perpetual differences, not only between the Maráthás and the Nizam, but between the Company and both those Powers.

"To have divided the country into three equal portions, allowing the Maráthás (who had borne no part in the expense or házard of the war) an equal share with the other two branches of the triple alliance, in the advantages of the peace, would have ben unjust towards the Nizam and the Company; impolitics as furnishing an evil example to other allies in India, and dangerous as effecting a considerable aggrandizement of the Maráthá Empire at the expense of the Company and the Nizam. This mode of partition, also, must have placed Chitaldrug and some of the most important northern fortresses in the hands of the Maráthás, while the remainder of the fortresses in the same line would have been occupied by the Nizam, and our unfortified and open frontier in Maisur would have been exposed to the excesses of the undisciplined troops of both Powers."

Proceeding, then, to state that the Maráthás had no claim to any portion of the conquered territory, Lord Mornington added:

"It was, however, desirable to conciliate their goodwill, and to offer them such a portion of territory as might give them an interest in the new settlement without offence or injury to the Nizam, and without danger to the frontier of the Company's possessions. On the other hand, it was prudent to limit the territory retained in the hands of the Company and of the Nizam within such bounds of moderation as should bear a due proportion to their respective expenses in the contest, and to the necessary means of securing the public safety of their respective dominions."

Lord Mornington then proceeded to declare how, acting on the lines thus laid down, he would deal with the territories which lay, without a recognised sovereign, prostrate at the feet of General Harris. To the representative of the ancient Hindu dynasty, then a body five years old, he would reserve a portion of the country, including the capital, the plateau of Bangalore, and other districts towards the sea cost, but the nearest served from the sea by a distance of fifteen miles, the whole yielding then (though it has since more than doubled) an annual revenue of about £5000,000. During the minority of the Rájah the resources of the country should be controlled and husbanded by a British Resident, and, on attaining his majority, the Rájah should be under the suzerainty of the British. To the British and the Nizam, portions of territory of equal value, yielding revenues to the amount of about £250,000 annually, would be assigned; whilst the Maráthás were to obtain a tract somewhat more than half the value of that assigned to the Nizam. But it was not the amount of revenue which constituted the main value of the territories obtained by the British. In coming into possession of the districts of Kanará, Koimbatur, Darapuram, and Mujnad, with all the territory laying below the gháts, between their possessions in the Karnátik and those in Malabar, they acquired valuable districts assuring uninterrupted communication between the eastern and western coasts of the Peninsula, the entire sea-coast of the kingdom of Maisur, and territories constituting the base of all the eastern, western, and southern gháts. To these were added the forts and posts forming the heads of all the passes above the gháts on the table land, with the fortress, city, and island of Seringapatam. The occupation for a term of about twelve years—the period of the minority of the young Rájah—would, moreover, assure to the English the time, which more than any other nation they have known how to employ, of procuring to the inhabitants, by the development of industrial enterprises, alleviation from the miseries they had suffered from years of misrule.

So far as this related to the British and the Nizam, there was complete understanding regarding the terms of the Treaty. But the condition on which the Peshwá should be invited to become a party to it differed, as I have already shown, in almost every particular form which concerned the Nizam. Lord Mornington thought, then, that high policy forbade him to offer to the Maráthá Prince, without something in the shape of an equivalent, territory as a reward for mere nominal service. The Peshwá had not put a man in the field, nor had he spent a rupee in preparations. He had been absolutely passive. In return for this, the action of the British and the Nizam had secured for him a peaceful neighbour on his south-western frontier in exchange for a neighbour who had been one of the greatest enemies of his race. If the Peshwá, then, were to obtain anything in the shape of territory, in addition to that sense of security, Lord Mornington thought that he should be asked to give something in exchange. That something might be shadowy, but it must possess the appearance at least of value, sufficient to constitute the basis of a contract. Carrying out this view, Lord Mornington proposed that in return for the territory which he was prepared to cede from the conquered kingdom of Maisur the Peshwá should guarantee the inviolability of the new kingdom; that he should constitute the East India Company arbiter of his disputes with the Nizam; that he should not admit Europeans into his service; and that he should enter into a defensive treaty against the French in case they should invade India. It seemed to Lord Mornington that as he was offering a solid substantiality in the shape of territory producing an annual revenue of about Rs. 12,00,000, in return for which he demanded only a few words, which, his Indian experience of little more than a year must have proved to him would only be binding so long as no strong temptation to break them should arise, the Peshwá would hasten to agree; that at the most he would only require a modification on the subject of the admission of Europeans into his service. But he was deceived. The Peshwá peremptorily demanded equal partition of the conquered territory with the Company and the Nizam, and declined to render any counter-gift of promises. As for the smaller portion with the conditions annexed to it, he indignantly refused it. That portion was, therefore, divided between the Nizam and the British.*

One word must be said as to the reasons which prompted Lord Mornington's policy to restore the Hindu dynasty of Maisur, instead of permitting the succession of a son of the deceased Sultán. It might have been argued that as the Governor-General had recognised Típu, had even been prepared to treat with him regarding the rearrangement of his frontier, and would most certainly have recognised a member of his family as his successor had Típu died before hostilities had broken out, it was reasonable that he should now pursue a similar course. But in Lord Mornington's opinion the schemes perpetrated by the deceased Sultán—schemes aiming at the expulsion by any means of the British

---

* The fate of the portion of the Maisur territory assigned to the Nizam is curious. In the first division he received districts yielding annually about 24,00,000 Rs. To these were subsequently added two-thirds of the territory offered to but rejected by the Peshwá, amounting to about 8,00,000 Rs. more. But all the territories thus acquired, as well as those acquired by the Treaty of 1792, and yielding altogether an annual revenue of about 100,00,000 Rs., were, in 1800, ceded to the British in perpetuity to defray the expenses of the subsidiary force, then augmented to 8,000 infantry, 1,000 cavalry, and a proportion of artillery. It was stipulated in this Treaty that, in the event of war, 6,000 infantry of this force with the cavalry and artillery, joined by 6,000 foot and 9,000 horse of the Nizam's own troops, should be under orders to march against the common enemy. (*Vide Aitchison's Treaties,* Vio. V.) The practical result, then, of the covenant made by Lord Mornington with the Nizam was that the spoils obtained by the latter from Típu Sultán in the wars of 1789-92, and of 1799, purchased a British guarantee for the Nizam's dominions, as they had been in 1789; and placed him absolutely in the position of a protected prince, bound to follow the fortunes of the British

from India—were so ingrained in his family that it would be in the highest degree impolitie to recognise a successor, born and brought up in those ideas, who sooner or later would develop similar idiosyncracies. It was true that the parcelling out of a considerable portion of the dominions of the Sultán would deprive his successor of much of the power for mischief which Típu had enjoyed. But if that successor was a son of Típu there would be perpetual brooding over past losses; a continuous searching for an opportunity to retrieve the disasters of 1799; the necessity would consequently be imposed upon the British Government to remain in a perpetual state of watchfulness, perhaps even, should war occur with the Maráthás, of alarm. To place upon the vacant throne, on the other hand, the representative of the dynasty which Haidar had removed, would be to secure a ruler who would be bound to the British by ties of gratitude; who would be acceptable to the Hindu races who constituted the vast majority of the population of Maisur; and who represented the ancient Royal line, endeared to them more miseries they had suffered at the hands of the tyrants who had expelled it. Influenced by these considerations, which he set forth at great length in a despatch to the Court of Directors, dated August 3rd, 1799, Lord Mornington appointed Commissioners to instal the young Rájah on the *masnad** This ceremony was performed with great pomp on June the 30th of the same year.

The reader will not fail to notice the wisdom of the policy which ditated this action. Not only was an inveterate enemy of the British race removed for ever from the control of territories which had been used before, and might be used again to the detriment of the Company; not only was that hostile family replaced by another family bound to be as hostile to it as it must be dependent on the British; but to guard against possibilities that new family was not entrusted with the power of peace or war. It was forbidden to maintain an army. For an annual subsidy of £280,000, the British

* *Masnad*, a throne, a royal cushion.

Government undertook to secure the defence and protection of the restored territories. The British likewise expressly reserved to themselves the right, which was exercised in 1831-2, of interfering in the management of the internal affairs of the country whenever high policy should demand such interference; and, further, of increasing when it might be necessary, the amount of the subsidy to be paid by the Rájah. Meanwhile, until that prince should obtain his majority, one of the ablest political officers of the day, Sir Barry Close, was appointed to reside in his capital as Resident, whilst the troops necessary to keep in the country for the maintenance of order were placed under the command of Colonel Arthur Wellesley.

Thus, within thirteen months of his arrival in India, the successor of a *doctrinaire,* Lord Mornington had settled two important, I might say indeed with truth, two vital questions, which he had found awaiting him, and which the policy questions, which he had found awaiting him, and which the policy of "masterly inactivity" of his predecessor had caused to assume enormous proportions. He had found Southern India smouldering; its independent princes ready to pour forth their hordes upon the English; the English unprepared even for a light attack; Anglo-Indian statesmen unwilling to make preparations lest thereby they should provoke a contest. The danger was vast, imminent, pressing, the more so as the greatest military power of Europe, in alliance with a native prince whose hostility to the English was inveterate, was occupying at the moment the country which was the halfway house to India. By a policy patient yet farseeing, mainly, direct, and statesmanlike, Lord Mornington averted both those dangers. He had scarcely landed in India when he recognised that his hands were tied. The danger was in Southern India, and the army in Southern India was not in a condition to fight. He had to meet two dangers the danger from the contingent of the Nizam, commanded by Frenchmen; and the danger from Típu Sultán. Till he was strong enough to meet the lesser of these he temporised and made preparations. In five months he had made himself strong enough to meet the Nizam's case. Acting then with the directness of purpose which was his great characteristic, he disposed off for ever that danger. He treated the Nizam as in 1871 Prussia treated the German princes; he deprived him, whilst guaranteeing his dominions, of all power of treating with foreign nations. He was not then quite ready for the inveterate enemy of England. He had ample proof of his treachery and hostile intentions; and he knew that any sudden action on the part of the French, then always possible—for France had still a navy—might add enormously to the difficulties of the situation. Still he waited again patiently, exercising a forbearance which, under the knowledge he possessed, must have chafed him sorely. He did more. He strove with all his might to effect a peaceful solution of the question. When his preparations were sufficiently advanced to enable him to speak without any fear of the consequences of speaking plainly, he acquainted the doomed prince with his knowledge of his plots and his intrigues, set before him his danger, and offered still to treat on terms which would have left him by far the greater part of his territories. It was not till his offers, first received with silence, had been finally responded to with insult, that he showed his whole hand to his enemy. Showing it, he still offered terms. But the enemy was bent on war. Típu precipitated by twenty-four hours the hostilities which were about to break out, and, rushing upon his fate, lost alike his throne and his life. Lord Mornington had, by his statesmanlike action, not only averted the second danger, but made a second settlement, which, like the first, has lasted till our own day—a settlement which secured the permanent predominance of the British in South-Eastern and in South-Western India. In the hands of such a man, from whatever quarter danger or difficulty might arise, British interests, it was clear, were safe.

6

Wellesley's Problems

Tanjur, Surat, Haidarabad, The Karnatik, Oudh, Persia, Kabul, Egypt. 1799-1801

Lord Wellesley's rewards and his disappointment—State of affairs in Tanjur—Removal of Amir Singh, and conclusion of a treaty with the Rajah—Settlement of the Surat difficulty—Rejection of Lord Wellesley's proposals by the Nawab of the Karnatik—Discovery of his intrigues with Tipu—Death of the Nawab and conditions of the treaty with his successor—Regulation of our relations with the Nizam—Disorderly condition of Oudh—Missions of Colonel Scott and Mr. Henry Wellesley—Surrender of the Nawab-Wazir—The Governor-General at Kanpur—Persia and Afghanistan—The French excluded from Persia—Danger from the Isle of France and Bourbon—Difficulties in the way of their capture—Summary of Lord Wellesley's foreign policy.

Henceforth we must think and write of the famous Governor-General as the Marquess Wellesley. For the services he had rendered in Southern India the Houses of Parliament unanimously passed a vote of thanks to him, as well as to Lord Clive, Mr. Duncan (Governor of Bombay), and the army engaged in the war. The East India Company passed resolutions expressive of their admiration of the important services rendered to them by their servants in the East. King George III testified his sense of the Governor-General's conduct by raising him to the dignity of Marquess in the peerage of Ireland. Pitt wrote to him: — "At this moment, my dear Lord, you are the admiration of all Europe. May you long enjoy the glorious laurels you have gained, in health, happiness, and every domestic blessing. . . I hear Lord Cornwallis talks with rapture and surprise of your noble administration in India, and he is a good judge." He received letters of similar import from all his friends.

Still, it cannot be concealed that Lord Wellesley was disappointed at the nature of the reward bestowed upon him by his Sovereign. Knowing better than any one in Europe, the greatness of his success, he felt that the recompense fell far short of his deserving. In a letter, dated April 28th, 1800, to the address of Mr. Pitt, he wrote that he could not describe his anguish of mind in feeling himself bound by every sense of duty and honour to declare his bitter disappointment at the reception which the King had given to his services, and at the ostensible mark of favour which he had conferred upon him. In England, as in India, he went on to say, the disproportion between the service and the reward would be imputed to some opinion existing in the King's mind of his being disqualified by some personal incapacity to receive the reward of his conduct. He left him (Mr. Pitt) to judge what the effect of such an impression was likely to be on the minds of those whom he was appointed to govern—and more to the purport. To a private friend he wrote that he would never have health or happiness till this outrage was required. There can be no doubt that he did regard this Irish Marquisate as an outrage, and he felt it so to the end of his life. Writing, many years later, to Lord Harris, when the Government tardily recognised the services of that excellent officer by bestowing upon him a peerage (1816), Lord Wellesley said that none of the subsequent triumphs of his life could drive from his memory the recollection of the scurvy manner in which he had been treated in 1800. He had, I think ample reason for his dissatisfaction. His services had been immense; his reward was, to use his own expression, "pinchbeck."

It deserves to be recorded that in the distribution of the plunder of Seringapatam, Marquess Wellesley had displayed the greatest self-abnegation. The army, sensible that to his foresight, his preparations, his energy, the triumph that had been achieved was mainly due, had expressed a desire to present to him a star and badge of the order of St. Patrick, composed of Tipu's jewels, but Lord Wellesley from motives of delicacy had declined the present; nor was it till the Court of Directors begged him to accept the star and badge, "as a testimony of the very high sense which they entertain of the distinguished services to the Company of the Most Noble the Marquess Wellesley, by the superior wisdom and energy of whose counsels the late war in Maisur was brought to so speedy and glorious a termination," that he was prevailed upon to take them. He declined, however, the donation of £1000,000, offered by the Court, "from the spoils taken at Seringapatam." "I am satisfied," he wrote to the President of the Board of Control, "upon reflection, you will perceive that the accepting such a grant would place me in a very humiliating situation with respect to the army; and, independent of any question of character, or of the dignity or vigour of government, I should be miserable if I could ever feel that I had been enriched at the expense of those who must ever be the objects of my affection, admiration, and gratitude, and who are justly entitled to the exclusive possession of all that a munificent King and an admiring country can bestow." Subsequently, the Court of Directors voted him a pension of £5,000 a year for twenty years. With that, and the "double-gilt potato," as he styled it in a letter to Pitt, the Irish Marquisate, he had to be content.

But, deeply though in this respect the iron had entered into his soul, the mortification in no degree affected the zeal and energy which the Marquess brought to bear on the administration of Indian affairs. Prominent amongst those which demanded his attention had been the State of Tanjur.

The affairs of that State had for some years caused anxiety to the Madras Government. In 1786, the ruling Rajah, Tulijai, had died, leaving an adopted son, Sarboji, then in tender years, to succeed him. The succession of Sarboji was, however, disputed by the half-brother of the deceased prince, Amir Singh, and the question was referred to the Madras Government for decision. The conduct of that Government was characterised by a childish unwisdom which did not augur favourably of the ability of its members to deal generally with affairs. They appointed Amir Singh to act as regent during the minority of his rival. Meanwhile they nominated a council of pandits to decide the question of succession according to Hindu law. The natural consequences followed. Although, according to the law which had been invoked, the claims of Sarboji were beyond question, the pandits, influenced by the man who held in his hands the power of the State, decided in favour of Amir Singh.

Amir Singh was, in the worst sense of the word, a tyrant. No sooner had his claim been recognised than he began a career of oppression, which very soon compelled the Madras Government to interfere. The party of Sarboji was still strong in the State. Sarboji, the widows of the late Rajah, and their prominent partisans, had therefore been especially made to feel the jealous dislike of the tyrant. The first step of the Madras Government, after its attention had been repeatedly called to their complaints was to remove the boy and the ladies to the Presidency. There the question of the boy's right to the throne was again brought forward, and, after some delay, was referred by the Madras Government to the then Governor-General, Sir John Shore. Sir John, in his turn, consulted the pundits in different parts of India; finally, those of the holy city of Banaras. These gave an unreserved opinion in favour of the rights of Sarboji. The papers on the question were then transmitted to England, and the Court of Directors ordered that Sarboji should be placed on the throne of Tanjur, though they left the time and mode of carrying their decision into effect to be determined by the Governor-General.

Such was the position of the Tanjúr question when Marquess Wellesley had arrived in India. He had well considered it on the voyage out, and he had decided not to deal with it until the more pressing affairs of the Nizam and of Tipu Sultan should be settled. In the autumn of 1799 that conjuncture had arrived, and Lord Wellesley at once took up the dropped thread of Tanjur. That country had been reduced by the misgovernment of Amir Singh to the worst throes of misery. The wretchedness of its distressed and despoiled people, ground down by the minions of the ruling prince, can scarcely be exaggerated. To transfer these unfortunates, like so many cattle, from a prince, who had reduced them to their miserable condition, to a young man, who, however amiable he might appear, possessed neither talents nor experience of governing, and who was almost certain, therefore, to drift into the worst ways of his predecessor, was a course against which the generous mind of Lord Wellesley revolted. Indian governors have very often been placed in the cruel position of having to perpetrate acts, apparently demanded by strict legality, but really fraught with misery to thousands of human beings, lest by refusal they should bring upon their heads the vials of wrath of inexperienced sentimentalists. In such circumstances a weak man will succumb; a strong man will act according to his conviction of right. Lord Wellesley was a strong man, and he acted accordingly. He removed Amir Singh; but unable to find it in his heart to place the people of Tanjur under the irresponsible sway of a zenanabred boy, absolutely without experience of the world, he made with him a Treaty, whereby the civil and military administration of the country should be vested in the British Government; an allowance of the equivalent of £10,000 per annum reserved for Aamir Singh, and one of £40,000 for the Rajah, who likewise was to receive all the honours attached to his position. This arrangement, Mr. Thornton justly remarks, was undoubtedly beneficial to the interests of Great Britain. No one who knows aught of India can fail to agree with that historian when he adds:— "but it is no exaggeration to say that it was far more beneficial to the people of Tanjur. It exonerated them from the effects of native oppression and European cupidity. It gave them what they had never before possessed—the security derived from the administration of justice." The Treaty, embodying the provisions stated, was concluded October the 25th, 1799, and ratified by the Governor-General in Council November the 29th following.

Another case of deadlock, the case of Súrat, had likewise been awaiting the settlement of claims more pressing. The town of Súrat on the Taptí had been one of the first which had attracted the commerce of Great Britain. Her merchants had built a factory there in 1612. Subsequently, the factors and writers of the Company had aided the native inhabitants to defend the town against the great Maráthá, the renowned Sívájí—a service which procured for them the thanks of the Mughul Governor. A century later, upon the invitation of the most powerful party in the country, they took possession of the castle and of the native fleet, as the *de facto* administrators of the town and its immediate surroundings, and this act was shortly afterwards confirmed by the Imperial Court of Delhí. I should add that, to this transfer of authority, the ruling Nawáb, whose power was thereby curtailed, had been a consenting party.

Had the Mughul authority at Delhí continued to exist in all its pristine vigour, it is probable that the Nawáb would have continued to acquiese in an arrangement which not only relieved him from great responsibilities, but secured the safety and prosperity of the town. But the fall of the Mughul Empire seemed to open out a new career to every petty princelet throughout India, and the Nawáb of Súrat was unable to resist the impetus which had carried away so many others. Step by step he began to assert his independence of his western coadjutors. At length he proceeded to decline to furnish the funds absolutely necessary for maintaining, in a state of efficiency, the military and naval forces required for the protection of the place. Entreaty and remonstrance met alike with refusal. As the Company was dependent on the

Nawáb for the requisite funds, his refusal to contribute naturally produced a deadlock. Matters were in this unsatisfactory state when, in 1799, the Nawáb died. Death is a great leveller of difficulties, especially when the material force is in the hands of a disputant who survives. The continuance of the *status quo* had become impossible, because, of the two parties whose co-operation was necessary to propel the State vehicle, one had refused his assistance. Lord Wellesley had long seen that "a dual control," to be exercised by two parties, whose interests pulled them in opposite directions, must terminate in failure. He determined, then, to put an end to it. Fortune singularly favoured him. A very short time after the death of the Nawáb his only son followed him to the grave. The next heir was the uncle of the deceased, and the uncle could not inherit without the permission of the British. Lord Wellesley had, then, the game in his own hands. He used the opportunity wisely and well. The lines upon which he acted were the lines of Tanjúr. He made a Treaty with the incoming Nawáb, by which "the management and collection of the revenues of the city of Súrat, and of the territories, places, and other dependencies thereof, the administration of civil and military justice, and generally the whole civil and military government of the said city and its dependencies should be vested for ever, entirely and exclusively, in the Honourable East India Company." A lakh of rupees was set aside annually for the maintenance of the Nawáb, who was to retain his honours and dignities. These arrangements were embodied in a Treaty which was signed by the consenting parties on May the 13th, 1800.

There remained still the Nawáb of the Karnátik. For many years the relations between the Madras Government and the ruler of the territories so denominated had been very unsatisfactory. The Nawáb, utterly careless of the engagements entered into by his father and himself for the maintenance of a subsidiary force, was becoming every year more and more involved in debts, which he took not the smallest pains to discharge. Europeans, unprincipled but shrewd, carried on the vile intrigues at his Court and with his connivance. The revenue was badly managed, the people were oppressed, and ruin was fast overtaking the country which he professed to administer. Unfortunately, the last Treaty made by the British with the Nawáb, the Treaty of 1792, had contained a clause which secured to the Nawáb absolute control over the territories thereby secured to him. Not only, then, did he meet the proposals made to him by Lord Wellesley after the conclusion of the war with Típu, and which had for their object the cession of a portion of his territories as a set-off against his debts, by a reference to the Treaty of 1792 and a question as to whether the terms of that Treaty were still binding; but he added thereto a demand to participate in the distribution of the territories just then severed from Maisur. Though Lord Wellesley was able to treat this demand with the indifference it merited, he was puzzled how to deal with the "*non possumus*" with which the Nawáb replied to every request to give valid security for reform. That he recognised the course which ought to be pursued and yet felt most strongly the difficulty in the way of pursuing it, is proved by his correspondence at this period with the Court of Directors. In a despatch to that august body, dated March the 5th, 1800, he wrote:— "The double government of the Karnátik is a difficulty which continues to present the most serious and alarming obstacles to every attempt at reform. . . I am thoroughly convinced that no effectual remedy can ever be applied to the evils which afflict that country, without obtaining from the Nawáb powers at least as extensive as those vested in the Company by the late Treaty of Tanjúr." But from the ruling Nawáb, who had succeeded his father, the notorious Muhammad Alí, in 1795, there was no hope that he would ever obtain the smallest concession. He was, however, comparatively old, given to debauchery, and his life as precarious. Lord Wellesley could only hope, then, that on his death he might be able to make conditions with his successor which would enable the paramount power to remedy the crying evils which characterised the administration of territories so closely adjacent to the possessions of the Company.

The Nawáb having repulsed, in the manner already described, the attempts made by Lord Wellesley to reform his administration, that lord, precluded by the Treaty of 1792 from attempting forcible entry, had almost abandoned the task in despair, when there arrived, at Madras, boxes containing the correspondence found in the archives of Típu Sultán, at Seringapatam. The perusal of this correspondence, which was officially examined by two officers of the highest honour, Colonel barry Close and Mr. Webbe, made it abundantly clear that for many years past the Nawáb and his father had been carrying on a treasonable correspondence with the Sultán of Maisur; that they had communicated to Típu such secrets regarding the British preparations and the British objects as had been entrusted to them; that they had, in fact, acted as secret friends and true allies of the prince, who, they knew (as the correspondence revealed), was endeavouring to form a league with the princes of India and the French for the expulsion of the English from India.

The revelation of this correspondence cleared the way for the action which Lord Wellesley had already hoped to put in force when a just opportunity should offer. But, in such a matter, it was above all necessary to show no indecent haste. Lord Wellesley waited, then, until due investigations had been made regarding the correspondence; he then considered it in council; then referred it, with his own comments, to the Board of Control. The Board of Control and the Court of Directors coincided in the views he had set forth. Then, and then only, did Lord Wellesley acted on those views. In a despatch to the Madras Government, dated May 28, 1801, he recounted the perfidy alike of the Nawáb and of his father; showed from the correspondence that the actual Nawáb had been confederate with his father in the machinations secretly carried on against the British; that as a party, likewise, to the Treaty of 1792, with the British, which he had negotiated, he was subject to the same conditions which his father had accepted. He concluded by directing the Governor of Madras, Lord Clive, to propose a new Treaty to he Nawáb, requiring him to cede the civil and military government of the Karnátik to the East India Company. Lord Wellesley wrote at the same time to the Nawáb himself, informing him of the discoveries which had been made, and referring him to the Governor of Madras for information as to the footing upon which his position would be placed in the future. That letter was never read by the Nawáb. When it reached his palace at Arkát, that prince was dying, nor, had he been physically sound, would the state of his mind have permitted him to understand its contents. Those contents were, therefore, mercifully withheld. But when, on July 15th following, he died, and his reputed son declined to accept the succession on the new terms offered by the Governor of Madras, Lord Clive made the arrangement, directed by Lord Wellesley, with another relative of the deceased, Azímu'd daulah. With him a Treaty was concluded, whereby the territories known as the Karnátik should be administered by the Company; whilst the title of Nawáb, with a suitable income for the maintenance of its dignity, should be secured to the holder of that title, and to his successors. Order thus replaced disorder; good government, bad government; justice, oppression. Yet, naturally enough, this transaction, which rebounds to the honour of the Marquess Wellesley, has been used by doctrinaires and sentimentalists to hold him up to reprobation. One of the ablest of this impractical body has gone so far as to insinuate that he caused the incriminating letters to be forged. The charge has only to be made to be repelled with indignation and disgust. If, it has been well observed, the documents were forged, not only must the Governor-General have been the grand mover of the forgery, but General Harris, General Baird, Colonel Arthur Wellesley, Colonel Close, the Hon. Henry Wellesley, Captain Macaulay, Mr. Edmonstone the interpreter, and Mr. Webbe the secretary to the Government, must have been "the vile instruments" of this "unmanly fraud."*

---

* The expressions used by Mr. Mill.

In the third chapter, I have related how, by the prompt method of dealing with the Nizam's French contingent in October, 1798, Lord Wellesley had converted that prince from the position of possible enemy to that of a dependent ally. I have also been told how the Nizam had been rewarded for the aid he had rendered to the British in the war of 1799, against Típu Sultán, by receiving, first, districts yielding an annual revenue of 6.07,332 pagodas; subsequently, two-third of the territories which had been offered to, and refused by, the Peshwá. The Maráthá chiefs had noticed with the greatest dissatisfaction the conduct of the British on the morrow of the short and glorious campaign they had made against a prince whose father had forced the haughty islanders to sue for peace. The feeling displayed at Puná formed one reason why, in the opinion of the Marquess Wellesley, the bonds which united the Nizam to the British should be drawn still closer. He accordingly, with the concurrence of the Nizam, resolved to increase the British contingent in the service of that prince by adding to it two battalions of infantry and one regiment of cavalry. Then came up for consideration the mode in which the subsidiary force should be paid. Experience had proved that engagements with the native princes, for the payment of a fixed annual sum to defray expenses incurred on their behalf, generally terminated by the default of the native prince, and, eventually by the cession to the debtor of the whole of his dominions. Two cases of this kind, the case of Súrat and the case of the Karnátik, have been recorded in this very chapter. It was then in the interest of the Nizam that Lord Wellesley proposed that there should be no open account between the contracting parties; that, in lieu thereof, the Nizam should cede to the British the territories he had acquired by their aid in the two last wars with Típu whilst opportunity should at the same time be taken to make some exchanges of territory to secure a well-defined boundary. These proposals were accepted by the Nizam, and embodied in a Treaty, dated October 12th, 1800. This treaty regulated, likewise, the duties on which the subsidiary force was to be employed; secured the Nizam in the sovereignty of his dominions; prohibited his entering into political negotiations with other states; and made the British Government the arbiter of his disputes with other powers. In a word it made more binding still the obligations on the contracting parties which had been shadowed forth in the Treaty of September 1st, 1798.

Having thus, by the union of an intellectual power, wide enough to grasp all the points of a difficult and complicated situation, with a strong of will sufficient to execute his conclusions, restored peace, order, and prosperity to Southern India; having, by the exercise of the same qualities, satisfactorily settled the Súrat difficulty; Lord Wellesley had leisure to take in hand the affairs of a province, the treatment of which had constituted the one great problem which had exercised his predecessor, and which threatened again to give trouble. In the second chapter, I have related how Sir John Shore had settled for the moment the difficulties which had occurred regarding the succession to the vacant *"masnad"* of Oudh, by recognising the claims of Saadat Alí. I added, that this recognition, though based upon legality, had left in the province a strong party which viewed with great disfavour the interference of the British.

It is possible that, notwithstanding this feeling, Saadat Alì, had been a man of capacity and character, would have succeeded in obtaining the affection of his subjects and the respect of the paramount power. But, like all the representatives of the family, which the break-up of the Mughul empire left in possession of one of the fairest provinces of India, Saadat Álí lived merely for the gratification of his own passions. With him the ruling passion was avarice; his mental failings were cowardice and irresolution. He trusted no one—neither his ministers, nor his troops, nor his courtiers. A veritable miser, a hoarder of wealth, he may be said to have hated those to whom it was absolutely necessary upon occasions to pay money. Such a man can never possess friends; and Saadat Álí had not one.

The disordered state of the country, the consequence or the government of such a man, had attracted the notice of the Governor-General when his mind was occupied by the more pressing dangers threatening Southern India, and he had addressed to the Nawáb-Wazír of Oudh more than one serious remonstrance. Lord Wellesley had to bear in mind that an invasion on the part of Zamán Sháh was always possible. Sometimes even it appeared imminent, and, although the Maráthás might be expected to bear the first brunt of it, their state of unpreparedness seemed to indicate that their resistance would be comparatively feeble, and that the reported richness of Lakhnao might invite the conquerors of Delhi. Saadat Álí had so neglected his army that against the hard warriors of Kábul he could put in the field only an ill-armed and disorderly rabble, whose drilling had been utterly neglected, and whom the withholding of their pay had rendered disaffected. So much had Lord Wellesley been impressed by the danger of having such a body of men on the flank of his northernmost position, that, in 1799, he addressed a letter to the Nawáb-Wazìr, recommending him to disband his rabble, and to allow it to be replaced by a British subsidiary force. To enforce his views in this respect, and to point out the extreme danger of his position to the Wazír, Lord Wellesley despatched the Adjutant-General, Colonel Scott, an officer in whom he had great confidence, to Lakhnao.

Saadat Álí did not like the proposition. It is true that the cost of the subsidiary force would not have exceeded in nominal value the cost of his own rabble, had he paid them. But he did not pay his rabble, and he knew he would have to pay the British contingent. Hence he hesitated long; he gave no decided answer; he always replied that he was preparing a counter-proposition. When, after many delays, he at length presented this proposition, it was found to be merely the expression "of an earnest desire to relinquish a government which he could not manage with satisfaction to himself or advantage to his subjects." Colonel Scott, believing that this renunciation would be agreeable to the Governor-General, transmitted it to him with all haste. But Lord Wellesley had a clearer grasp of the true bearings of the situation than was displayed at a later period by his successors. He had no desire to annex Oudh. He preferred that province, stripped of the additions made to it in the north-west, should be well administered, under the nominal rule of a native sovereign. He proposed, then, an arrangement similar to that which he had inaugurated at Tanjur, *viz.*, a native ruler with a fixed income and all the paraphernalia of sovereignty; the administration to be in the hands of British officers. This proposal the Nawáb-Wazír at once rejected. It would seem, too, that in a conversation with Colonel Scott he endeavoured to explain away his former offer. He did not intend, nor had he intended, to abdicate in favour of the British, but merely to shift the burden of sovereignty on to another member of his family, so that he might enjoy, in a private situation, the wealth he had amassed. Rightly did Lord Wellesley regard such an explanation as the veriest trifling, "as intended to defeat, by artificial delays, the proposed reform of his Excellency's military establishments." With characteristic resolution, he pressed with all the more vehemence the necessity of arriving at a conclusion which should ensure the end he had in view—the formation of a disciplined force for the defence of a province, the safety of which against an invader was necessary for the security of the British dominions. If he could not obtain that result by introducing the Tanjúr system, he was ready to accept that which had been inaugurated in the territories of the Nizam. Still, Saadat Ali refused. He hoped by pleading the eternal *non possumus* to ward off for ever an interference which seemed to threaten his ability to indulge in his favourite passion. Little did he know the character of the man with whom he was dealing. When the Marquess had exhausted every other mode, when his patience was tired out by continued pleas for delay, then, and then only, did he take decided step to bring the negotiations to a conclusion. He despatched his brother, Mr. Henry Wellesley*, to Lakhano, with instructions which should leave no doubt on the mind

* Afterwards Lord Cowley.

of the Nawáb-Wazír as to his determination. Mr. Henry Wellesley was equal to the occasion. Saadat Álí recognised that the day of delay passed. He accepted then an arrangement analogous to that concluded with the Nizam. On November 10th, 1801, he signed a Treaty by which he ceded to the British Government lands in the Duáb* yielding an annual revenue of one crore and thirty-five lakhs of rupees (£1,350,000), including expenses of collections. In consideration of this cession, the British Government agreed to commute the subsidy till then paid, to pay the pensions accruing to Banaras and Farrukhabad, and to maintain a force for the defence against external enemies of the territories of the Nawáb-Wazír. The Treaty provided likewise that the Nawáb-Wazír should reduce his troops to four battalions of infantry and one of Najibs (police), 2,000 cavalry, and 300 gunners; further, that he should introduce a system of good government into his remaining territories.

This Treaty having been concluded, the Governor-General proceeded to Kánpúr. There he was met, on January 10th, 1802, by Saadat Álí, who accompanied him to Lakhnao. In that city, after some discussion, various matters arising out of the Treaty were arranged. Amongst these was an agreement by which the Nawáb of Farrukhábád transferred to the British the civil and military administration of his territories, receiving in return an ample provision for the maintenance of his honorary dignities. The Nawáb submitted reluctantly to this arrangement, but he did submit.

The rumours which had prevailed regarding a possible invasion of India, by the ruler of Kábul, had not yet died away. Indeed they assumed, from time to time, a consistency which lent force to the belief that at any moment such an invasion might occur. It was, repeat, in view of such a possibility that the Marquess Wellesley had endeavoured, by

---

* The "Mahalls" (districts) included in this cession were those of Koráh, Kariah, Itáwah, Kehr, Farrukhábád, Khairagarh. Ázamgarh, Gorákhpur, the Subah of Alláhábád, Barelí, Nawábganj, Mohul, and others of less importance.

his action in Oudh and at Farrukhábád, to put his frontier house in order. But such a preparation, however well designed, it might be, to meet an invasion, would have no effect in averting one. Delhi, Ágra, Áligarh, were held by the troops of Scindhiá, and, judging the present by the past, Lord Wellesley might well believe that these would be quite insufficient to stem an invasion made in the fashion of that conducted by the father of Zamán Sháh. To avert such a calamity he must have recourse to other means. Turning over the matter in his prolific brain, the Governor-General arrived at the conclusion that the best mode of preventing an Afghan invasion was to provide occupation for the ruler of the Afghans at home. With this view, early in 1800, he despatched Captain Malcolm,* of whose sterling worth he had experience at Haidarábád, to Persia, to negotiate a treaty with the Sháh. Malcolm acquitted himself of his task with an ability and a success which left nothing to be desired. Persia had always coveted that portion of Khorásán which had formed, alternately her boundary in the north-east, or, as it does in the present day, the frontier of Afghanistan to the north-west. Malcolm experienced but little difficulty in persuading the Sháh to renew his attack upon that debatable land. To enfeeble still further the ruler of Kábul, the Sháh stirred up his brother, Mahmud, to make war against him. These tactics succeeded almost beyond expectation. Mahmud defeated, made prisoner of, and deposed his brother. But he had laid up a store of domestic trouble for himself. Thenceforth, there was no occasion to dread an invasion from Kábul.

But there was yet another anger recognised by the far-reaching mind of the Governor-General. The Czar of Russia, Paul Petrovitch, had made no secret of his desire to invade India from the north. His plans were ready; and he was but awaiting the opportunity to put them in execution. At this conjuncture the young conqueror of Italy, just became virtual master of France, had known how to captivate the soul of

---

* Afterwards Sir John Malcolm.

Paul. How dangerous to the tranquility of India would be an alliance of these ambitious and powerful potentates, Lord Welleslely at once recognised. He endeavoured to provide as far as he could against the danger by enlisting the Sháh of Persia on his side. Malcolm, under his instructions, succeeded then in adding a clause to the treaty he made with that prince, by which the French were forbidden to establish themselves in any portion of the Persian territories.

Those who know only the British India of the present day naturally experience some difficulty in imagining a British India held under conditions varying in almost every respect from the India of their experience. Not only, I repeat, was the India of Lord Wellesley's day not the predominant power; but the traditions immediately preceding told of war waged, not always successfully, with native princes, and of native princes largely assisted by troops sent from France. Only fifteen years before the arrival in India of the Marquess Wellesley, that is, in 1783, a French fleet under the famous suffren had captured Trinkamali, and a French force, three thousand stronger, led by the once renowned Bussy, had joined Haidar Ali. The animosities between the two nations, England and France, were pale at that period compared with what they became during the war of the Revolution. Between 1793 and 1800 there always existed the possibility of an invasion on a scale larger than any which had been previously attempted. The reason for this, as a reason which considerably exercised the mind of the Marquess, deserves a paragraph to itself.

During the time the Marquess Wellesley ruled in India the route to India was the sea-route by way of the Cape of Good Hope. Capetown had been a Dutch Colony. The English had captured it in 1795, and they held it at the period of which I am writing. But there was a general impression that if a general peace should shortly ensue the colony would be restored to its original owners. That indeed happened when the peace of Amiens was signed. In 1800, then, the English held the Cape, recently conquered, by a precarious tenure.

But, not very far from the east coast of Africa, infact on the direct course between that coast and India, were to islands, held for many years by the French the isles of France and Bourbon, which had ever constituted the base of the French operations against India. Those islands constituted likewise places of arms, whence French ships could rally to prey upon British commerce. The fleets and light squadrons of England, numerous and well appointed as they were, were still not numerous enough to command at the same moment every sea. They were wanted in the Mediterranean, in the West Indies, in the Channel; they had to blockade the coasts of France; often the coasts of Spain; to protect our enormous commerce; to ward off threatened invasion from our shores. Large, then, as was the British navy, especially large in proportion to the navies of other European nations, it was not large enough to dominate at the same moment all the waters of the world. In the Indian seas France possessed the enormous advantage over England, in that she possessed a base for naval operations in the mid ocean, far nearer to India than the temporary and precarious base which England had secured at the Cape, and which did not offer a safe anchorage in all seasons. The result of this difference is shown in the tables below,* compiled from the official record of the five years prior to the arrival in India of the great Marquess. With such figure before him; with the knowledge of the negotiations of Típu with the Governor of the islands; and with a tolerably correct insight regarding the actual ruler of France; Lord Wellesley might well be alarmed, in 1800-1, at the fact that at a period when France had humbled all Europe, England alone accepted, she should possess a base of operations, so valuable to her, so dangerous to the commerce of England, so dangerous even to the position of England in India, as that which the occupation of the isles of France and Bourbon afforded her. With characteristic decision; with a directness of purpose which always struck at the end to be obtained; Lord Wellesley resolved to despatch an expedition to secure that base for England. Early in 1801, then, he directed the concentration of an English force at Trinkamalí, composed of three regiments of the line, and detachments from two other corps, a corps of Bengal native volunteers, and two companies of European and native artillery with lascars attached. The command of this force he gave to Major-General Baird,* commanding the Dánápúr division. He instructed that very distinguished officer to proceed first to Java and capture that island; to remain there as Lieutenant-Governor; whilst his second in command, Colonel Arthur Wellesley, should proceed with the bulk of the force to drive the French from the islands of France and Bourbon.

	Merchant ships taken by the French from the English	*Merchant ships taken by the English from the French*
* In 1793	261	63
In 1794	527	88
In 1795	502	47
In 1796	414	63
In 1797	562	114
	2266	375

being a proportion in five years of more than six to one. Capetown was taken by the English, September 25, 1795.

All at once a difficulty arose. To ensure the success of the expedition, Lord Wellesley had requested the co-operation of the British admiral commanding in the eastern seas. He had not the smallest doubt but that such co-operation would be freely rendered. But it is not given to all British admirals to possess that disregard for punctiliousness which distinguished a Nelson. The Admiralty, not possessing the gift of prescience, had not specially instructed the admiral on the eastern station, Admiral Rainier, that he was to take part in an expedition against Java and the two French islands. Not possessing a specific order to aid in such an operation, Admiral Rainier then refused his co-operation. But already,

* Afterwards Sir David Baird.

while Lord Wellesley was digesting this refusal as best he might, plans had been formed for an even more important expedition against the French. General Baird had not left the Ságar Roads on his way to trinkamalí when the governor-General received a despatch from Mr. Dundas, informing him that a British force had been directed to proceed to Alexandria for the purpose of landing there and co-operating with the Turkish army assembling in Syria for the explosion of the French from Egypt; and that it had been thought expedient "that a force should also be sent from India to act in such a manner as might appear conducive to that essential object," from the side of the Red Sea. The force which had been warned, then, to act against the islands, was now, with some changes in its composition, diverted to Egypt. Consisting of about a thousand European and four thousand native troops, it was escorted to the shores of the Red Sea by a squadron of the Company's ships commanded by Admiral Blankett. With the order for the despatch of the expedition the responsibility of the Governor-General in its action ceased, but the Marquess Wellesley did not fail to take the deepest interest in the progress of an expedition till then unique in the history of the world.

Hitherto I have dealt only with the foreign policy of the Marquess Wellesley. I have endeavoured to set out in detail, as they occurred, the measures which, during a period of four years, he had prescribed and carried out to secure the safety of the territories entrusted to his care. It is not too much to say that in those four years he had effected a complete change in the situation he had found existing. He had found Southern India trembling before the native sovereign of Maisúr—dreading, unprepared, an attack, and yet fearing to arm lest it should provoke one. He had found the Nizam halting between two opinions, hesitating whether to cast his lot with the French or with the British; he had found Tanjúr, Súrat, the Karnátik, and Oudh in desperate

* Afterwards Sir David Baird.

need of a reminder that for them, at all events, the British power must be paramount; and, lastly, he had found India threatened by an invasion from Afghanistan. In four years not only had he dispelled all those dangers, but he had derived from every one of them advantages of a decisive and permanent character for England. He had made of the Nizam's dominions a protected State, with no voice in the direction of its external policy, for he had allied its fate with the fate of the British. He had smitten Tipu to the earth, annexed a large portion of his territories, and so dealt with the remainder that danger from Maisúr was eliminated for ever. He had placed in British hands the administration of Tanjúr, of Súrat, of the Karnátik. He had added to the British dominions two-thirds of the territory till then ruled by the Nawáb-Wazír of Oudh, and he had located in the remaining third a contingent officered by British officers. Finally, he had rendered invasion from the north impossible; and, changing his defensive attitude into an attitude of offence, had despatched a force to aid in driving the French from Egypt. In every instance the policy pursued was marked by clearness of vision, by directness of aim, by thoroughness inaction. Scrutinise as strictly as one may all his measures, it is impossible to detect a single error. The general plan, the modes of execution, the management of the details stand out faultless. Every one of the acts mentioned has stood the test of time. Haidarábád, Maisúr, Tanjúr, the Karnátik, Súrat still remain, with the differences only which his system was certain to evolve, just as Lord Wellesley made them .Oudh remained so, likewise, till 1856, when she, too, was brought, in a manner which Lord Wellesley would never have sanctioned, within the British family. His plan of securing the two islands in the Indian Ocean was carried out a few years after he had quit India. Finally, the despatch of Indian troops to Egypt, unique, as I have said, in the history of the world, constituted a precedent of which the genius of Lord Beaconsfield eagerly availed itself in 1878, and to which Lord Beaconsfield's successor, after denouncing it as unconstitutional, took recourse to three years later.

Lord Wellesley might well be proud of his foreign administration. He had done much for the security of British India. Much, however, remained still to be accomplished. Hitherto the Maráthá Powers had been deterred, by mutual jealousies and internal strife, from making any effort to stop his progress. But it was certain that Scindhiá, at least, would not notice unmoved the absorption of Farrukhábád and Rohilkhand within the British border, and Scindhiá was far more formidable than had been the ruler of Maisúr. But before I notice the course of Maráthá action, which gradually led to new complications and to a final settlement, I shall ask the reader to glance at those domestic measures which illustrated the administration of the accomplished statesman whose splendid administration I am recording.

7

Domestic Legislation

Sir John Shore had left the civil administration of the affairs of the East India Company in a plight almost, if not quite, as heart breaking as the condition of their military forces. During his rule, notwithstanding his peace-at-any-price policy, there had been a steady annual declension of the revenue until, in 1797-8 it had fallen to £8,059,880, whilst the charges, lightened by cheese-parings in the military expenditure, reached £8,178,626. The debt, meanwhile, had gone on increasing till "the Company's credit was at its lowest ebb, and money could not be borrowed in Bengal under twelve per cent."*

Nor were the civil and military services in the condition which a young, active, and resolute Governor-General could regard with satisfaction. The former seemed sunk in a torpor from which it would require very strong measures to rouse them; the latter, neglected and left in idleness, were in a state of semi-mutiny. The allowances for service at frontier stations not only differed from those sanctioned for inland stations, but they were ill-defined. The new system of officering native regiments, based on the system prevailing in the Royal Army, had but recently been introduced, and it had caused much intrigue and much heart-burning. Regimental committees, the existence of which was utterly subversive of discipline, had been formed in every battalion, to watch the rights of officers.

* Memorandum by Sir Arthur Wellesley in 1806, on his brother government of India.

The officers complained, and probably their complaints were founded on justice, that their services were unnoticed, and that even recommendations on their behalf forwarded to Leadenhall Street were disregarded.

Lord Wellesley was the last man in the world to permit the continuance of such a state of things. One of his first acts, after he had mastered the situation, was to insist on the dissolution of the regimental committees. Possessing, as the reader will have seen, a true soldierly instinct, and foreseeing how much the India of the British would have to depend upon its officers, he, whilst firmly recalling them to the strict line of discipline and duty, allowed them to see that he sympathised to a great extent with their position, and that their future would be safe in his hands. In the army, then, the order to abolish the committees, far from exciting discontent, was hailed as the beginning of a new line of policy in which the claims of the soldier should meet with due attention.

The other defects he had noticed in the actual condition of both services, Lord Wellesley met in a similar manner. In all that he did he could not help being "thorough." With that "thoroughness" there did not mingle a particle of meanness or parsimony. He recognised at the outset that services rendered should be well paid. But then he would see that the service was rendered. He grudged not recompense provided this condition were fulfilled. He wished to stimulate zeal amongst a body of men in whose minds along period of unenterprising and methodical government had introduced a profound lethargy. Yet his position was one of extreme difficulty. He had, on the one hand, to reform the army; to prepare it to meet the wars which he saw looming in a very near future; to rouse from the torpor in which they were sunk the bulk of the members of the civil service; on the other, to bring expenditure within the limits of the income, to restore credit, and to procure the money which would be necessary for the conduct of military operations on a large scale. He proposed, with a view to attain these aims, to apply himself in the first instance to a general revision of all public establishments in the three Presidencies. With the army he would deal in a different manner. There, no great reduction of numbers was to be thought of. One regiment of cavalry, taken over from the Chevalie de Boigne, would be transferred to the Nawáb-Wazír of Oudh. Further economy would be consulted by the abolition of the extra allowances granted to the garrison of Alláhábád. Finally, he would refer to specially appointed committees, under his own inspection, the revision of the several branches of the revenue and its collection.

Lord Wellesley was planning and partially carrying out these reforms when the discovery of the correspondence of Tipu Sultán with the Isle of France forced him to provide funds for the military preparations which had become absolutely necessary. If he had money, he would have solved the question without further delay; but in the south, in the west, in the east, the treasuries were alike empty.

For the moment money was found, and the success of the war which followed augmented alike the credit of the Company and its means of permanent supply. But the improvement did not come all at once. In 1800, the Treasury notes, bearing 12 per cent, were selling in the bazaar at a discount of 3 or 4 per cent. Silver was scarce, and in the hands of the native capitalist; and he would only sell it at a discount sometimes of as much as 7 per cent.

One of the special qualities of Lord Wellesley was his power to detect worth in others. He had picked out young Malcolm from the crowd before even he had seen him, judging merely from some letters of the young soldier which had come under his eyes. To aid him in his financial difficulties, to restore order and credit, he now selected a Bengal civilian, M. Tucker, to fill the office of Accountant-General. He had known Mr. Tucker when that gentleman was on sick leave at Madras, prior to, and during, the Maisúr war, and he had formed a high opinion of his capacity as a financial administrator. There could not have been a better selection. Recognising that the financial embarrassment and its consequences were due to the lowness of the Company's credit. Mr. Tucker, as soon as he could spare time from the exigencies of the hour, pressing upon him from the three Presidencies, inaugurated a bold and soundly based system, which, in a short time brought about the desired result. Thence-forward the finances of India worked with a magical regularity.

Amongst other subjects which had greatly exercised the mind of the Governor-General, was the regarding the observance of the Sunday in India. Up to his time there had been no intermission of trading or work on the seventh day. To the Hindu population and to the Muhammadan shopkeeper the day had no religious significance, and the European settler had fallen in with the ways of the people of the country. But few things had more struck the keen mind of Lord Wellesley than the observance of the ceremonies which formed part of their religions by the Hindus and the Muhammadans. He had noticed how such observances entitled those who strictly kept them to the respect of their fellow men; how, also, neglect in particular on the part of the English had led to a very general impression that they had no religion—none, certainly, that regulated their conduct—and that they were regarded therefore by the native community as little better than pariahs or outcasts. In Bengal and Bihar the English had from the time of Clive been the paramount power. By the action of Lord Wellesley they had become so in Southern India. It was not fitting then, he thought, that they should continue to subject themselves to the reproach which till then had been freely cast on them in the matter of religion. Accordingly, shortly after his return from Madras, Lord Wellesley inaugurated the germ of his future policy by directing that the Government of India should make a public profession of its faith. He ordered that a day should be set apart for a public and general thanksgiving for the various successes which had attended the British arms. The day fixed was February 6th, 1800. On that date the Governor-General proceeded on foot from

Government House to the Church of St. John, accompanied by the leading members of the Government and of the community. He followed up his action by directing, in an order in the *Gazette,* the observance of Sunday as a day of rest, and by prohibiting Sunday newspapers. But, whilst he thus publicly announced that the English had a religion and that he, as the Head of the State in India, desired to set an example in the observance of the authorised ceremonies of that religion, he did not depart a single hair's breadth from the practice of toleration. The Hindu and the Muhammadan were allowed the most complete liberty of action in the exercise of their religious observances. The one point upon which Lord Wellesley insisted was that the paramount power should not show itself ashamed of the faith which it professed.

His dealings with the native press were characterised by the same combination of firmness and prudence which had marked his transactions with native princes. Naturally, he was in favour of unrestricted freedom of the press. But he felt that, although the influence of Great Britain might be paramount in Bengal, in Madras, and in Bombay, there was a large portion of India, comprehending the imperial cities of Delhi and Ágra, and the important centres of Puná, Nágpúr, Indúr, Gwáliár and Barodah, subject to the unsubdued Maráthás, who, more openly than the English, laid claim to the succession to the Mughul. The native press within the British territories was, even in those days very licentious. It was represented, then, to Lord Wellesley that in the independent native states the comments, the unrestricted comments, of newspapers published under the shadow of the English Government were liable to be mistaken for the comments of the Government itself. That such an impression should prevail at a time when Europe was in arms, when India was always liable to attack from without, when a jealous and susceptible rival was watching from Puná the tendency of the action of Calcutta, was dangerous to the maintenance of peace. Acted upon by these considerations—which even in our own time have not been without their weight—Lord Wellesley established a mild censorship, which, without interfering with legitimate comment, prevented the ill consequences which absolute freedom of utterance might have caused.

In February, 1801, the complete satisfaction of the Crown with the mode in which the Marquess was administering England's great dependency was manifested by the bestowal upon him of the rank of Captain-General and Commander-in-Chief of all the Forces in the East Indies. A year later, the Ottoman Porte, to testify its high appreciation of the manner in which the Marquess had co-operated for the expulsion of the French from Egypt, bestowed upon him the Order of the Crescent of the first rank. The first of these appointments caused the most unbounded satisfaction throughout British India. There was not an officer in the army who did not feel that the success which had been obtained in Southern India had been due in the first instance to the splendid initiative of the Marquess Wellesley; that it had been he, who, against advice and remonstrance from the highest quarters, had insisted, amid great financial difficulties, in putting the army on a war footing; that he, too, had planned the campaign which—a contrast to the previous campaigns against the same enemy and his father—had been brought to a successful issue within three months; that he then had declined to diminish the spoil due to the army by refusing to accept the proffered donation of £100,000. He was their paladin, their hero. His nomination to that high, and till then unbestowed, office was hailed by all classes as an honour fittingly conferred upon the most deserving.

In consideration of this supreme command over the armies of India, the Marquess Welleslely took possession of the house in Barrackpúr Park, which had always been occupied by the Commander-in-Chief. Here he found the rest which was denied to him in the crowded quarters of Fort William—quarters at no time befitting the master of nearly one-third of India. That the Marquess had long felt the unfitness of the; residence assigned to the Governor-General of India which had been evidenced not very long after his return from Madras, by the designing and laying the foundations of a building which should be more worthy of England's representative. He had noticed, as a matter of no little significance, the importance which the natives attached to display as it was a part of his policy to indulge them in it to their hearts' content. With them he was the "great lord," the living embodiment of the Company's power, "the perfect representative of the might of England." The outer manifestations of his grandeur, in the building of a new and magnificent palace, of a splendid barge, of a richly-attired *entourage,* seemed to them to be the fitting demonstration of the greatness which characterised all his acts of government, and they rejoiced at them accordingly. Never was pageantry employed to a more useful end.

But, amidst the pomp and glittering circumstances of war and its concomitants, the Marquess neither forgot nor neglected the subject of education, of the education especially for the English public servants, to whose hands would be entrusted the working of the measures of the Government. His views on this point are contained in an elaborate minute bearing the title, "Notes by the Governor-General in Council." In this State paper he pointed out that the civil servants of the Company could no longer be considered as the agents of a commercial concern; that they were, in fact, the ministers and officers of a powerful sovereign; and that they must be viewed in that capacity with reference to their real occupations. Proceeding to show that they were thus required to discharge the functions of magistrates, judges, ambassadors, and governors of provinces, in all their complicated and extensive relations of those sacred trusts and exalted stations, sometimes under circumstances of great difficulty, he laid down the kind of education they were bound to acquire before starting on the race for distinction.

"Their education," he wrote, "should be founded in a general knowledge of those branches of literature and science which form the basis of the education of persons destined to similar occupations in Europe. To this foundation should be added an intimate acquaintance with the history, languages, customs, and manners of the people of India, with the Muhammadan and Hindu codes of law and religion, and with the political and commercial interests and relations of Great Britain in Asia. They should be regularly instructed in the principles and system which constitute the foundation of the wise code of regulations and laws enacted by the Governor-General in Council, for the purpose of securing to the people of this Empire the benefit of the ancient and accustomed laws of the country, administered in the spirit of the British constitution. They should be well informed of the true and sound principles of the British constitution, and sufficiently grounded in the general principles of ethics, civil jurisprudence, the law of nations and general history, in order that they may be able to discriminate the characteristic differences of the several codes of law administered within the British empire in India, and practically to combine the spirit of each in the dispensation of justice, and in the maintenance of order and good government. Finally, their early habits should be so formed as to establish in their minds such solid foundations of industry, prudence, integrity and religion, as should effectually guard them against those temptations and corruptions with which the nature of this climate and the peculiar depravity of the people of India will surround and assail them in every station, especially upon their first arrival in India."

To carry into action these views, the Marquess issued orders (July 10, 1800) for the foundation of a college, which should be called the College of Fort William. The regulations of this college required that the provost, that is, the immediate governor of the college, should receive the junior civil servants on their first arrival at Fort William; should superintend and regulated their general morals and conduct; should see that they duly attended the several courses of instruction, of which a list was given; that the civil servants arriving after the date of its formation, as well as those who had not already served three years in India, should be attached to the college for three years; that the junior military servants of the Company should be admissible to the college under such terms and regulations as might be deemed advisable. There were also further regulations for public examinations, bestowal of degrees, and the arrangement of other matters affecting its well-being.

Well intended and loudly called for by the existing defects in the public service as was this scheme, it was not to be. Lord Wellesley had been gifted by nature with an order of mind far more capacious, a genius for administration far more brilliant, than were to be found amongst his masters in Leadenhall Street. Although these, not too openly to discredit him, professed to applated the design of the college, and to sanction the principle upon which the Governor-General had acted in constituting it, they declared it to be too vast, too expensive, for the purpose. The vexation of the great Proconsul on receiving this unlooked-for disapproval is not to be described. He did not recognise at the moment the fact that the opposition of the India House was dictated mainly by a desire to check his autocratic tendencies; to signify, without saying it, that they constitued a body which had the right to be consulted before action was taken, and not a Directorate merely to register his decrees; but, believing that in his original proposal he must have omitted some argument necessary to convey conviction, he sat down and penned a despatch containing a hundred and forty-two paragraphs, in which, in classic sentences, he unfolded the unanswerable reasons why his original plan should be sanctioned. To support his arguments with the Court, he solicited the assistance of the Board of Control and of several members of the Ministry. In reply to Lord Wellesley's arguments, the India House continued to plead poverty. Finally, on the intervention of Lord Castlereagh, a compromise was arrived at, really acceptable to neither party, and for the moment the college was saved. It did not, however, in its original form, survive the departure of Lord Wellesley from India.*

The disagreement about the college was not the only disagreement which the far-seeing but high-handed Proconsul had at this period with his uncongenial masters. The world's history gives examples without number of the difficulty with which genius works under mediocrity. Cromwell was forced to dissolve his Parliament; Napoleon to upset the fictious Directory; Wellesley, unable to follow in their footsteps, experienced a repugnance amounting to disgust at finding his actions controlled and then annulled by men whose intellectual requirements were of the smallest, and for whose political knowledge and parsimony he had learned to feel only contempt.

Before the year 1802 had dawned, he had received instructions from them, some of which, if he had literally carried them out, would have placed English interests in India in the greatest peril. For instance, whilst four of the Maráthá Powers were still indignant at having been debarred from their share of the plunder of Maisúr, and the astutest among them were deliberating how best to deliver a counter blow to the foreigner whom they now recognised as their

---

* "It is but justice to the Honourable East India Company," writes Mr. Pearce, "to say that, after the heat of these discussions had passed away, in a magnanimous spirit they took up the plan of Lord Wellesley, and put it into execution with so much success that many have doubted, and still doubt, whether the maintenance of Fort William College as originally designed would have been more useful to the servants of the Company than the College of Haileybury." The scheme was strongly supported by some of the best men in England, amongst others by Wilber force, who condemned the parsimony of the Company in withholding its sanction. The bitterness of Lord Wellesley's feelings may be gathered from a letter which he addressed to Lord Castlegraph on the subject in 1804, in which he speaks of his "unqualified contempt and abhorrence of the proceedings and propensities of the Court of Directors."

only possible rival for empire, the Court peremptorily instructed the; Governor-General to reduce his military strength. Again, the same controlling authority rudely interfered with the staff salaries he had authorised for the new political appointments which it had been necessary to create on the close of the Maisúr campaign. Among these was the salary of the Governor-General's brother, Arthur Wellesley. Further, Lord Wellesley had nominated Colonel Kirkpatrick, the same with whom he had journeyed from the Cape on his voyage to India and who had rendered him then and subsequently the most valuable services, to be Secretary to the Government in the political department. The Court brusquely ordered him to rescind that appointment. He had nominated Colonel Scott, whose services in negotiating with the Nawáb-Wazír of Oudh had been eminently useful, to be Resident at Lakhnao. The Court ordered him to revise the appointment "with a view to rescind it." The Court had further interfered with his patronage by directing him to bestow upon one of its *protégés* an appointment for which, in the judgement of the Governor-General, he was not qualified. This last order, following upon the implied disapproval of the nomination to high political office in Maisúr of his brother, Arthur, was regarded as peculiarly offensive. By the confession even of his enemies, the principle upon which the Marquess Wellesley had acted in his selection for staff employment was one which ought to prove a standing rule for all governors. Solicited by many, he selected only those whom he believed deserving, and to them he gave all his confidence. It is worthy to be noted that all his selections stood the test of time and trial.*

---

* Mill, who has done his best to disparage the great Proconsul, thus wrote regarding his selections for offices; "The Governor-General, amid the talents for command which he possessed in a very unusual degree, displayed two qualities of primary importance. He has seldom been surpassed in the skill with which he made choice of his instruments; and, having made choice of his instruments, he communicated to them, with full and unsparing hands, the powers which were necessary for the end they were employed to accomplish."

These several annoyances, crowned by the cavalier rejection of his scheme for the college, so irritated Lord Wellesley, that on January 1st, 1802, he intimated to the Court of Directors his desire that they would select some one to replace him the following October. The moment he had been selected for making this request, tranquillity reigned throughout India. The revenues of the British provinces were showing signs of great improvement. Communications between their component parts had been opened out, and were being vigorously pushed forward. Information had reached India leading to the belief that the negotiations for peace in Europe, then pending, would prove successful. There was not a cloud on the horizon.

About ten weeks later, when at Banáras, he received from Lord Hobart a letter, dated Downing Street, October 12th, 1801, informing him that Articles of Peace had been exchanged at Amiens between Lord Hawkesbury and M. Otto, and that hostilities had ceased. Lord Wellesley, conceiving that this announcement added force to his previous request, wrote at once to the Court (March 13th, 1802), to reiterate it, merely deferring his time of leaving from October to December, or the month following. The reply of the Court was a request to the Marquess to defer his departure for a year, that is, to the beginning of 1804. How Lord Wellesley would have acted had no complications arisen in India as it may not be difficult to surmise. But, long before he received the reply, the struggle for Empire between the two rival powers in India, the British and the Maráthás, had commenced.

The definitive Treaty of Peace with France was not signed till March 27th, 1802. In compliance with one of its clauses instructions were transmitted to the Marquess Wellesley "to restore to the French and Batavian Republics respectively all the countries, territories, and factories, with the exception of the Dutch possession in the island of Ceylon, which belonged to them, respectively, in India, and which had been occupied or conquered by His Majesty's forces, and," added Lord Hobart, "you will take the necessary measures for placing the subjects of the French and Batavian Republics in India upon the same footing on which they stood at the commencement of the war." These directions involved the retrocession of Chandranagar, Pondichery, Chinsurah, Mahe, and Goa.

In the November following, circumstances having arisen in Europe which tended to show that the peace would not last, Lord Hobart enclosed to Lord Wellesley a cypher letter, from the Admiralty to himself, informing him that Commodore Linois, having on board one of the ships of his squadron the new French Captain-General for India, was about to sail from Brest, to be joined *en route* by another squadron, and instructing him to defer the reduction of the force in India till he should receive further orders. Two days later, Lord Hobart wrote directing him still to execute the instructions he had received regarding the immediate restitution of the French possessions to the commander of the troops of that nation.

Well may Mr. Pearce write that "a man of less firmness than the Marquess Wellesley would perhaps have obeyed thee commands." So precise were they that it required a very strong man indeed to disobey them. But, reading between the lines, Lord Wellesley clearly discerned that the Peace of Amiens was but an armed truce; that it had recognised the French Republic as the virtual mistress of continental Europe, and would afford that Republic facilities for extending her power in Asia and in Africa. He took upon himself, then, the responsibility of declining for the moment to direct the restitution of the French possessions. When, then, in due course, the squadron of Commodore Linois appeared before Pondichery, Lord Clive, acting upon orders from the Marquess Wellesley, informed the French commander that he had not received instructions to surrender the place, and referred him to the Governor-General of India.

Pondichery, then, was not restored to the French. A few months later, a despatch from Lord Hobart (March 19th) completely justified the previous of the great Marquess. That despatch contained enclosures which made it abundantly clear that the armed truce was virtually at an end. On May 17th following, Lord Hobart announced the recall of the British ambassador from Paris, and the renewal of hostilities. The despatch containing this announcement urged upon Lord Wellesley the duty of recapturing "any forts or possession which the French may have in India." Happily, the firmness and prescience of Lord Wellesley had rendered it unnecessary to fire a shot to effect that object, for, thanks to him, the French had no forts and no possessions in the country.

Before the war with France had been renewed, and whilst the British possessions in India were enjoying peace and the consequences of peace, Lord Wellesley publicly inaugurated the opening of the new Government House. Occasion was taken to make the *féte*, which was then celebrated, a *féte* of rejoicing for the cessation of hostilities in Europe. It took place January 26th, 1803 and, like everything to which the Marquess Wellesley put his hand, was in all respects magnificent. It should be borne in mind that at that period the knowledge that peace had been signed in Europe was comparatively fresh news for the residents of Calcutta, the peace having been signed only at the very end of March. Other rejoicing followed, and these rejoicings gave place in turn to the consideration of remedial measures affecting the country. Amongst these was a measure by which might be prevented the practice prevalent among the Hindus of allowing the wife of a deceased nobleman to be burnt alive on the funeral pyre of the husband. The din of war came, however, to interrupt the Governor-General in the midst of this work.

I have already stated that twice in the year 1802 had the Governor-General, annoyed beyond measure at the parsimony and short-sighted policy of his masters in Leadenhall Street, tendered the resignation of his high office. In reply to both these offers he had been requested to remain another year. But, meanwhile, the relations between himself and the Court of Directors did not improve. They seemed to take a special delight in the display of suspicion and distrust. In his dealings with the Nawáb-Wazír of Oudh, Lord Wellesley had derived the most important assistance from his brother, Henry, afterwards Lord Cowley, placed by him in a high position at the Court of that prince. The Court of Directors had objected to the appointment of a gentleman not in their covenanted service, as one outside the power of the Governor-General to bestow. This annoyed him greatly. There, however, the Court were, strictly speaking, within their rights. But, about the same time, there came from them a despatch, which, whilst revealing their petty suspicion of their representative in India, placed them completely in the wrong.

When, at a critical period of the war just concluded, Lord Wellesley had despatched Indian troops to Egypt, he had sanctioned the chartering of three private ships, that is, ships not the property of the Company, to convey stores to the Red Sea. The Court of Directors, who jealously guarded as their most precious possession the monopoly of trade with India, seized the occasion to accuse him of abusing his discretionary power for the purpose of enriching private shipowners at the expense of the Company to the extent of 30,000 tons. It was not difficult for Lord Wellesley to prove that he had employed only three ships, the united tonnage of which did not exceed one-tenth of the amount stated by the Company. And he proceeded further to justify his action. That action, he stated, had been adopted "under an irresistible exigency of the public service at the most critical period of the war." In the letter to Lord Castlereagh, in which that expression is used, Lord Wellesley expatiated on the difficulty of defining the precise boundaries of the discretionary authority vested in the Governor-General. "On the due and firm exercise of that discretion, however," he added, "the stability of the empire must principally depend." In such a matter much must depend on the degree of sympathy between the employer and the emloyed. Between the genius of Lord Wellesley and the halting and suspicious mediocrity of the Court of Directors there could be none. Lord Wellesley's letters abound with expressions of the loathing, the contempt, with which he regrded the inmates of Leadenhall Street.

Stung by the vexatious opposition to his best thoughtout schemes, the Marquess Wellesley once again, in 1803, expressed to the Court his desire to be relieved of his office, so as to enable him to return to Europe some time in the following year. But when this despatch reached England there were signs that the discontent long seething in the minds of the Maráthá princes was about to burst into action; and the Court, in reply, requested the Marquess to remain at his post until the nascent excitement should be appeased. Lord Wellesley, bitterly as he felt and keenly as he resented the indignities which had been heaped upon him, could not bring himself to abandon the state vessel in the hour of danger, and he agreed to remain until that danger should be averted.

That danger was upon him before his thoughts had expressed themselves in words.

8

The Maratha Wars—I

Lord Wellesley, besides enlarging the dominions of the Company, and extending their influence by the treaties with the Nizam, the Rajah of Mysore, and the Princes of Tanjore, the Carnatic, and of Oude, carried his military and diplomatic policy beyond the sphere of India. In order to aid in the expulsion of the French from Egypt, where they were a menace and danger to the British power in India, he was able to furnish the British armies in Egypt with a very respectable contingent, under Sir David Baird. He was also able to excite disturbances in the rear of Zemaun Shah, so as to distract him from the invasion of India, which he had threatened and commenced; and he succeeded in obtaining from the Persian monarch a defensive alliance against the Afghan Sultan. The Persian Government undertook, in case Zemaun renewed his attacks on India, that the Persian army should invade the Afghan dominions, and that no peace should be concluded which did not include a stipulation for abandoning all designs of attack on the British territories; in return the British bound themselves, incase of attack on Persia by the Afghans or the French, to furnish military aid, and particularly cannon, warlike stores, necessaries, and provisions. Zemaun Shah, who had penetrated as far as Lahore, was compelled by the disturbances at home to retreat, and never ventured to renew his attempts against India.

Lord Wellesley's policy, upto this point, had not only been eminently successful in rescuing the dominions confided to him from the perils which he found them exposed to, but met with almost universal approval in India and in England. 'We find him next engaged in the prosecution of schemes still more vast, in which, as will in the sequel be seen, he was also no less successful, but as to the propriety and prudence of which there was great controversy. His policy was ably criticized by Lord Castlereagh, though with no unfriendly hand, and was as ably defended by the fraternal zeal of Sir Arthur Wellesley (afterwards Duke of Wellington), who himself had a great part in securing its success.

From the time of Lord Wellesley's acceptance of the office of Governor-General, he appears to have had what the French call. "des idées fixes," on two subjects, one, the necessity of obtaining a footing in the Maratha empire, the other, the necessity of excluding Frenchmen from the armies and councils of the native princes, and shutting up every avenue through which French forces could find their way into India. The possession or absolute control of the whole sea coast was involved in the latter object.

The Maratha empire was of vast extent, as large in proportion to India as the whole of the old German empire was to Europe. Lord Wellesley appeared to have regarded the Marathas with much the same apprenhension as French statesmen recorded the power of Charles V., when Emperor of Germany and King of Spain. It was by no means an improbable contingency, that an able and ambitious *Maratha* potentate might be able to weld the whole of that mass of states into one empire, or to obtain such a complete ascendency, as to be able to wield the whole military resources of that which was in theory, and to some extent in practice, a confederation. Lord Wellesley looked with great misgiving at the probability of a French and *Maratha* alliance. There were several French adventurers of military skill in the service of more than one of the Maratha chiefs, employed in training and disciplining their troops. The raw material with which he French officers had to deal, was at least as good as that out of which the Bengal Sepoys had been made what they were. The number of European troops on which the Anglo-Indian Government could count was very small; and the English power of reinforcing them very limited. If the French could succeed in introducing anywhere into India a powerful army, with artillery and stores, and cold from a cordial alliance with a *Maratha* Emperor, all conditions under which the great combat between clive and his French rivals had been fought, would be changed. Under such circumstances and conditions, the expulsion of the English from India would be much more probable than the destruction of the French power would have seemed at the commencement of the former struggle.

Treaties with the *Maratha* powers, by which they could be induced to admit English subsidiary forces, and to submit their disputes with the Nizam and with one another to English arbitrament, were therefore from the first the favourite scheme of Lord Wellesley's Indian policy. The conception was his, the execution was his, and he succeeded in it beyond his utmost expectations, not only without aid or countenance from home, but in defiance of the known ill-will of the Court of Directors, who loved neither his ambitious policy nor the somewhat haughty and overbearing independence of his administration. He thought it right in his despatches to tell them what he had done, and why he had done it, but does not seem otherwise to have taken much heed of their counsels or suggestions.

In execution of his scheme he had introduced into his treaties with the Nizam, stipulations for admitting the Peshwa into a participation in the spoils of conquest on certain conditions. The Peshwa, under the advice or rather under the control of Saadat, who was all powerful at Poonah, resolutely refused the English offers, but "Heaven soon granted what the Peshwa had denied."

In the first place, the Guicowar, one of the *Maratha* powers whose dominions it will be recollected lie above

Bombay, being attacked by another chief called Mulhar Rao, and unable to defend himself, applied for assistance to the Bombay Government, and received it, on the usual condition of admitting a subsidized English force into his territories, and on the cession of some territory in Surat, but the importance of this event was soon lost sight of in the course of the more striking and momentous events which shortly afterwards happened.

In order to have a clear conception of the entangled web which Lord Wellesley had to unravel, it is necessary always to bear in mind that there was no such thing in India, except perhaps under the vigorous rule of Hyder and of Tippoo, as a sovereign in the European signification of the term. The state of society was an exaggeration, almost to caricature, of the worst times of the feudal chaos in Europe. Every little lord was absolute despot in his own territory. There was no administration of justice as between him and his subjects, or as between him and his neighbours. There was no recognition of a sovereign as the fountain and dispenser of justice in public law or in public opinion. There was, however, an understanding that the lord owed tribute and military allegiance to some one or the other, and a Rajah or Nawab grew or diminished in power, according to the number of the subordinate chiefs, who, for the time being, were coerced to acknowledge his right to the tributes from their territories. Every person, however, who captured a country by the sword, sought to give a colour of legality to his possessions by a title from the Great Mogul, as in Europe under the same circumstances, titles were eagerly taken from the emperor. The titles Nawab, Vizier, Nizam, speak for themselves; they all mean lieutenant or minister; the Company themselves were Dewans or Stewards; even the Marathas followed the same habit. The Peshwa, who was, as we have seen hereditary Prime Minister, and, therefore, Viceroy over his Sovereign, was also Vaquel-ul-Mutuluck, Regent or Viceroy of the Great Mogul.

The family of Scindiah, orginally an officer in the Peshwa's army, had come to establish themselves as permanent rulers under the Peshwa, and Doulat Rao Scindiah, the Scindiah of our narrative, who was deputy to the Peshwa in his office of Vaquel-ul-Mutuluck. But this chain of delegation did not rest there; under Scindiah again was M. Perro a Frenchman, who had succeeded to the command of a very large force of regular infantry, disciplined by European officers after the manner of the Sepoys of the British. M. Perron in nominal subordination to Scindiah, and nominally for the purpose of paying the latter's troops under his command, had established himself really in absolute sovereignty over a vast dominion, extending towards the left bank of the Indus through the Punjab, and comprehending a large portion of the Doab, between the Jumna and the Ganges, including Agra and Delhi. It has been estimated that the annual revenues of M. Perron's dominions were not less than 1,700,000*l*, sterling. As the general of Scindiah, M. Perron had not only Delhi in his guard, but also possession of the person of the unfortunate Shah Alam, who was kept in the most abject subjection, and whose name and nominal authority M. Perron used whenever, and in whatever manner, it suited his purpose. M. Perron affected to call his army the Imperial army, and himself, the servant of the Great Emperor; the latter, however, was not only deprived of all power, but seems not even to have been treated with any of the outward respect ordinarily paid to the possessors of imperial name and title.

Scindiah's virtual possession of the power of the Peshwa's office was not submitted to willingly by the Peshwa himself, nor by the great *Maratha* chief, the Rajah of Berar, who asserted a better right to the office of Peshwa, by virtue of his descent from the founder of the Maratha Empire. In the Peshwa's own family, there was a brother Amrut Rao, with considerable influence, ready to usurp his place; and in the Rajah of Berar's territory again there were several subordinate rajahs or chiefs, who were very restive under his yoke. It will be recollected that there was, as there still is, the considerable *Maratha* principality of Holkar on the Nerbudda to the north-east of Bombay. On the death of Tuckojee Holkar, which had occurred some time before the events we have to narrate, his son, Cashee Rao, was acknowledged as successor by Scindiah; but there was another claimant, one Khundah Rao Holkar, who had been seized by Scindiah, and kept in confinement by him.

To add to the ingredients of mischief in this cauldron, there were throughout the Maratha states, Pindarees, who were then the freebooters which the *Marathas* had been; like the Black Bands or Companions in European History, sometimes soldiers, at all times robbers, sometimes acting as independent plunderers, and at other times ranged as mercenaries under the banner of some great prince or chief. Something of the same kind, and bound together by the tie of a mystic religious fraternity, were the sikhs, who swarmed in the territories upon the Sutlej, and thence over the Punjab, and had already in great degree passed from the condition of freebooters into that of permanent masters of the districts overrun by them.

This being the state of things, there appeared on the scene a very active and energetic adventurer, Jeswunt Rao Holkar, a natural son of Tuckojee Holkar, who raised its standard, and soon gathered together very formidable host, with which he sought to establish himself under some name or title as the real possessor of the power of the Peshwa. With this army he defeated the forces sent against him by the Peshwa, and he subsequently defeated in a decisive battle the combined armies of the Peshwa and Scindiah, who attempted in vain to intercept his march on Poonah, which capital he took and occupied. The Peshwa fled for protection into the British territory, and asked for British aid. He was only too glad now to comply with all Lord Wellesley's conditions, and a treaty known as "the Treaty of Bassein" was made between the Peshwa and the Government of Bombay on the 31st of December, 1802, by which in consideration of a British force and the British guarantee of his dominions, very considerable territories were ceded to the British, and some old claims of the Peshwa's upon some territories already in their possession were given up. The Peshwa further stipulated to discharge all Europeans of any nation at war with England; to abstain from any attack on the British or any of their allies, or any of the principal branches of the *Maratha* Empire or any power whatever; and to submit all disputes between himself and the Nizam and any other power to the arbitrament of the British. The treaty formally ratified the treaty which had been made with the Guicowar, and contained the stereotyped clause that the Peshwa "should not enter into any negotiations with any other power, without previous consultation with the Company's Government, and that the Company should have no manner of concern with any of his children, relations, subjects or servants, as to whom he was absolute."

No time was lost on the part of the English in performing their part of the treaty. In the Nizam's territory, in the Presidency of Madras, and in that of Bombay, armies were put on foot ready for action.

The first military operations were under Major-General Wellesley (the Duke of Wellington), who commenced his march on the 9th of March, 1803, from the Mysore frontier, and crossed the Toombucram river on the 12th. He displayed the judgement and skill for which he was afterwards so conspicuous, in preventing plunder and every excess, and in making such arrangements for his supplies as to prevent injury to the people of the districts through which route was directed, and so to protect and conciliate them. He consequently was able to obtain abundant supplies along his whole march. He was welcomed by the population, and so far from meeting with opposition was joined by most of the chiefs of the country. They relied implicitly on his assurance, that those who deserved well should be recommended to the particular favour of the Peshwa. Several who had been under the displeasure of the latter were induced to co-operate with General Wellesley, on his promise that the influence of the British Government should be exerted to restore them to the favour of their sovereign. On the 15th of April he effected a junction with the subsidiary force and native troops of the Nizam. On news of its advance Jeswunt Rao Holkar fell back, and with the main body of his army retreated 130 miles north-east from Poonah, which was left to Amrut Rao and a body of 1500 men. As General Wellesley advanced towards Poonah, he received intelligence that Amrut Rao intended to plunder and burn the city as soon as the British were in sight; and the Peshwa sent him the most pressing entreaties to provide for the safety of his family, who still remained at Poonah. General Wellesley was sixty miles from Poonah on the 19th April, and placing himself in person at the head of the British cavalry and some of the Peshwa's *Maratha* troops, marched the sixty miles through a rugged country in thirty-two hours, and arrived unexpectedly at Poonah. By the celerity of this march he took Amrut rao by surprise. The news of his approach preceded the English General only a few hours, and on hearing of it on the morning of the 20th, Amrut Rao precipitately retired leaving the city in safety. The general and his troops were welcomed as deliverers by all who had remained, and those who had deserted their homes and fled to the hills during Holkar's usurpation, immediately returned to their houses and resumed their ordinary avocations.

Lord Wellesley writes with just pride:—"It is a circumstance equally honourable to the British character and propitious to the British interests in that quarter of India, that the first effects of the British influence in the *Maratha* dominions should have been displayed in rescuing the capital of the Empire from impending ruin, and its inhabitants from violence and rapine." On the 13th of May, the Peshwa, attended by a numerous train of *Maratha* chiefs, entered Poonah and resumed his seat on the Musnud, his restoration having been effected in two months from the commencement of the British march, without spilling a drop of blood and to the great satisfaction of the people.

These proceedings and the Treaty of Bassein were regarded with very different feelings by the great *Maratha* powers. Scindiah and the Rajah of Berar temporized at first, and expressed no disatisfaction with the treaty; indeed, Scindiah, who had in fact nominated the minister of the Peshwa by whom the treaty was negotiated, on being pressed by the English Resident, expressly declared that he saw no objection to it, and that not the contrary it provided for the greater security of the chiefs in their relation to the Peshwa. Information, it is true, had reached the Governor-General that messages had been sent by Scindiah to various *Maratha* chiefs and commanders, commanding them to hold their troops in readiness for a combined attack on the British ;but these were disavowed with such apparent earnestness by Scindiah, that the Resident was satisfied that no hostile designs were entertained, and Lord Wellesley was only too willing to believe, that at all events the *Maratha* potentates would not venture to commence a conflict with a power so strong as the British then was and had shown itself to be.

It would have been very strange if the two great *Maratha* powers, Scindiah and Berar, had really acquiesced without a struggle in the quiet establishment of a British Protectorate at Poonah. It was wholly subversive of their own respective schemes of aggrandizement; and as to Scindiah, it was in effect the complete emancipation of the Court of Poonah from his control. He was willing enough to call in the British assistance against the irresistible power of Jeswunt Rao Holkar, and that the Peshwa in his distress should promise the required price; but when the service had been rendered the real extent of the price came to be weighed; and so far as it affected Scindiah, the price comprehended the whole spoil of his long aggressive policy towards Poonah. The Rajah of Berar's views were no doubt antagonistic to Scindiah, for he claimed for himself the post; but each probably thought, and not without reason, that the other would be a less formidabel antagonist to deal with in the future, than were in the present the British, of the tenacity of whose hold India had furnished so many examples. It was therefore very natural and very legitimate that they should come to an understanding, not only amongst themselves but with Holkar, to postpone their own dissensions and to concert measures to get rid of the British intruders into the *Maratha* country.

It was as natural and as legitimate that Lord Wellesley, on the other hand, should take and keep the hold which circumstances had given him. But for the British power the Peshwa would have remained a dethroned exile, Scindiah having failed in his attempt to assist him, and the Rajah of Berar having not even made an attempt in his favour. As far as the chiefs and people of the Peshwa's own particular dominion were concerned, they were not dissatisfied. The Treaty of Bassein certainly gave the British at least as legal and good a title to their protectorate over the Peshwa, as any which Scindiah could allege for the control he had usurped, or the Rajah of Berar could advance for the control he hoped to usurp. It was open to the *Maratha* powers, Scindiah and Berar, if they had been so minded, and if they had been content therewith, to repudiate the central authority of the Peshwa, as one which by submitting to a foreign protectorate, he had in truth abdicated; and such a proceeding would not have afforded the slightest legitimate excuse for hostilities on the part of the British.

Lord Wellesley was not at all desirous of having a quarrel with the confederate *Marathas*. Wars were expensive, and unprofitable in their result, and had always to be justified in an apologetic tone in the despatches to the Directors, who saw in them only fresh peril for their dividends, great risk of loss, with no probability of gain. Lord Wellesley would, therefore, have been only too glad to be able to announce to the Home Government that he had effected the restoration at Poonah, and carried out his favourite scheme of policy at that Court without firing a shot. Peace would have been to him unqualified success, but was fatal to all the ambitions and hopes of Scindiah and the Rajah. It is, therefore, with undoubting confidence that we may rely on Lord Wellesley's representations, that he was forced into the hostilities which ensued.

Soon after the restoration at Poonah, Scindiah gathered together a large army on the frontier of the Nizam's territory, in an attitude evidently hostile. It was impossible to suggest any motive for the assembling of an army there, other than a preparation for an attack either on the English or their ally. When it was found that the Rajah of Berar, after communication with Scindiah, had also left his own dominions at the head of his army, and was proceeding to join Scindiah, and accounts came in from all quarters of hostile preparations, and of attempts to seduce the allies of the British into the league which was being formed, the situation of affairs became very serious. At length, in answer to the repeated applications of the British Resident for a positive explanation of the real object of the military movements and preparations, Scindiah said, "I will give an answer when I have talked with the Rajah of Berar, and then you shall know whether it is peace or war." It was impossible to disregard this plain intimation of the real designs of Scindiah; but it was still thought expedient to give the *Marathas* an opportunity of peace ably withdrawing from the prosecution of their hostile enterprise. General Wellseley, to whom the conduct of the British affairs in that quarter was confided, after many evasions on the part of the confederates, at length peremptorily required that they should each withdraw his army into his own territory, pledging himself thereupon to withdraw his from the advanced position he occupied into its proper cantonments. Some show of complying with this requisition was made, but with such affected delays and so delusively, as to show to demonstration that they were merely intended for delay and in the hope of amusing the English, while the *Maratha* princes were completing their hostile preparations and alliances. Under these circumstances, General Wellesley was satisfied that it was his duty to resent their proceedings, and to bring the matter to ahead before the confederates were further strengthened. Hostilities were not, however, actually commenced until the 8th of August, 1803, when General Wellesley commenced his march towards Ahmednugur, and on the same day he attacked and carried by escalade the town. On the 10th reopened his breaching batteries against the fortress, which on the 12th surrendered; and by the 21st all the districts around Ahmednugur were taken possession off.

The forces of the combined armies were as follows:

Scindiah, Cavalry, 18,500; Infantry, 11 battalions. Rajah of Berar, Cavalry, 20,000; Infantry, 600. They had, besides, 35 pieces of heavy ordnance, 205 field-pieces, and 500 camel guns.

General Wellesley's entire force consisted of 384 European Cavalry, 1347 Native Cavalry, 1368 European Infantry, 5631 Sepoys, 173 Artillerymen, and 1000 Artillery lascars and pioneers; and he had with him 2400 Cavalry of the Rajah of Mysore, and about 3000 Marathas. There was marching to his support a force under Colonel Stevenson, of 8500 men, of whom there were 778 Europeans, all Infantry.

The two British armies having approached, it was arranged that they should, on the 24th of September, make a combined attack on the enemy. General Wellesley, however, ascertained that the enemy were moving to clude his attack, and going towards one of the passes into the Nizam's country, and he found that he must either attack alone, before Colonel Stevenson could effect a junction, or allow the enemy to escape. He determined to attack alone. He found the enemy strongly posted on the bank of a river, near the village of Assaye, and directed his attack against the infantry. His infantry advanced under a very hot artillery fire, the execution of which was terrible, and after a severe engagement the enemy's infantry line gave way in all directions, and his whole army retreated, leaving ninety pieces of cannon in the hands of the victors. Thus ended the battle of Assaye, one of Wellington's victories, achieved with great loss. Although the enemy retreated, they were not routed or dispersed, and General Wellesley and Colonel Stevenson had to proceed with their campaign.

While these operations were going on in the west, a British force, under Colonel Harcourt, attacked Cuttack, a seaboard province of the Rajah of Berar on the east, which interposed between the territories of Bengal and those of Madras, and contained the great temple of Juggernaut. Colonel Harcourt rapidly overran and subdued the province, where he was welcomed by the native Hindoo population, and found no difficulty in bringing into alliance with the British many of the inferior rajah, zamindars, and others amongst the *Marathas* themselves who owned nominal allegiance to the *Maratha* Rajah. Colonel Harcourt's campaign on the side of India was eminently successful, and the results great.

The fort and city of Baroch, a *Maratha* port on the Bombay coast, were taken by assault by another force despatched for that purpose. The capture of this place was considered a great moment by the Governor-General, as closing access from the sea to Scindiah; but the greatest interest of the *Maratha* campaign attaches to the operations and proceedings of General (afterwards Lord) Lake, the Commander-in-Chief. To this General Lord Wellesley communicated in the fullest and most unreserved manner his policy, his wishes, and his own views of what might be obtained, and then left him to act according to his own judgement and decision, assuring him of his most cordial support. General Lake showed himself in all respects worthy of the confidence reposed in him. The instructions given to General Lake pointed out (to use his own summary of them) the expediency of destroying the French power and authority in Hindostan; of seizing their arsenals, military stores, and strong places; of taking possession on account of the British Government of that extent of country which is situated between the Ganges and the Jumna, called the Doab; of securing a line of forts on the north-western banks of the Jumna, to protect the navigation of that river; of taking under the protection of the British Government his Majesty Shah Alam; and of forming such connexions with the independent rajahs and petty princes to the north-west of Hindostan, as would secure their friendship and form a barrier against the power of the *Maratha* states.

As soon as Lake heard of the actual commencement of war between General Wellesley and Scindiah, he put his army in option. The Governor-General had previously, by proclamation, warned all British subjects, and all natives of British India, serving in Scindiah's regular army, of whom there were many, to leave his service. This proclamation being coupled with offers to take them into the English service or otherwise to compensate them for their loss, produced a considerable effect in weakening the enemy. The French general, M. Perron, had himself, before the outbreak of hostilities and from personal considerations, expressed a wish to retire from Scindiah's service and his position in India, and had applied for a safe conduct for himself and his wealth through British territory, which had been granted him.' As soon, however, as war actually broke out, M. Perron, with proper soldierly feeling, resolved to stand by his nominal master, or at least by his own army, and took the field at their head.

General Lake, on the 29th of August, 1803, found Perron strongly posted near the fortress of Aligarh, on which his right rested, his entire front being protected by a deep morass. By a considerable détour the British General turned the left flank of the enemy, dislodging a body of troops posted in a village in their front. He then moved forward with his cavalry in two lines, supported by a line of infantry and guns, and the enemy after a very few shots from the guns with the cavalry, which did some little execution, retired, making a very rapid retreat from the field. The British loss in men and horses was inconsiderable and did not comprise a single officer. The loss of the enemy was also small. Their army consisted entirely of cavalry, except a few matchlock men, and "they were" (writes Lake) "so quick in their retreat the moment we attempted to charge them, that there was no possibility of catching most of them." But this battle, so little sanguinary, was in effect decisive of the campaign; Perron with his body-guard retired towards Agra, leaving M. Pedron in the fort of Aligarh.

The natives had hitherto always thought Perron invincible, but most of them now left him; and the very next day Lake was able to inform the Governor-General that the inhabitants were coming in fast, manifesting a wish to place themselves under British protection. The English General immediately caused it to be made known to the head men of the villages, that it was not his intention to molest either the persons or properties of the inhabitants who should claim his protection. The people of the town of Coel, who had fled the day before on his approach, returned fast to their homes, and the town was already nearly re-inhabited, under the protection of a battalion which was posted there to prevent plunder, so that very little loss was sustained by the inhabitants. On the same day Lake was able further to report, that the country in his rear was in a state of perfect tranquillity; that the horse had all retired, as he believed, to their own homes, as no depredations had been committed, and that not a horseman was to be seen or heard of in that part of the Doab, or in any of the British districts; and in fine the congratulated the Governor-General on the full possession of the Doab. Lake immediately summoned the fortress of aligarh to surrender; and after spending some days in fruitless endeavours to obtain the surrender of the fortress by purchase, finding that the garrison persisted obstinately in their determination to resist, and in their rejection of his overtures, he determined to try an assault.

The assault was given accordingly on the morning of the 4th of September. The assaulting force consisted of four companies of the 76th Royal Regiment, one battalion of native infantry, and a detachment from another native regiment. With this force, Colonel Monson, leading his men on under a most galling fire of musketry and grape, almost immediately carried the fort, hitherto deemed impregnable and defended on all sides with the utmost obstinacy. Although the entire loss of the British was from the rapidity of the attack not great (223 rank and file), the nature of the task may be estimated from the loss of officers. The 76th Regiment had its colonel and its major wounded, a captain, adjutant, and three lieutenants killed, and two other lieutenants wounded. The fortress which was thus taken was found armed with seventy-eight pieces of artillery; and besides the ordnance actually mounted, there were found 26 brass and iron guns, and 182 iron wall-pieces in the arsenal. From the great breadth of the ditch and its depth of water the attack was only practicable on the gates, three of which it was necessary to burst open. The gates were uncommonly strong, and the road to them was completely covered by batteries and other strong works in the fort, from which the enemy did much execution.

Lake after this halted two days only in his position at Coel; and leaving a garrison in the fortress and detaching a brigade of cavalry (one royal regiment and two native regiments) to deal with a force of the enemy's cavalry, which had made an irruption into the British territory, he marched rapidly on with the remainder of his army. On the 11th of September he encountered a very large force, both of cavalry and infantry, with a numerous artillery under the command of one of Perron's officers, M. Bourquin, or as he was generally called M. Louis. After a long march of eighteen miles in the morning, the British having learnt that M. Louis had crossed the Jumna from Delhi to attack them, had hardly encamped when they found their outposts assailed by a strong body. On reconnoitring, Lake found the whole army drawn up in order of battle, and immediately ordered out the whole line and advanced to attack the foe in front. The enemy at first oppose to them a tremendous war of grape and chain shot, from the numerous artillery, uncommonly well served, and causing great loss, which did not, however, check the British advance. A charge of bayonets by the latter caused a most precipitate retreat, and the enemy left the whole of their artillery in Lake's hands. The British cavalry pursued the fugitives to the Jumna, causing great havoc; and numbers were drowned in attempting to cross.

The completeness of this victory was principally due to the steadiness and coolness of the infantry, who advanced to within one hundred paces of the enemy without taking their firelocks from their shoulders, when they fired a volley and rushed on with the bayonet to the charge, which the enemy were unable to face. The English loss was 197 Europeans (including one major, one captain, and two lieutenants, ten non-commissioned officers, and thirty-nine privates killed) and 288 Natives, (including ten officers and thirty-eight privates killed). The whole British army did not consist of more than 4500 men, including only one European regiment of cavalry and one European regiment of infantry, on whom, as will be seen from the loss, the brunt of the fight must have fallen. The enemy were upwards of four times that number, supported by nearly one hundred pieces of cannon, many of a very large calibre. The General might well therefore write, "The more I reflect on the glorious affair of the 11th,[1] the more forcibly I feel the bravery and intrepidity displayed by every individual composing my army." The garrison left in Delhi on bearing of the rout of their army, after plundering the city, left it precipitately; and they, as well as the remains of Louis's army, dispersed in different directions. The country people were so enraged at their plundering them, that they retaliated by plundering and killing those who fell into their hands; and the French officers were obliged to seek their personal safety by delivering themselves up to the British on the 15th of September.

Shah Alam had for a number of years in the past been under the power and control of the French faction. "The oppressive and degrading manner" (writes Lake) "in which they had exerted their authority, their insulting conduct to the royal family, the state of rigorous confinement in which it had been detained, and the extreme indigence to which it was reduced by French rapacity, were all circumstances which rendered this monarch eager to receive the British protection, and made him view its approach with joy and exultation. Every effort, which the liberty he had now obtained gave him the power of exerting, was employed in affording the British army the means of crossing the river into Delhi, and in testifying the extreme satisfaction of himself and his dependents at the success of the British."

The Governor-General, however, had been careful that the Shah should not be deluded by any vain hope of restoration to this imperial power, or to any power. Lord Wellesley had furnished general Lake with a letter to "His Majesty, Shah Alam," which after many expressions of respect concluded by offering the monarch an asylum with adequate provision for himself and his household;[2] and the unfortunate monarch was, after all he had suffered, only too glad to avail himself of the promised protection and provision.

General Lake lost no time in executing his successful march, first to Muttra and then to Agra, a very strong place on the Jumna, with a fort regularly constructed with a deep ditch and high walls, deemed amongst the natives of extraordinary strength. On the 10th of October Lake drove the enemy from the town and from deep ravines near by. By the morning of the 17th the breaching batteries were ready, and in the course of that day they did so much execution that the garrison of 5000 men capitulated, and on the 18th marched out, leaving the fort to be occupied by the British. The only terms required by the garrison, consisting of the best of Perron's sepoys, were protection to their persons and private property, which were of course granted.

While these military operations were going on with such brilliant results, the political negotiations were making no less progress. Rajah after Rajah, chief after chief, gave in their adhesion to the British and entered into treaties of alliance which were more or less after the same stereotyped form; that is to say, treaties by which they accepted the protection of the English control in all matters of foreign relations and disputes with other powers, and undertook to be governed by English advice in all domestic matters.

There was neither love nor fear in these alliances; so far as they had any preference, these petty potentates probably preferred the English to any other master, having more confidence in their pledge word; and as they were obliged to have some one in the position of master or suzerain, they of course took the protection and placed themselves under control of the power which appeared so great, and whose European soldiers must have been deemed by the natives invincible. Of course a tie so easily made was liable at any moment to be as easily loosened. Nor has there ever been any delusion in this respect in the councils of the British. It was well understood, that the native chiefs would be faithful, so long as the British power was and showed itself strong enough, to punish those who were unfaithful, and to protect those who were faithful to their engagements, and no longer.

One great cause of the marvellous facility with which the English took towns and annexed provinces, was the strict discipline which the commanders enforced. Lord Wellesley repeats more than once with legitimate pride, the following extract from the General's despatch. "It is with a mixed sentiment of pride and pleasure that I inform your lordship that all the inhabitants of this place, who for a time fled, returned to their habitations last night on perceiving that no ravages had been committed by the troops. I am informed from all quarters that the inhabitants behold with astonishment this proof of the discipline and good conduct of the army; all declare that hitherto it has ben unknown in Hindostan that a victorious army should pass through a country without destroying by fire, and committing every excess the most injurious to the inhabitants, but on the contrary, from the regularity observed by us, our approach is a blessing, instead of bringing with it all the horrors of war attended by rapine and murder; that their cattle remain in their fields unmolested and the inhabitants in their houses receive every protection. The favourable opinion the inhabitants have formed of us cannot fail of producing the most beneficial consequences."[3]

Just before the fall of Agra, Scindiah made one great effort to recover the possessions of which he had been deprived by Lake. He gathered together the force of infantry which remained with him in Hindustan, and a considerable body of cavalry, with which he took up a position about thirty miles to the rear of the British encampment before Agra. As soon as the surrender of the fortress released the British forces detained there, Lake marched to seek the enemy and force them to an engagement. It was all-important to prevent the enemy, who retired after the fall of Agra, from eluding the attack. Leaving his heavy guns and most of his baggage behind him, Lake, on the mornings of the 30th and 31st October, 1803, marched forty miles, although the climate was extremely unfavourable to rapid movements by his European troops.

Receiving certain intelligence that the enemy were encamped about twenty-five miles in his front, and intended by a very long march the next day to frustrate his intention, Lake set out at midnight with his cavalry, desiring his infantry to follow him with all expedition, starting at three in the morning. He succeeded with his cavalry in coming up with the enemy just as they were moving at daylight, having in forty-eight hours accomplished a march of sixty-five miles. He immediately attacked with his cavalry, and so succeeded in detaining the enemy until noon, when the infantry arrived. He then at once made a general attack with his whole line, and the result was the great and crowning victory of Laswary.

It was while it lasted a desperate conflict. The enemy offered a most vigorous resistance until he lost his guns; and then abandoned his post. The left wing did not then fly, but attempted to retreat in good order, but two regiments of cavalry—one European, the 27th, and one native, under Colonel Vandeleur—succeeded in breaking in upon the retreating column, who were all cut up or made prisoners. With the exception of 2000 prisoners few of the enemy escaped the general slaughter. The enemy's army comprised seventeen regular battalions of infantry—the whole residue of the troops which had been disciplined by the French. General Lake had therefore to congratulate the Governor-General on the complete annihilation of the whole of the regular force in Scindiah's service commanded by French officers, which had been so long the subject of apprenhension to the British Government, not indeed without cause. "These battalions" (writes the General) "are most uncommonly well appointed, have numerous artillery as well served as they can possibly be; the gunners standing to their guns until killed by the bayonet. All the sepoys of the enemy behaved exceedingly well, and if they had been commanded by French officers the event would have been, I fear, extremely doubtful. I never was in so severe a business in my life, or anything like it, and pray to God I never may be in such a situation again." The brunt of the engagement fell as usual on the Europeans, of whom there were killed or wounded 39 officers, 38 sergeants, and 315 privates. It was not then without great reason that Lake did earnestly "wish for more men from England."

On the other side of India, General Wellesley and Colonel Stevenson were pursuing their career of victories and successful storming of towns. At length, on the 30th of November, 1803, General Wellesley was able to bring the combined armies of the Rajah of Berar and of Scindiah to a general engagement at Argaum. After a long day's march on a very hot day, the English General was preparing to encamp his troops, when he perceived a long line of infantry, cavalry, and artillery, regularly drawn up on the plains of Argaum, about six miles from his intended encampment. Although late in the day, and not withstanding the fatigue of the long march, General Wellesley determined to attack the army at once. A large body of Pathans, who attempted an attack on the 76th and 78th Regiments as these were advancing, were destroyed; and Scindiah's cavalry, which charged a battalion of Sepoy infantry on the left, were repulsed. Dispirited by these failures, the whole army retired in disorder before the British troops, leaving in their hands thirty-eight pieces of cannon and all their ammunition. The lateness of the hour prevented the rout being so complete as it would otherwise have been, but the British, Mogul, and Mysore cavalry pursued the fugitives for many miles, continuing the pursuit by moonlight, destroying great numbers, and taking many elephants, camels, and baggage.

The British loss was not great, but as usual fell disproportionately on the small European force, of whom there were 15 killed and 145 wounded, to 31 killed and 147 wounded out of the large number of native soldiers.

After the victory of Argaum, General Wellesley lost no time in commencing the siege of Gawilgurh, a strong fortress situated in a range of mountains near the sources of the Taptee and the Purna. From the 7th to the 12th of December, the heavy siege ordnance and stores had to be dragged by the troops by hand, over mountains and through ravines, by roads which the troops had previously to make for themselves. On the night of the 12th breaching batteries were placed in position. On the 13th the fire opened, on the 14th, at night, the breaches in the outer wall were declared practicable, and the next morning the assault was given, and the outer wall was soon carried. The inner wall had not been breached, but a party of light infantry of the 94th Regiment, under Captain Campbell, succeeded in mounting it by ladders, getting into the place, and opening the gate for the storming party; and the strong fortress was shortly in the possession of the British.

With this brilliant achievement the *Maratha* campaign closed. Scindiah and the Rajah of Berar were beaten at every point by a series of military operations, over a theatre of war, the extent of which may be estimated from the fact, that from Cuttack to Baroch is in a straight line 1000 miles, and from Ahmednagar (where General Wellesley broke ground on the 12th of August) to Delhi, more than 700 miles.

They sued for peace; the Governor-General was in a position to dictate his own terms; and on the 17th of December, 1803, the Rajah of Berar's minister and General

Wellesley signed a treaty, the important provisions of which treaty were:—

1. The cession of the province of Cuttack, including the post and district of Balasore, and of all the Rajah's territories to the westward of the river Wurda, of all of which he had been joint owner with the Nizam.
2. The renunciation of all claims on the Nizam.
3. An engagement by the Rajah not to take or retain in his service any Frenchman, or the subject of any European or American power at war with the British, or any British subject.
4. A confirmation of the treaties made by the British with the Rajah's feudatories.
5. A renunciation of the confederacy formed by him with Scindiah and other *Maratha* chiefs, to attack the Company and their allies.

The Company on their part undertook to mediate and arbitrate according to the principles of justice, in any disputes between the Rajah and the Company's allies, the Nizam and the Peshwa, and not to give aid or countenance to any discontented relations, rajahs, zamindars, or other subjects of the Rajah, who should fly from or rebel against his authority.

On the 30th December, General Wellesley also signed a treaty with the ministers of Scindiah. By this the Maharajah ceded the territory in the Doab, and all that he had to the northward of Jaipur and Joudpoor, the forts of Baroch and Ahmednagar and their territories, and all to the south of the Adjuntee Hills, including all his districts between that range of hills and the Godavery; and he renounced all claims of every description on the Company and their allies the Nizam, the Peshwa and Guicowar, reserving to himself and to certain of his chiefs the rights of property free of all payment to the

Government, in certain districts which were alleged to be his ancestral property, or to have been given to the chiefs for their support. He confirmed all treaties made by the British with his feudatories, renounced all claims on them, and declared them to be independent, provided that his should not extend to any of his territories to the southward of Jaipur, Joudpoor and Gohun. He renounced all claims on his Majesty Shah Alam, and engaged to interfere no further in his affairs, and entered into an engagement, similar to that which the Rajah of Berar had entered into, as to the employment of Frenchmen or other foreigners or British subjects. By a special article, the option was given to Scindiah to acceede to the treaties of general defensive alliance between the Company, the Nizam, and the Peshwa, and on his making such option, which he afterwards did, the Company were to furnish him with a subsidiary fore of seven battalions.

By these treaties a vast accession of territory was made. But the more important results in Lord Wellesley's view were, that the whole sea-coast was now in the hands of the British and their dependent allies, so as to preclude all access to any European enemy; that the great *Maratha* states of the Peshwa and Scindiah were placed under the protection of the Company; that by the treaties with almost the whole body of the smaller powers of India, confirmed by the general treaties with the *Maratha* potentates, and the very general agreements to submit disputes to the arbitration of the Company's Government, the power of any *Maratha* chief to establish a real *Maratha* Empire or to increase his dominions was effectually precluded; that the French party was wholly annihilated; and that with the possession of the person of the Shah, as pensioner of the state, the power and influence which the use of the Imperial name might still have given, was, if not actually vested in the British, at all events prevented from being turned against them. The British had now become substantially the sovereigns of India, and had succeeded to far more than the power, which had even been really acquired by any Great Mogul.

Lord Wellesley claimed as one of the results of his policy the elevation of the fame and glory of the British nation in India, by the splendid achievements of the war, and by the clemency, moderation, and public faith which distinguished the British counsels on the conclusion of the peace. His hopes were sanguine that the British power would now be enabled to control the causes of that internal warfare, which, during so long a series of years, had desolated many of the most fertile provinces of India, and had formed an inexhaustible source for the supply of military adventurers, prepared to join the standard of any turbulent leader for the purpose of ambition or plunder; and he trusted "that a general bond of connexion has now been established between the British Government and the principal states of India, on principles which render it the interest of every state to maintain its alliance with the British Government, which preclude the inordinate aggrandizement of any one of those states by an usurpation of the rights and possessions of others and which secure to every state the unmolested exercise of its separate authority within the limits of its established dominion, under the general protection of the British power." He was a little premature and a little over-sanguine as to the new reign of peace; the results obtained, however, were very great. Is there any ground for imputing to the British Government that they were obtained improperly or unfairly, or as the fruits of an ambitious and aggressive policy, or for charging the Governor-General with a violation of the spirit or the letter of the express legislative declaration and enactment denouncing and forbidding aggressive wars, and all schemes for the extension of the British territorial possessions in the East? The British nation sincerely dreaded and disliked all territorial extension in India; and the Court of Directors and the Government fully shared the national feeling. No great proof could be found of this than a despatch, in which they requested Lord Wellesley to consider again whether it would not be better to give back everything he had gained from the *Marathas*, and intimated pretty clearly their inability to furnish the requisite military force for the defence of the empire which he had created.

Lord Wellesley for himself always indignantly denied that he was in the slightest degree actuated by any vulgar ambition of increased dominion. He was personally satisfied, as he well might be, with the glory of the Mysore war. He was on bad terms with the Court of Directors, who had in many ways and on many occasions slighted, thwarted, and in an offensive manner overruled him, and he was really anxious to return home at the very time when the events occurred which led to the *Maratha* campaign, which made it his duty to remain at his post until he had brought the matter to a conclusion. He had plainly intimated, that while it was his inclination and his duty to manifest prompt obedience to the orders of the Directors, it was his primary duty to look into all hazards to the security of the British possessions, and that he should have in constant remembrance that the law had invested him "with a trust for the Company and for the British empire, as well as for the Court of Directors."

In this he really understated his case. He had another and a higher trust, a trust imposed on the British nation themselves, for the people of British India. It was his duty to do what a just, good, and competent sovereign would have done, if that sovereign had been a native and hereditary monarch, instead of being a foreigner, exercising the powers of a temporary proconsulate. Tried by that, the only true test, nothing was done by Lord Wellesley which it was not his full right and bounden duty to do.

To have allowed a lawless and unscrupulous adventurer like Jeswant Rao Holkar to establish himself at Poonah, would have been an act of culpable neglect. Such an adventurer would probably, if not interfered with have had as little difficulty in establishing a powerful *Maratha* kingdom, as Hyder had in building up his formidable power in Mysore; and in league with the 40,000 disciplined regular troops under Perron and it's French officers he would have been irresistible, and under no restraint in carrying on wars either of aggression or devastation. How formidable he was even alone, if not to the British power, to the poor inhabitants, whom the British were bound to protect will be seen in the sequel. Every consideration of self-defence against an imminent peril, therefore, rendered it imperative on the British to take up the cause of the expelled Peshwa. Starting from that point, the Treaty of Bassein was a just and proper treaty, and nothing was exacted from the Peshwa that was not consistent with justice, or not required by the exigencies of the situation. In their dissatisfaction with that treaty Scindiah and the Rajah of Berar became clearly the aggressors, and their attitude of unmistakable hostility, with the moral certainty, afterwards fully confirmed, of the offensive league into which they had entered and sought to bring the other Indian powers, rendered the political and military measures, which were taken to defeat their designs a matter of absolute necessity.

In considering the perils of the position in which Lord Wellesley found himself, it is necessary to bear in mind, what his military strength and resources actually were, and the real weakness which he had to supply by promptitude and vigour of action. The whole European force over the whole India territory consisted of six batteries of artillery, four regiments of cavalry, thirteen regiments of royal infantry, and three of the Company's infantry. The latter were very indifferent in those days, and the deductions for sick were very heavy, not less than a fourth of the force, and it was very difficult to keep up the nominal strength by recruiting. The sixteen regiments of European infantry would probably have never turned out 11,000 effective bayonets. Sixteen regiments of cavalry, and fifty-nine regiments (118 battalions) of infantry, made up the sum of his native force. From England he had received the unwelcome news, that it was scarcely possible to obtain recruits even for the necessary defence of the British Isles. Hesitation while the enemy were gathering strength, and might possibly be tampering with the native troops, would have been in ruin. After the great and brilliant successes obtained against the confederacy, to have allowed them to go unpunished would have been mere imbecility. The sacrifices demanded and the terms imposed were as moderate as they could be consistently with the objects which it was the Governor-General's bounden duty to effect:— that is, to deter, if possible, from a repetition of the offence, and to diminish effectually the power of repeating it with success. Nor was there any one who could truly allege that any wrong was done to him, that any real or just right of his was invaded. Scindiah was himself a mere usurper and conqueror; the Rajah of Berar's power was hardly a generation old, and as the power of the sword; M. Perron was an alien adventurer, who had just obtained his dominions by the abuse, for his own purposes , of the military powers which Scindiah had gathered to aid his aggressions; and there was neither rajah nor chief, zamindar nor ryot, who was not glad to try a new master, or who owed loyalty to the old one.

The feudatories, with whom the treaties were made, made them voluntarily. As to the poor Mogul, it would have been a folly and a crime to the real people of India, the Hindoos, had there been any attempt to restore the power of an oppressive Mohammedan dynasty, which had become effete. Nor did the British Government attempt to derive from the charge of protecting and supporting the monarch, the means of employing the nominal imperial power for the assertion of claims upon the provinces composing the Mogul empire.

The arrangements made for the support of the king and the royal family were such as to secure them the enjoyment of every reasonable comfort and convenience, and every practicable degree of external state and dignity compatible with the extent of the British resources, and the state of dependence in which they must thenceforth live. It may well be doubted, whether the Governor-General was not rather misled by the desire of appearing in the eyes of India, and of the world, as the magnificent protector and benefactor of the great Mogul, the representative of Timur. It was not necessary to preserve, as was done, the imperial name and state, the sovereign power over the city of Delhi, and the royal domains assigned for the support of the family. No good could come from keeping before men's eyes in India this phantom of departed imperial power, and evil might, and in fact long afterwards did, come of it. Ninety thousand sicca rupees a month were assigned to the monarch and his family, with an addition of 10,000 rupees annually on certain festivals, agreeably to ancient usage; and a provision for an additional monthly sum of 40,000 rupees of the revenue, if the assigned districts should there after admit of it. Having regard to the then value of money at Delhi, and to the state of almost privation in which the Mogul's family had been previously kept, the allowances were not only ample, but magnificent. It would, however, have been really kinder, as well as a more prudent policy, if preserving the titular rank during the old man's life, the members of the family had been at once reduced to their true position of wealthy nobles, with such social distinction as might be due to their princely birth and high lineage. It is difficult to conceive any worse position for men to be brought up in, than as the idle titular princes at the court of a titular emperor, with all its mock ceremonial and pageantry.

II

The *Maráthá* Empire, if I may so term the five States ruled by *Maráthá* chiefs, with the Peshwá as their nominal head, which, at the period of which I am writing, dominated Western, Central, and North-Western India, founded in the middle of the seventeenth century by Sívájí; tending to decay under his son, Sambají; restored by the efforts of Mulhárjí Holkar and Ránojí Sc indhiá; had been humbled to the dust by the complete defeat its armies sustained on the fatal field of Pánípat, at the hands of the ruler of Kábul, Ahmad Sháh Abdálí, January the 6th 1761. There fled, however, from that field, sorely wounded, a member of the house of Scindhiá, Mádhájí by name, who, recognised shortly afterwards as the head of that house, devoted all his intellectual power, which was extraordinary, and his energies, which were untiring, to restore to his race the influence and the position which it had lost. He succeeded. In 1771, he entered Delhi—the titular Emperor, Sháh Álam, in his train—as a conqueror. In 1778, he had his first contest with the English, a contest in which not only had the Maráthás all the advantage in the field, but they forced upon their enemy the shameful and humiliating Treaty of Wárgaum (January 14th, 1779). Warren Hastings, however, who then guided the fortunes of British India, was not the man to allow such a disgrace to pass unavenged. Disavowing the Treaty of Wárgaum, he sent Goddard and afterwards Camac to Central and Western India, and these commanders soon retrieved the reputation which had been lost in the disastrous campaign.

Mádhájí, indeed, fought not unequally with Goddard, and baffled two successive attempts to force him to a general action (April 3rd and 19th, 1780). But meanwhile, Captain Popham had surprised and captured the strong fortress of Gwáliár. The following year, however, Mádhájí came up with a small force under Colonel Camac at Sironj, and drove it for seventeen days before him. But on the eighteenth day Camac, suddenly turning, surprised the Maráthá chieftain in his camp. His great superiority in cavalry saved Mádháji however, from much damage, and during the rest of the year he compelled the English to remain inactive. Finally, perceiving he had everything to lose from carrying on a contest within his own territories, he concluded (October 13th, 1780) a treaty with Colonel Muir, who had joined Camac, by which he bound himself to neutrality, agreed to exercise his good offices to bring about a peace with the other Maráthá powers, recovered all his territories except the fortress of Gwáliár, and obtained from the English a promise that they would recross the Jamnah.

Warren Hastings was conducting at this time the last and desperate war with Haidar Álí, and he wished by all the means in his power to make peace on fair terms with the Maráthás. He succeeded, by the aid of Mádhájí, in May, 1782, in inducing the Peshwá to agree, at Salbai, to a treaty by which the contending parties were, with respect to their territories, restored to the positions they respectively occupied before the war. This treaty was ratified June the 6th, and the rectifications were exchanged with the Peshwá on February the 24th following. The Maráthás were thus left free to consolidate their fortunes in Western, Central, and North-Western India.

In the attempts which they made to this end, Mádhájí Scindhiá took a very decided lead. First, by an arrangement with the native chief to whom the English had made over Gwáliár, he recovered that fortress. Then, having ascertained that the English would not interfere with any plans he might put inaction for obtaining possession of the imperial cities of Ágra and Delhí, he joined the Imperial Court, then a prey to contending factions, near the former city; speedily obtained a complete ascendancy in the councils of the Mughul, and accompanied it to Delhi. There he accepted for the Peshwá the title of "Vicegerent of the Empire;" for himself that of Deputy to the Peshwá. From this period to the occurrence of the event immediately preceding the action forced upon Lord Wellesley, and which I am about to describe, the Maráthá power, as exercised by the house of Scindhiá, was supreme in the two imperial cities, and in the districts immediately dependent upon them.

To establish and maintain his power in North-Western India, and to prepare for the decisive struggle with the English, which he not only saw looming in the future, but which he was resolved to provoke at an opportune moment, Mádhájí organised bodies of troops on the European model, under the immediate command of adventurers from all parts of Europe, but mostly from France. His policy was to destroy the power of the smaller princes who should prove irreconcilable, to conciliate those who would be conciliated; then, when his power in North-West and Central India should be firmly consolidated, to proceed to Puná; obtain the ascendancy he required in the councils of the Peshwá; to induce, then the independent native chiefs of India to join the confederacy which he was forming against the foreigner;

and finally to enter upon a decisive struggle for empire with the English. Had he lived two years longer he would have had a great chance. He would have had to do with a Governor-General who would have moved neither hand nor foot until he were attacked, and it is impossible to say that he might not have succeeded. When the year 1794 dawned he had accomplished most of his objects. He had consolidated his power in North-Western and Central India; he had obtained the ascendancy he required in the councils of the Peshwá; he was engaged in arranging for a general combination against the English. But, just as success seemed within his grasp, he was attacked by fever and died (February 12th, 1794).

He was succeeded by his grandnephew, a boy of fifteen. This boy, Dáolat Ráo by name, was suddenly called upon, with a character unformed, to deal with problems which called for the wisdom of an experienced statesman.

The first problem was caused by the death of the Peshwá. On October the 25th of the year following, Madhu Ráo Peshwá, a young man of considerable promise, deliberately threw himself, in a fit of melancholy, from the lofty terrace of his palace to the ground. Two days later he died from the effects of the injuries he then received. The misfortune was not so much that a Peshwá had died, but that the nearest heir to the Peshwá was a young man so unscrupulous, so deprived, so intriguing, and so cowardly, that his succession could not fail to prove a misfortune to his family and race.

After much manoeuvring, this young man, whose name was Bájí Ráo, did succeed to the vacated seat. His first aim was to rid himself of the powerful vassals who surrounded him. The first whose influence he neutralised, was his predecessor's minister, Náná Farnáwís, the partisan of alliance with the English. Then he turned his attention to Dáolat Ráo Scindhiá, the successor of Mádhájí, and who still remained at Puná. He began by doing all in his power to lessen his popularity, to weaken his influence, to exhaust his treasury. Then he encouraged Jeswant Ráo Holkar to attack the dominions of Scindhiá in Central India. Hostilities in consequence broke out between the two Maráthá princes. After some preliminary successes Holkar was totally defeated by Dáolat Ráo, in a battle fought near Indúr, October 14th, 1801. Had Dáolat Ráo followed up this victory the career of Jeswant Ráo had been finished for ever. But Dáolat Ráo delayed to amuse himself, whilst Jeswant Ráo, hurrying off with fresh troops to Khandesh, turned suddenly upon the army which, led by one of Scindhiá's Generals, as leisurely following him, and inflicted on it a crushing and decisive defeat near Puná, October 25th, 1802. From this defeat arose the conjuncture which brought the Peshwá in close contact with the British, and gave the Marquess Wellesley the opportunity, of which he availed himself with rare ability, to carry out the policy which he had fixed in his own mind as the only policy which could ensure absolutely the security of the British in India.

Impatient of the yoke which Scindhiá had long imposed upon him, the Peshwá, Bájí Ráo, had for some time past been listening, not without indifference, to a proposal made to him by the British Resident at his Court, Colonel Barry Close, for the location, near to, but not within his territories, of a British force which he might call to his aid in case of need. No arrangements had been actually arrived at when the rival Maráthá armies came into each other's presence, near Puná, on that morning of October 25th. The Peshwá, confident that Scindhiás troops would gain the day, had actually set out from the city with his own following for the purpose of taking part in the action. But the battle had joined before he reached the ground, and, naturally a coward, he became frightened by the noise of the firing, and turned off to the south, there, at the distance of three or four moles, to await the result. As soon as he had ascertained that Holkar had gained the day, dreading that chieftain far more than he had dreaded Scindhiá, he fled with about seven thousand followers to the fort of Singarh, eleven miles from Puná, and despatched thence to Colonel Close a preliminary engagement, binding himself to subsidize six battalions of sipáhis, and to cede twenty-five lakhs of rupees of annual revenue for their support. He stayed three days at Singarh; proceeded thence twenty-one miles further, to Raigarh; thence to Mahar. From this place he despatched letters to the Bombay Government, requesting that ships might be sent to convey himself and his follower to Bassein. Hearing, before he could receive a reply, that Holkar's troops were approaching, he required to Severndrug; stayed there till a fresh alarm arose; he crossed over to Rewadanda, and, embarking thence in an English ship, provided for his reception, proceeded to Bassein, where he arrived on December 6th. He was met there by Colonel Barry Close, armed with full instructions from the Marquess Wellesley; and there, on December 31st, he signed the important Treaty, known as the Treaty of Bassein. By this treaty the Peshwá entered the list of protected princes. He bartered his independence for security. The titular chief of the Maráthá confederacy became virtually the vassal of the nation, which he had regarded till then as his rival for empire.*

In May of the following year, the Peshwá accompanied a British force, which, under the provisions of the treaty, was assembled, in a manner presently to be described, to reseat him in Puná. Holkar, who till that time had occupied that capital, fled on its approach, acquiescing for the moment in an arrangement which he did not feel himself strong enough to prevent. Dáolat Ráo Scindhiá was not so easily reconciled to the position. He had now attained the age of twenty-three. During the seven or eight years which had followed the death

* By the Treaty of Bassein, the Peshwá was to receive a subsidiary force of six battalions with guns, and was to cede for their payment territory of the value of 26,000,000 rupees. He was to refer to the British Government all his disputes with the Nizam, and his claims against the Gaikwár. and was to be re-established by the British Government in his full rights as the head of the Maráthá confederacy. A portion of the territory thus ceded was afterwards exchanged for part of these Peshwa's possessions in Bundelkhand. These arrangements were embodied in supplementary Articles to the Treaty, on December 16, 1803. *Vide* Aitchison's *Treaties*, vol. iii.

of Mádháji, he had some rough schooling. Some glimmering of the wisdom of the policy entertained by his prescient great uncle, had forced itself on his intelligence. He recollected that opportunity had been offered twice to him for preventing the catastrophe: once, when he had beaten Holkar at Indur; again, when after the defeat of his General, he might have marched with an overpowering force to the aid of the Peshwá. The Treaty of Bassein took him completely by surprise. He was not ready for the contest which he now foresaw would be waged under conditions far less advantageous for the Maráthás than would have been possible before the signature of that treaty. Invited to acquiesce in its conditions, he at first hesitantingly agreed, then as abruptly refused, and sent messengers to two other Maráthá chiefs, Holkar and the Bhonslá,* to endeavour to persuade them to enter into a confederacy against the foreigner. Jeswant Ráo, influenced probably by jealousy; believing that, in the event of victory, which he did not doubt, the main advantages would accrue to Scindhiá; received the messengers coldly. The Bhonslá on the other hand, professed himself willing to discuss the matter at a personal interview.

The action of the Peshwá in throwing himself on the generosity of the British Government, and in invoking its protection corresponded entirely to the hopes which Lord Wellesley had long entertained as constituting the best solution of the Maráthá question. "The most effectual arrangements for securing the British Government against any danger from the Maráthá States," he had written, "appear to be an intimate alliance with the acknowledged sovereign power of the Maráthá empire, founded upon principles which should render the British influence and military force the main support of the Power. Such an arrangement appeared to afford the best security for preserving a due balance between the several states constituting the confederacy of the Maráthá empire, as well as for preventing any dangerous

* The Márthá prince who ruled at Nágpúr: otherwise called the Rájah of Berar.

union or diversion of the resources of that empire." And now, without any prompting on his part, "the acknowledged sovereign power of the Maráthá empire" had solicited, with an earnestness which would not take refusal, permission to place himself and his territories in the very position which Lord Wellesley had declared to be "the most effectual arrangement for securing the British Government against any danger from the Maráthá states." The arrangement, it is true, was one which, through his agent at the court of the Peshwá, he had been constantly suggested, and which, by that means, had become familiar to the mind of Bájí Ráo. oppressed by the superiority affected by Scindhiá and Holkar. When the hour of trial came that prince had clutched at it, as his one hope of protection against men of his own race and kin, little knowing that by his action he was signing the death-warrant of the Maráthá empire.

For the Marquess Wellesley, through in all his actions, had resolved, when he accepted the propositions of the Peshwa, and directed Colonel Close to sign the treaty of Bassein, to leave nothing in the carrying out of its provisions to chance. Jeswant Ráo Holkar, flushed with victory, was still occupying Puná with his army. It was always possible that Scindhiá, placing the interests of the Marátha race above personal feeling, might, at a conjuncture the like of which had never before occurred to blight his plans of empire, join his forces to those of Holkar, and that the fate of the two rival powers might be decided at Puná. The Marquess, then, had to take care that the army which should reconquer Puná for Bájí Ráo, should be an army strong enough to meet any possible opposition. Whilst, then, he communicated to the other Maráthá princes the conditions of the Treaty of Bassein, and suggested their adherence to those of its provisions which secured the Peshwá against external attack, he directed that his brother, Major-General Arthur Wellesley, should march upon Puná with 15,000 troops from the south. At the same time he urged upon the Nizam to send his contingent in the same direction, to be joined at a fixed place by his brother; and he intimated to the Commander-in-Chief in India,

General Lake, that it was necessary he should be ready at any moment to commence hostilities.

General Wellesley responded with alacrity to the orders he received. With a force consisting of one regiment of European and three regiments of native cavalry; two regiments of European and six of native infantry; a proportion of artillery; and 2,500 Maisur horses, he set out from Harihar, on the frontier Maisur, on the 9th of March, and, pushing on with all possible haste, effected a junction with the Nizam's contingent on April 15th. As he advanced the detached troops of Holkar's army fell back, without engaging, before him. When he was still some seventy odd miles from Puná, Holkar quit that city, and, leaving there a garrison of 1,500 men, retired to Chandaur, a town distant from it about a hundred and thirty miles. Information of this movement having been promptly brought to Wellesley, he detached General Stevenson, with about a third of his own force and the Nizam's contingent, with instructions to post the latter at Gardur, within the Nizam's territories; to join the his own troops to those of the Haidrábád subsidiary force; and to await further instructions on the Bhima river, near its junction with in structions on the Bhima river, near its junction with the Mota Mola. Warned, at the same time, by the Peshwá, that the small garrison left in Puná would probably plunder the Peshwá's palace and then fire the city, Wellesley pushed on at the head of his cavalry, marched sixty miles in thirty-two hours, and appeared before Puná on April 20th. The garrison evacuated the place as he approached it, and he took possession of the Peshwa's capital without firing a shot. That prince, meanwhile, had remained at Bassein. But, on hearing of Wellesley's movements, he quit that place, escorted by British troops, and accompanied by the British Resident (April 27th). On the 13th May following, he re-entered his palace, under a salute fired by British guns.

So far, the success of Lord Wellesley's policy had been complete. There was, at the moment, no reason to despair of the acquiescence, sullen though it might be, of Scindhiá.

Holkar, it was clear, was not prepared to enter upon hostilities. The Bhonslá was believed to be indifferent and apathetic, and was far less formidable than either of the others. Lord Wellesley, then, had reason to hope that Dáolat Ráo Scindhiá, feeling that he was isolated, would hesitate to imperial his own vast possessions by being at war with the British, for an idea which their recent action had rendered impossible of realisation. But Dáolat Ráo was yet young. He had an army partially modelled on the European system, and officered to a certain extent by European officers. By degrees he had been realising how possible it had been for him, had he employed the preceding nine years more wisely, to realise the dream of his great-uncle. Acquiescence in the Treaty of Bassein would render that dream for ever impossible of realisation. It was worth fighting for. He was ready for war, and he would fight. He declined, therefore, as I have told previously with some asperity, to become a party to the Treaty of Bassein. To the remonstrances of the British Resident, Colonel Collins, he replied:—"After my interview with the Bhonslá you will know whether it is to be peace or war."

On June 4th, Scindhiá met that prince at Mulkapur, on the confines of the Nizam's dominions. On the 8th, he had with him a prolonged interview. At the close of the conference Colonel Collins again pressed him to declare his intentions, but received only the reply that it was necessary that he should have another interview with the Bhonslá before he could give a definite answer. It would seem as though the two chieftains had agreed to try once again to induce Holkar to embrace the common cause, and the evasive answers each in turn gave were intended to gain time. For some weeks Collins displayed the most exemplary patience. When, however, he could elicit no satisfactory reply, the Governor-General, anxious to know for certain whether the two chieftains were really determined on war, directed his brother, about the middle of July, to address a letter to Scindhiá, requesting him to separate it's army from that of the Bhonslá, and to retire across the Narbadá; in which case, he was informed, the British troops would return to their cantonments. To this request again an evasive answer was provided. Practically it was refused, for the armies of two chiefs remained united. It became, then, clear that the two chiefs were bent on war, though neither would declare it. In the actual state of affairs in India, the Marquess Wellesley could not afford to allow the continuance of a situation so fraught with danger. There must either be peace or there must be war—a middle course was impossible. With a patience which seemed to hope everything, the Governor-General had allowed the two Maráthá chieftains more than two months' time to make up their minds as to which course it should be. They had met on June 4th, Scindhiá having previously declared that after the conference he would give a definite answer. Up to August 1st he had evaded a clear reply. His last had been so unsatisfactory, alike in its spirit and expression, that Colonel Collins informed him that, finding it useless to continue negotiation, he should leave his camp. He quit accordingly on August 3rd. His departure, which Scindhiá took no means to prevent, was the signal for the commencement of hostilities.

The Marquess Wellesley, meanwhile, as Captain-General of India, had made arrangements to meet the issue which had now practically occurred. On June the 28th, he had instructed General Lake, who was at the frontier station of Kanpur, to put the army under his command in a position to take the field at the shortest notice. To his brother, Arthur Wellesley, he transmitted at the same time instructions to advance on the territories of Scindhiá to the south of the Godávarí as soon as negotiations should be broken off. He would do all that was possible to maintain peace, but, should the conduct of the Maráthá chiefs force war upon him, he was determined to prosecute it until such a settlement were effected "as would afford a reasonable prospect of continued peace and security to the British Government and its allies." With characteristic boldness and grasp of view, he thus expressed the objects which he was determined to accomplish in the two spheres in which he was about to operate, in the north-west and in the south-west. "The first of the military objects was to conquer the whole of that portion of Scindhiá's dominions which lay between the Ganges and the Jamnah; destroying completely the French force by which that frontier was protected; extending the Company's frontier to the Jamnah, and including the cities of Delhí and Ágra, with a chain of posts, sufficient for protecting the navigation of the river, on the right bank of the river." His second object was to acquire Bundelkhand, or, at least, that portion of it which was necessary to secure his hold upon Ágra. The political objects he aimed at securing by a successful war were not less important. By the conquest and permanent occupation of Delhí he would obtain possession of the representative of the Mughul, the unfortunate, Sháh Álam, kept virtually as a State prisoner by Scindhiá, and, with his person, of the authority attaching to his name. It would be easy, he conceived, to make such an arrangement with that prince as would secure his personal comfort without awakening his ambition. Then, in the south, he would trust his brother to secure the position of the protected allies of the British, the Nizam, the Peshwá, and the Gaikwár, by defeating the combined armies of Scindhiá and the Bhonslá. When they had been sufficiently humbled, he would then take measures to secure the British position, by compelling the former to surrender the port of Baroch, with the adjoining district on the coast of Gujrát: the latter to cede the one province which connected Bengal with the south-eastern districts known as the Northern Sirkars, the province called Katak.

Such were his aims, bold, practical, statesman like, necessary for the consolidation of the British power in India, the complement to the measures by which he had secured permanent predominance in the south, and reduced the unwieldly proportions of Oudh. And—a most important consideration in the matter—he had not provoked the contest which promised to produce the magnificent results I have enumerated. He had, on the contrary, displayed a patience quite exemplary, a desire to avoid war so great as to have tried to the utmost a man who knew that war meant triumph, the increase, the consolidation, the permanent predominance and security of the British all over India, in the north as well as in the south. Promised on June the 4th a definite reply in four days to his very moderate proposals, he had waited more than eight weeks to receive it. Then only, when the demands of the allied princes rose with every day of delay, did he authorise his agent to declare to them, in the manner best appreciated by Orientals, that the day of grace was past; that, thenceforth, they must try the arbitrament of the court to which they had appealed. Nor, to refer for a moment to the antecedent incident, which converted the titular head of the Maráthá confederation into a protected prince, can the impartial historian find words too strong to express his admiration. It had been in the power of Scindhiá to prevent an event so galling to his pride by occupying the same position himself. The opportunity of the English had become possible because of his supineness. Here, too, the part played by Lord Wellesley was a part forced upon him. It was his merit that he had recognised the danger planned by Mádháji; that in quiet and calmness he had prepared the remedy; and that when the occasion arose he applied it with a skill and a courage indicative of a real statesman.

It is not necessary that I should describe the details of the campaign which followed the departure of Colonel Collins from the camp of Scindhiá. It will suffice to say that Arthur Wellesley, advancing with a force of about 9,000 men from Puná on June the 4th, took up a position on the frontier of Scindhiá's territories, which would permit of his acting whenever war should be declared. On August the 7th, the Governor-General issued a proclamation declaring that on the day previous he had directed the levying of war against the two Maráthá chieftains. On the 8th, his brother, who had been previously instructed, advanced against Scindhiá's fortress of Ahmadnagar, forced it to surrender the 12th, crossed the Godavari the 24th, and reached Aurangabad the 29th. There he was but forty miles distant from the Maratha army, for their allied forces had the same day ascended the

Ajanta Pass, and the day following were at Jalnah. Wellesley, then, despatching Stevenson against Jalnah, marched himself down the Godavari, and caught the Marathas on the banks of the river Kaitna, their cavalry resting on Bokardan, their infantry on Assaye, on the morning of September the 23rd. Without waiting for Stevenson, he crossed the Kaitna by a ford, attacked, and after a very hotly-contested battle, completely defeated the enemy. Pushing on after this, his first victory, Wellesley having meanwhile, by his lieutenants, forced the surrender of the important places of Asirgarh and Burhanpur, caught the enemy once again (November 29th) on the plains of Argaum. That same afternoon he attacked them, and inflicted upon them a second defeat, more decisive even than that of Assaye. That victory decided the war in Southern India.

Nor had Lake been less successful in North-Western and Central India. Marching from Kanpur with an army about 8,000 strong on August 5th, he had crossed the British frontier the 28th, defeated the enemy's cavalry before Aligarh, the 29; stormed the fortress of that name September 4th; beat the Maratha on the Jehna nullah, six miles from Delhi, on the 11th; entered that city, and released from confinement the blind Emperor, Shah Alam, the 14th; defeated the enemy in front of Agra, October 10th; compelled the surrender of that fortress on the 18th; and on the 27th started for Central India in pursuit of the best army of Scindhia—that which had been entirely drilled by foreign officers. He caught it with his cavalry at the village of Laswari, after a series of forced marches, the morning of November Ist, and at once attacked it. The enemy's position was, however, too strong, and was too well defended to be forced by cavalry alone, and Lake drew off to wait for his infantry. On these coming up, he gave them their dinner, and then renewed the attack, this time with complete success, though at a heavy expenditure of life. Laswari was one of the most decisive battles ever fought. It finished the war in Northern and Central India.

But it was the battle of Argaum, fought November 29th, and the events which immediately followed it which brought the two Maratha princes to ask for peace. Sixteen days after that battle Wellesley stormed the strong fortress of Gualgarh, believed by the enemy to be impregnable. It was the last blow. Two days later, the Bhonsla signed a treaty with the British by which he yielded the province of Katak and the port of Baleshwar; renounced all his claims on the Nizam, including those to the territory in Barar to the west of the Wardah river; and agreed to refer all disputes with that prince to British arbitration. Further, he promised to take no foreigners into his service without the consent of the British.

Thirteen days later, Daolat Rao signed with the British the treaty which is known as the Treaty of Surji Arjangaon. By this treaty he ceded to the British all his rights of sovereignty over the country between the Jamnah and the Ganges, and as well as over the territories belonging to the Rajahs of Jaipur, Jodhpur, and Gohad, with each of whom separate treaties were concluded. He ceded Baroch and Ahmadnagar, with the territories pertaining to both: and the territory between the Ajanta Hills and the Godavari. Finally, he renounced all claims on the Emperor, Shah Alam; upon the Nizam; upon the Peshwa; upon the Gaikwar; and upon the British Government. On the other hand, certain lands which belonged to the family of Scindhia, in the districts he was ceding, were to remain in the occupancy of their actual tenants; and in the same spirit, pensions assigned from similar lands, to the amount of seventeen lakhs a year, were to be paid as before.

Of the territories thus gained from the two princes, Lord Wellesley apportioned to the Nizam the territory to the westward of the Wurdah, and that between the Ajanta Hills and the Godavari; to the Peshwa, the town and territory of Ahmadnagar; the rest he retained. With the further view to place Scindhia, thus weakened by the war, in a position in which he could defend himself against Holkar, Lord Wellesley entered, two months later, into a supplemental agreement with Daolat Rao, to furnish him, in case of need, with a force of 6,000 infantry and the usual proportion of artillery. The expense of this force was to be borne by the ceded districts, but the force itself was not to be stationed within the actual dominions of Scindhia. This treaty was signed at Burhanpur on February 27th, 1804, but events moved too fast to allow of its conditions being acted upon.

It has always been something of a mystery why Jeswant Rao Holkar had not joined Scindhia in his struggle with the British. Their interests were identical. Jeswant Rao had been, moreover, in a position peculiarly favourable for the commencement of a war in alliance with Scindhia. He had held Puna. He had also troops trained by foreigners. He was daring even to rashness, and he resented, as much as did his fellow-Chieftain, the intrusion of the English into Maratha quarrels. When, from their encampment at Mulkapur, Scindhia and the Bhonsla despatched messengers to Holkar to endeavour to persuade that prince to become a party to the alliance, they had resolved to amuse the British agent until they could receive a reply. The reply came, and it was favourable. Holkar sympathised with the views of the two allies, and agreed to join them. But the rapid movements of Wellesley and Lake probably disconcerted his plans. The English were too successful from the very outset; and his preparations had been made when it was too late to interfere with advantage. Added to this, there may have been a jealousy of Scindhia, a desire to see him humiliated, a superlative confidence in his own ability to repair any damage. One fact is certain, viz., that although he took no part in the war, yet, no sooner was it concluded, than he showed himself resolved to provoke hostilities with the victor.

In December, 1803, Holkar had been quite ready. But by that time Laswari and Argaum had been fought, and Scindhia and the Bhonsla were suing for peace. Holkar then took up a position with his army on the frontier of Scindhia's dominions, with the intention of taking advantage of the weakness to which he had been reduced by the British to turn and plunder him. It was the view of such probable action on his part that induced Scindhia to conclude with the British that supplementary treaty of February 27th, 1804, of which I have spoken. Holkar, hearing of this treaty, changed his tactics. He endeavoured to persuade Scindhia to join him against the British, whilst he solicited from the latter permission to attack Scindhia. In both these attempts he overreached himself. Scindhia, smarting at having been left in the lurch in the late war, communicated to the British the overtures Holkar had made to him. The perusal of Holkar's letters, and the haughty, almost insolent tone assumed by that prince in his communications with the British officials, convinced Lord Wellesley that he was bent on war. He sent, then, to General Lake instructions to oppose with force any attempt Holkar might make on the dominions of Scindhia, and on those of the protected allies of the British.

General Lake, struck by the hostile attitude assumed by Holkar, had not, on the conclusion of the war with Scindhia, moved back at once, as he would have done under ordinary circumstances, into cantonments, but had remained encamped at Bana, fifty miles south-west from Agra. He was there when information reached him that Holkar had not only announced in his own camp his intention of making war on the British, but had barbarously murdered three English adventurers attached to his army, who had largely contributed to his success in his last war with Scindhia, because they had declared that whilst ready to fight against any other people, they would not bear arms against their own countrymen. Lake, believing that a strong demonstration would suffice, detached a force of sipahis, under command of Colonel Monson, to protect the city of Jaipur, which, he was informed, Holkar was threatening. He then marched back slowly to Kanpur.

Monson reached Jaipur just in time to prevent the city from being plundered by Holkar. That prince fell back in the direction of Kota, as if in dread of an attack. Monson followed him, first to Kota, thence through the Mokandara Pass to Sonara. Learning there that Holkar was encamped on the Chambal, some twenty-five miles distance, Monson, though he had, but three days provisions with him, started to drive him thence. On his way, however, he was persuaded by a traitor in his camp, one Bapuji Scindhia, to stay his hand, and to retreat. That retreat, known to this day as Monson's retreat, was one of the most disastrous, till then, experienced by any army. Begun on July 7th, some seven miles from Rampura on the Chambal, it terminated on August 30th and 31st, by the arrival at Agra "of wretched, footsore, half-starved, and dispirited fugitives," whose appearance "conveyed to the garrison some idea of the humiliation in every store for the General who retreats before a barbarian enemy."*

General Lake, however, speedily avenged this misfortune. Marching from Kanpur, on September 3rd, he reached Mathura on October 1st. There he had hoped to find Holkar. But that wily chief, having succeeded in drawing Lake to Mathura, had himself made a dash on Delhi. Delhi, feebly garrisoned, but animated by the lofty spirit of David Ochterlony held out till Lake, following close upon his enemy, compelled Holkar to raise the siege. Lake, then, finding that Holkar had made a dash into the Duab, followed him thither, leaving General Fraser to deal with the smaller force that remained. Whilst Fraser—and Monson, who succeeded to the command on his being mortally wounded—beat that force at Dig, Lake, pursuing his enemy by forced marches, caught him up, completely surprised and defeated him at Farrukhabad, and compelled him to flee with but a small retinue in the direction of Dig. Lake carried that place on Christmas Day; then set down to besiege Bhartpur.

---

* *The Decisive Battles of India* (W. H. Allen & Co., London), contains in full detail an account of this famous retreat, in which a force of four to five thousand sipahis, led by English officers, baffled a pursuing army of 75,000 men, of whom 60,000 were horsemen.

Here, after a long siege of fifty-three days, he was baffled. But he had not forgotten Holkar. Springing after him from the very walls of Bhartpur, he drove him before him through the north-west provinces, through the Cis-Satlej States, across the river Satlaj, till he compelled him to surrender "his whole kingdom on his saddle's bow,"* on December 24th, 1805.

REFERENCES

1. Known as "The Battle of Delhi."
2. See p. 233, vol. iii., of Wellesley's Despatches.
3. See p. 427, vol. iii., of Wellesley's Despatches.

* Holkar's very expression.

9

End of Maratha War

The peace which had been established by the treaties with Scindiah and the Rajah of Berar was of short duration, owing to the intrigues of Jeswant Rao Holkar, who had usurped the possessions of the Holkar family in the name of Khundah Rao, the pretender whom he had brought forward to the exclusion of Cashee the legitimate successor. It was no part of the British policy to interfere in these family disputes, or that there should be any interposition of British power, unless absolutely required for the security of the chiefs and states with whom defensive alliances had been contracted.

Both Lake and Lord Wellesley thought it highly improbable, as Holkar had not taken advantage of the opportunities afforded him in the midst of their arduous struggle with Scindiah, Perron, and the Rajah of Berar, that he would now venture to provoke a conflict with the British power, strengthened and consolidated as it had been by the results of the campaign. They were mistaken.

Although both the English Governor-General and Commander-in-Chief then looked upon a war waged by such a person as Jeswant Rao against such a power as the British as an act of folly, which it was scarcely possible a man of his craft could be guilty of, yet, looking back now, with the knowledge of the events which really happened, we feel that the Maharatta adventurer, or freebooter as he was called, was a man of uncommon talents, and that his schemes were formed with great ability, and carried out with great energy, as well as with the duplicity which in the East seems always to accompany ability.

In listening to the overtures of Scindiah and the Rajah of Berar for an active offensive alliance against the British, he had obtained not only substantial concessions of land and pecuniary means, but a recognition by the two greatest *Maratha* powers of himself as a power. He had ceased to be a mere captain of a horde of plunderers, and was now a *Maratha* potentate. Using the means and influence thus obtained to increase and strengthen his army, he stood aloof during the struggle. It did not suit his policy to be aiding as an humble ally the two other powers, who if they had succeeded would probably have broken faith with him as easily as he broke faith with them. When the contest ended, to the discomfiture but not to the ruin of the two *Maratha* powers, who were still left at the head of very considerable states, and when the English were tired of, and as he imagined exhausted by, an expensive war, Jeswant thought his opportunity had come, and seized it boldly. Assuming a haughty and insolent tone towards the English, he demanded of them, first, the concession of several large territories within their recent conquests, which, he alleged, had at one time belonged to the Holkar family; and, secondly, a treaty recognizing him as sovereign of the Holkar dominions, and guaranteeing him their possession. To these insolent demands was added a menace, that in the event of war, although unable to oppose the British artillery in the field, "countries of many hundred costs should be overrun and plundered and burnt; the Commander-in-Chief should not have leisure to breathe for a moment; and calamities would fall on lacs of human beings in continued war by the attacks of his army, which overwhelms like the waves of the sea." Nor was this menace altogether an idle one.

The charges of Holkar's troops greatly exceeded the resources of his usurped dominion, and had been defrayed by black mail on the profits of indiscriminate plunder; and continued predatory warfare was in fact the only thing his followers had to look to. Not only were these men ready for any enterprise of plunder, but the numerous bands of irregular troops, which had been thrown out of service by the peace, were naturally attracted to his banner. This made him formidable enough; but he was more than a bold freebooter; he was evidently a skilful diplomatist.

His agents intrigued successfully with many discontended chiefs and zamindars; and amongst others with the Rajah of Bhurtpore, a powerful, wealthy, and influential prince, holding a commanding territory with strong fortresses, particularly those of Deeg and Bhurtpore. Jeswant Rao, although himself a *Maratha* and a Brahmin, made skilful appeals to the Mohammedans, urging them to come out and expel the infidels. His friends and agents got a foot hold at the courts of Scindiah and the Rajah of Berar, and in their armies; and he found the means of tampering with corps in the British army itself. It was not therefore against a despicable foe that the Governor-General and Commander-in-Chief had now to exert their utmost energies.

Preparations were therefore made, in the autumn of 1804, for a combined attack upon Holkar and his dominions from all sides, by the Commander-in-Chief from the north-east, by General Wellesley from the south-west, by the Guicowar and by Scindiah; but these movements were necessarily delayed by the season, and by the impossibility of obtaining supplies in the countries to be traversed, which had been already stripped. During this delay, disasters befell the British. Another chieftain, Meer Khan, at the head of a considerable predatory force burst into Bundelcund. A small British detachment was wholly cut off, and the main body from which it had been detached, deceived by exaggerated reports of the strength of the invading bands, made a hasty retreat. This gave confidence to the enemy. Shortly afterwards Colonel Monson—described by the Commander-in-Chief as an officer brave as a lion, but wholly without judgement—at the head of a very considerable force (five battalions and six companies), already in an advanced position, thought himself strong enough to advance further, was attacked at a disadvantage by Holkar at the head of a large force, was beaten and obliged to make a precipitate retreat with greater part of his baggage to fall into the enemy's hands.

Taking up a fresh position, Monson found himself surrounded on all sides by the enemy's cavalry, and discovered moreover, that some of the native commissioned officers were in correspondence with Holkar. Two companies of Sepoys and 400 irregular cavalry actually deserted him, and went over; he knew not how far the contagion of treason might spread, and he had to retreat, fighting his way pursued by overwhelming masses of the enemy. Officers and men appear during this retreat to have behaved with great courage and discipline; and at length, after eight days' continued retreat, harassed by the pursuing foe in every direction, the severed corps reached Agra, much diminished in numbers, and with the loss of guns and baggage.

The disaster, though serious, was partly due to a cause not less disastrous. Bapojee Scindiah, commander of one of the principal divisions of Scindiah's army, had been despatched with ostensible orders to join the British in fulfilment of the treaty of alliance, and having joined Monson had at the most critical moment gone over openly to Holkar, and, as was suspected, not wholly without the privity of his master, although the latter strongly protested his innocence of the treason. The Rajah of Bhurtpore now openly took the side of Holkar, although he was one of the first of the princes who had sought the English alliance and protection, and had actually been rewarded with a grant of territory for his supposed friendship and loyalty. Exaggerated accounts of the disaster to Monson's corps spread over India; and Holkar's prestige was great as the conqueror of the British, who had been at last found not invincible by a *Maratha*. A little more, and Scindiah and the Rajah of Berar would have openly declared themselves as the allies of Holkar, who would have become generalissimo of all the *Maratha* forces. It was a time of grant peril for the British.

Holkar showed himself not deficient in activity in following up his advantage, and made a rapid march against Delhi, which was protected only by a very small British force, and was indifferently fortified. It was, however, after the usual fashion of British officers in India, resolutely defended by the gallant band within; and after three or four unsuccessful attempts at assault, Holkar, alarmed by Lake's approach, was fain to draw off. Lake was as active as Holkar; and luckily he had taken great pains in organizing and disciplining his cavalry, which was all-important against an enemy like Holkar, whose object was to make sudden attacks on many points, and to elude anything like a general engagement.

Having ascertained that Holkar with his cavalry was near, Lake marched out before daylight to attack him, and reached his camp just as day broke, but not before the alarm had been given. The horse artillery and the cavalry were able to do some execution; but the enemy, by a rapid flight, succeeded in getting off with little loss towards Bhurtpore. Besides his cavalry, Holkar had gathered together a very considerable force of infantry and artillery, partly his own, and partly those of his ally, the Rajah of Bhurtpore.

Determined to bring the matter to a rapid conclusion, Lake divided his small army into two; and placing the greater part of the infantry and artillery under General Frazer, to deal with the infantry and artillery of Holkar, he put himself at the head of the other division, determined to run down Holkar, and bring him to bay.

Frazer came into collision with his opponents, who were strongly posted near the fortress of Deeg. His division consisted of two regiments of native cavalry, and six battalions of native infantry, the park of artillery, one European Company's regiment, and above all, that which was to Lake what the 10th legion was to Casar or the old guard to Napoleon, the 76th Regiment of Royal Infantry, or at least so much of it as had survived the hard wear and tear of the previous campaign. The enemy's force, under Holkar's chief lieutenant, consisted of twenty-four battalions of infantry, a considerable body of horse, and 160 pieces of cannon. Frazer immediately made arrangements for attacking them, heading the 76th Regiment himself, but fell mortally wounded, and the command devolved on Colonel Monson. Range after range of batteries on the right of the enemy was carried by the impetuous advance over two miles of country, the enemy flying into a swamp and up to the very walls of the fortress of Deeg; then the British commander rapidly wheeled round upon the enemy's left, which in its turn fled precipitately into a lake hard by, where numbers of them perished. The enemy made no further opposition, but entirely quietened the field, flying in all directions. Many took shelter in the fortress in the greatest consternation, and, as was almost invariably the case with native armies after a defeat, began to desert in vast numbers. Lake, who was not present himself, writing privately and confidentially to Lord Wellesley, talks of it "as the great and glorious victory gained by Frazer and Monson, which I really do think appears to surpass anything that has hitherto been done in India," and writing a day or two afterwards, says, "I have every reason to believe that the action of the 13th was a very near business. The personal courage of Monson and others alone saved it."

Lake meanwhile himself pursued Holkar very closely, marching for seventeen days together, twenty-three or twenty-four miles a day. At length, hearing that Holkar was encamped under the walls of Farukabad, obtaining money and supplies from that place, Lake resolved to leave his infantry and baggage, and put himself at the lead of his cavalry and horse artillery. They had travelled thirty miles on the forenoon of the 16th of November; they proceeded nearly a similar distance in the course of the night and succeeded in surprising the enemy at daybreak the following morning. The horse artillery opened a most destructive fire, and the different regiments of cavalry instantly charged with impetuosity. The enemy were completely surprised, and at once thrown into confusion. Most of their horses were at the picket; and those who had mounted were unable to oppose the least resistance; great numbers were killed; and the rest dispersed in every direction, and were pursued over the adjoining country with great slaughter. This destruction of Holkar's cavalry, following on the rout of his infantry and artillery, was decisive of the campaign. All that were before ready to join him now hastened to abandon his fallen fortunes. Scindiah and the Rajah of Berar disallowed all alliance with him, and were only too glad that the Governor-General's policy was not to inquire too closely into what they had done. On the other or Bombay side the British and their allies were rapidly overrunning the Holkar dominions, and taking place after place.

The British now turned to punish the defection of the Rajah of Bhurtpore. His fortress of Deeg was soon stormed; but Bhurtpore itself was more lucky. Four successive attempts at assaulting it failed, and the British were preparing for further siege operations when the Rajah made his submission. His fortress of Deeg was taken from him in pledge for his good behaviour. The territory which had been given to him was resumed, and he was mulcted in a heavy fine for the expenses of the war. As his pecuniary resources had been much wasted in his unlucky confederacy with Holkar, he was allowed to discharge the fine by yearly instalments, with a promise that the last should be remitted, if his continued good behaviour should merit it.

Thus practically ended the campaign against Holkar; but some members of the conflagration had still to be stamped out. Meer Khan had to be hunted down, and some remains of Holkar's forces which gathered together had to be dispersed. Holkar himself with a small force took refuge with Scindiah, with whose minister he was on terms of intimate alliance, and over whose court he contrived still to exercise great influence. He had ceased, however, to be really formidable, and although the terms of peace were not actually signed until the end of the year, Lord Wellesley thought it in May, 1805, possible and desirable to make a settlement without further war; and the British army, ordered into cantonments, rested from their labours.

Lord Wellesley sailed for England in August, 1805. At the close of his administration the Indian dominions in the actual possession and under the immediate rule of the British comprehended the whole sea coast of the Peninsula from the mouths of the Ganges to Cape Comorin, and with the exception of the seaboard of the small dependent states of Travancore and Cochin on the south, and of the Guicowar's on the north, substantially the whole sea coast on the other side from Cape Comorin to the Gulf of Cutch. The British territory within this coast-line comprised the whole valley of the Ganges, except what was left to the allied Nawab Vazir of Oudh; the Doab or country between the Ganges and the Jumna; the extensive provinces which to this day constitute the Presidency of Madras; and the smaller but not insignificant countries under the Government of Bombay. Mysore was in the hands of a prince who owed his throne to the English, and their troops occupied the capital and stronghold of Seringapatam. Not only this prince, but the Peshwa and the Nizam had by the subsidiary treaties agreed to place themselves completely under the control of the Calcutta Government. The great seat of the Mohammedan Empire of India, Delhi, was occupied by the English, and the titular emperor, the representative of the line of Timur, was in their hands, a pensioner on their bounty.

The external commerce of India was centred in the three British ports of Calcutta, Madras, and Bombay, marts which owed their very existence to the English. There was no naval force but the British, with the exception of some piratical squadrons, which continued for a few years longer to infest the seas. In actuality, the Governor-General of India had, during Lord Wellesley's proconsulate, became completely and more absolutely the sovereign paramount of India than any of the Mohammedan emperors had been, with larger domains under his own immediate rule and government, and with more complete control over the princes of the other provinces.

The Anglo-Indian Empire was firmly established. In looking back at this great creation, we are struck with the smallness of the means by which the results were achieved. On the 1st of April, 1805, the whole of the royal regiments in India, including 2000 sick, did not exceed 12,778; the Company's European infantry were reduced to 717, and their artillery did not exceed 2393 men. In July of that year the Governor-General in Council wrote thus—"The Governor-General will not continue to be alarmed for the security of this empire, if the European establishments shall be completed to the extent, which his meeting in council has proposed for the continent of India, of sixteen regiments of his Majesty's infantry of 1000 men each, three regiments of the Company's infantry of the same strength, with four regiments of dragons at 640 men each, and a due proportion of European artillery." The native troops at the same time amounted to sixteen regiments of cavalry and fifty-nine regiments (118 battalions) of infantry. From the correspondence between Lord Wellesley and the home authorities, it appears that but faint promises were held out, that in the military state of England at that time she could afford the quota of European soldiers, which the Governor-General rather ventured to hope for than expected to have.

The revenues of India when Lord Wellesley assumed the government amounted to rather more than seven million and a quarter, and grew to thirteen and a half millions by the year 1806-7. Since that time we have become so familiarized with the expenditure of enormous sums for military purposes, and with the creation of gigantic debts, that it is very difficult to realize the full measure of alarm, almost of terror, which was produced at home when it was ascertained that the arduous wars, in which Lord Wellesley's whole period of administration was spent, had resulted in an augmentation of the Indian national debit by no less a sum than eleven million sterling.

Notwithstanding all the triumphs of Lord Wellesley's career, and the grant ability which he had displayed throughout, he had never really obtained the approbation or cordial support of his masters, the East Indian Company, with whom he was generally on bad terms. They resented his imperious and autocratic style, and his hardly-concealed disregard of and contempt for their wishes and opinions. On two of the points on which they were most susceptible, patronage in India and private trade, he had given them grave offence. The disputes as to the first are too trivial for further notice. The other reminds us again of the wonderful patience, with which the English nation and its rulers continued to submit to the trade monopoly of the Company, and to regard it as a thing so good, so just, and so natural, that the Company did not scruple openly to avow as a ground of quarrel with their Governor-General that he had endeavoured to do something for opening trade to the private traders from England, and to the native-built shipping of India. But apart from these wretched grounds of discontent with his proceedings, they had other more legitimate causes of dissatisfaction. They had a create disinclination to all schemes of conquest and affectation not a feigned or hypocritical affectation of motivation on their part, but a dread as real as it was natural and legitimate in their position. As a Company they could never hope to obtain any benefit from the growth of the Anglo-Indian Empire. Their annuity was fixed at a certain sum, which was not likely ever to be exceeded, but which might fail if the resources of India and the profits of the trade should be unable to meet the expenses of a warlike policy, fertile in glory to the Governor-General and his commanders, but barren of profit to the Indian exchequer.

The Governor-General's successes might dazzle the multitude, but to the Directors they afforded no compensation for his heterodox notions on that which was then to them the greatest of all questions—the question of private trade. They distrusted, reasonably enough, his calculations, as they have distrusted every succeeding Governor-General's calculations, of the profits to be derived from conquered territories; they dreaded least the swollen Empire should it break down under its own weight; and they had a prudent, almost instinctive, foresight of the dangerous entanglements, in which they might find themselves involved by the subsidiary alliances and treaties of dependence and protection, in which their Governor-General had bound them and the native powers. If they had been permitted by the Board of Control, the Directors would have sent a despatch entirely condemnatory of Lord Wellesley's policy and measures. Although he was supported, not very cordially, by the Government and by Parliament, he was almost unanimously condemned by the Court of Proprietors, who resolved, by a majority of 928 to 195, that—

"This Court do most highly approve [the conduct of the Directors in their efforts] to restrain a profuse expenditure of public money, and to prevent all schemes of conquest and extension of dominion, measures which the legislature had declared to be repugnant to the wish, the honour and the policy of the nation."

The financial state of India for the next few years appeared indeed to justify the apprehensions of the Company as to the result of the ambitious policy of their Governor-General. Deficit after deficit continued to aggravate their financial difficulties. A cold fit followed in India itself the hot fever of martial ardour. Economy, retrenchment, peace, and non-interference became the watchwords of the English policy. Territories which had been ceded by the Peshwa in Bundelcund were eagerly given up to the native princes, and excuses, not always creditable or honest, were found for relinquishing the honour and, so escaping the burden of the alliances—alliances of dependence and protection—with some of the minor powers. The policy of leaving the princes and leaders of India to manage their own affairs, to settle their own quarrels, to fight their own battles, was ostentatiously proclaimed as the rule of conduct thenceforth to be pursued by the British. They were ready and willing to abdicate the Imperial dignity and power which had fallen into their unwilling hands; and the Company would gladly have returned to the quiet pursuit of commercial gain, and made it their only care to increase their store and to keep their Governor-General at home in their old dominion of Bengal, which was in truth large enough to content any moderate ambition.

10

The Fourth Mysore War

In September, 1793, Lord Cornwallis resigned the Government to Sir John Shore, and left India in the full assurance, that he had by the Treaty of Seringapatam established permanent peace throughout the south of India by a well-arranged balance of power. The British Government to Madras had no designs upon the territories either of the *Marathas* or the Nizam, and had no reason to anticipate any hostile proceeding on their side. The alliance between them for mutual defence against the ambition of Tippoo Sultan was so natural, and so obviously dictated by the commonest prudence and by a sense of their common interest, that it had every reasonable prospect of continuance. On the other side, Tippoo, although still formidable from the extent of his remaining dominion and his commanding central position in the highland plateau of Mysore, had, it was to be hoped, been so reduced by the last war, as to make him loth to enter into conflict with the united strength of the allies. It was hoped that the Nizam, the Peshwa, and the British would retain their possessions in peace and tranquillity, and that the apprehension of Tippoo's power and designs would have prevented the Nizam and the Peshwa from destroying one another.

The expectations of peace, reasonably based on these considerations, were doomed in a very few years to be disappointed. Again we find a tropical rapidity of growth and of decay. The Treaty of Seringapatam was signed on the 18th of March, 1792, but by the year 1798 the following startling changes had been made in the state of Southern India. Madhoo Rao, who was Peshwa at the time of the treaty, had a very able minister, Nana Furnavese, by whose kill it was at one time feared, that such great weight might be thrown into the scale, as to enable the Government of Poonah to wield the whole united force of the colossal *Maratha* empire; but on Madhoo Rao's death, Nana, following the usual practice of Indian Prime Ministers, attempted to disturb the regular course of succession by intruding an adopted child upon the throne. This led to a succession of intrigues and revolutions at Poonah, which ended in the establishment of Badjes Rao as the reigning Peshwa, though still for a time overshadowed by the power and influence of Nana. In the meantime the Nizam had been engaged in a disastrous and disgraceful defeat of the former at the battle of Kurdla, by which the military power of the court of Hyderabad was reduced to the lowest point of degradation. The Nizam was compelled to sacrifice a large portion of his territory, to engage to pay a fine of three crores[1] of rupees, and to submit to the captivity of his minister, Azim-ul-Omra, who was carried a prisoner to Poonah. Azim, although a prisoner, was able to take a distinguished part in the revolutions of Poonah in support of Nana, who, in return, agreed to relinquish all the concessions made by the Nizam by the Treaty of Kurdla. The Peshwa, to get rid of the overgrown power of his minister, Nana, called in the assistance of Scindiah, the *Maratha* Rajah of Gwalior, by whose persuasion the Peshwa violated the engagements made with Azim-ul-Omra, and insisted upon, and obtained, a cession of one-fourth of the territory, and the payment of one-fourth of the fine stipulated by the Treaty of Kurdla.

In addition to these heavy losses of power and honour the internal resources of the Nizam's state were still suffering from the derangement occasioned by two serious rebellions, the contest with the *Marathas*, and the detention of the minister Azim-ul-Omra at Poonah. In order, as he hoped, to strengthen himself, the Nizam had formed an army of Sepoys, officered by Europeans. In 1798 these amounted to a body of not less than 14,000 men, under the command of a Frenchman, M. Perron. Besides field-pieces to each regiment, a park of 40 pieces of ordnance (chiefly brass), from 12 to 36-pounders, with a well-trained body of artillerymen, including a number of Europeans, was attached to Perron's forces, and a foundation was being laid of a body of cavalry to act with the corps of infantry. The chief officers of the corps were Frenchmen, and many of the privates had been Sepoys in the French army at Pondicherry. The whole corps was, in fact, an armed French party of great power, zeal, and activity, whose whole efforts naturally were to magnify the power, resources, and success of France, to depreciate those of England, and to excite the Indian princes against the latter. The entire ordnance of the Nizam had been entrusted to the French commander, whose corps constituted the only efficient part of the Nizam's army, and was paramount in the state, the Nizam's Government being wholly unable to control the overbearing spirit and formidable power of the French faction. M. Perron maintained a correspondence with a powerful faction at the Nizam's court, opposed to the minister, Azim-ul-Omra, which had been long connected with Tippoo Sultan; he was also in direct correspondence with his own countrymen in the service of Tippoo and of Scindiah; and French military adventurers were arriving continually at Hyderabad to officer and discipline his corps. Such an armed body became naturally a source of terror to the Hyderabad Government, which had so rashly created it. Azim-ul-Omra, the able minister, dreaded the growth of a force which he could no longer restrain within the bounds of moderation, and which had already threatened to subvert his power. Such a force could obviously at pleasure dictate the succession, which was likely at no distant time to come in question, and even destroy the throne itself. Such was the position of affairs at Hyderabad; and Scindiah, taking advantage of the weakness of the Nizam, was preparing to attack him.

The situation of the Peshwa's affairs was not more promising. He had called in Scindiah, and by his assistance had succeeded in overthrowing his minister, Nana, who was imprisoned. But Scindiah, having during the revolutions at Poonah alternately taken part with Nana and the Peshwa, at length and in fact overpowered both, and remained as real master in the territory of the Peshwa. The power and authority of the Peshwa as the head of the *Maharattas* were thus superseded, under circumstances which menaced the abolition of his office, and the elevation of Scindiah to the real chieftainship of the Marathas.

Scindiah had in his service a considerable body of soldiers, disciplined and officered by Frenchmen. Scindiah was, moreover, the *Maratha* power who had possession of Delhi and of the person of the great Mogul. Powerful, however, as he seemed, and formidable as he really was to the Nizam and to the Peshwa, there were elements of weakness in his seeming strength, which placed him almost at the mercy of the British in the north-east. In his aggressions upon the Nizam and the Peshwa he had left his government of Gwalior; and behind him was a spirit of faction and revolt in his own dominions. By the ungovernable excesses of his temper he had got disgusted all the ancient friends and connexions of his family, and all his respectable adherents; the other great *Maratha* powers disliked him, and feared his aggressions; he was surrounded by an army clamorous for pay, was destitute of pecuniary resource, and unsupported by any one respectable friend. His principal minister even had expressed to the British resident at Poonah his entire disapprobation of Scindiah's conduct, his wish for an accommodation with the Peshwa under British mediation, and his desire for the return of Scindiah to his own dominions. These too were at that time threatened from Afghanistan; Zemaun Shah, the head of the Mohammedans there, having openly expressed his intention to invade Hindustan, to restore the Mohammedan power in India, and wholly to expel the *Marathas*.

In the meanwhile Tippoo Sultan's kingdom had been enjoying a state of internal tranquillity nearly uninterrupted; while the allies of the British had been distracted and exhausted by faction, rebellion, revolution and war, he had been diligently and successsfully employed in improving the discipline of his armies, and repairing his resources. The British Government at Madras had no money in their treasury; their credit was exhausted; they had no magazines or stores or depots; and they were even afraid, after the public exhibition of Tippoo's hostility, to concentrate their dispersed forces for the defence of the Carnatic and for watching the Malabar coast, lest they should give the alarm to Tippoo, and provoke an immediate attack from an enemy, "whose resources were more prompt than their own, and a great part of whose army was supposed to be in a state of field equipment."

At this time, too, the strength and resources of the British in Europe were strained almost to the utmost by their contest with revolutionary France. The latter had just sent the expedition under General Bonaparte to Egypt, with the intent, after taking possession of that country, thence to attack the British in India. The importance of their Indian possessions to the latter as a source of wealth and strength was then, as it has always been, strangely exaggerated by the French, who thought that by expelling their rivals from their Eastern dominions, they would inflict a deadly blow on them. Emissaries from the French Government and General found a ready ear at Seringapatam, where the most exaggerated statements of the prowess of the French arms and the strength of the French Republic met willing credence. Tippoo Sultan thought this a favourable opportunity to gratify his hostility against the English, and sent ambassador to the French Governor-General of the Mauritius. There was so little secrecy observed as to this hostile movement, that the latter actually issued an official proclamation as follows—

"This prince desires to form an offensive and defensive alliance with the French. He promises to furnish everything necessary. He declares that he has made every preparation to receive the succors which may be sent to him. In a word, he only waits the moment when the French shall come to his assistance to declare war against the English, whom he ardently desires to expel from India. As it is impossible for us to reduce the number of soldiers of the 107th and 108th regiments and of the regular guard, we invite the citizens who may be disposed to enter as volunteers to enrol themselves, and to serve under the banners of Tippoo. The prince desires to be assisted by the free citizens of colour; we therefore invite all who are willing to serve to enrol themselves."

Some troops were enrolled under this proclamation, with whom the ambassadors returned to Mangalore, a port of Tippoo's on the Malabar coast. It was also known that Tippoo had sent an embassy to Zemaun Shah to invite him to invade India, and had sent circulars to the native princes to join him in effecting the expulsion of the English. He had even sought to induce their allies, the Nizam and the Peshwa, to desert them and to join him in an alliance against them; it was more than suspected that he had an understanding with Scindiah; and he was in secret communication with the English dependant, the Nawab of Arcot.

This was the state in which Lord Mornington, afterwards Marquiss of Wellesley, found India, when he arrived at Madras on the 26th of April, 1798. The situation was in the highest degree critical, but the news of Nelson's victory of the Nile in great degree removed the immediate apprehensions of danger. Lord Wellesley (as we shall hereafter call him, as his best known title) felt justly, that so flagrant an act of hostility on the part of Tippoo Sultan, in direct violation of his treaty engagements, could not be passed over with impunity. He determined to extract from him full reparation for the wrong done, and to take from him effectual security against its repetition. The terms, which he proposed to extract and was willing to be satisfied with, were the cession of the sea-board, so as to shut Tippoo off from those reinforcements from France, from which the greatest danger was apprehended; the possession of the passes; the dismissal of all Tippoo's French officers and soldiers; and a pecuniary indemnity for the expenses of the preparations which the English had been obliged to make. Lord Wellesley was in some degree at first hampered by the instructions of a very peaceful character, which he had received on leaving England, where the Home Government dreaded any extension of territory as an incumbrance, and were very loth to risk the financial embarrassments which were sure to be occasioned by fresh hostilities in the East; and it was almost in terms of deprecatory apology that he wrote to England. "My ideas are that on the one hand we ought never to use any high language towards Tippoo; nor ever attempt to deny him the smallest point of his just rights; so on the other where we have distinct proofs of his machinations against us, we ought to let him know that his treachery does not escape our observation, and to make him feel that he is within the reach of our vigilance."

The proclamation of the Governor of the Mauritius had in the meantime reached England, and on the 15th of October, 1798 (such were the delays in communicating in those days) Lord Wellesley received from England a despatch written in June, which by anticipation approved of the vigorous policy, which he had on his own responsibility meanwhile determined on.

It was not altogether an easy task to take the immediate and decisive measures which the crisis demanded. The forces at the disposal of the Governor-General were not large, and his treasury was anything but overflowing. Some idea of his financial difficulties may be gathered from one of his despatches, in which he is able to congratulate the Court of Directors that—

"The zeal, alacrity and public spirit of the bankers and commercial agents at Madras, as well as of the most respectable of your civil servants there, enabled me within a few weeks to raise a large sum of money by loan for the public service. Previous to my departure from Bengal I had remitted twenty lacs[2] of rupees in species for this Presidency.

I now sent for a further supply, and the extraordinary exertions of his Excellency the Vice-President in Council, assisted by the diligence and ability of Mr. Thomas Myers, the Accountant-General of Bengal, furnished me with an additional aid of twenty lacs, within so short a time, that the movement of the army was not delayed for an instant on account of a deficiency of treasure, and Lieutenant-General Harris was provided with a sufficient supply of species to maintain his army in the field until the month of May."

It may now excite a smile to think of a grand British army of invasion with such a military chest; and that by the "extraordinary exertion" of the Government, and by the diligence and ability of the Accountant-General, so large a sum as "two hundred thousand pounds," had actually been raised in so short a time as to merit the grateful mention of it by the great Governor-General of the British Empire in India, supposed by the world to be the great unfailing source of England's wealth. Lord Wellesley did in fact take decisive measures as promptly as his necessary preparations and the nature of the Indian seasons permitted; and he took them with great vigour, and with rare skill and ability. He first by skilful negotiations made sure of the Nizam. He undertook to furnish him with an English contingent, to be maintained at his expense, on his agreeing to dismiss at once his French troops, and for ever to renounce all employment of European or American auxiliaries for the future. Acting on this arrangement with great promptitude, Lord Wellesley threw an English force into the Nizam's territory, to whom M. Perron and the French officers were obliged to surrender themselves on honourable terms, and the whole dangerous corps lately commanded by them was forthwith disbanded and disarmed. This was a great advantage gained; and the Nizam undertook to fulfil the terms of the old treaty of alliance, and to join in the demonstration, and, if necessary, the coercive measures against Tippoo. The Peshwa was also to some extent secured, and a promise of his co-operation was obtained. His conduct was vacillating, uncertain, and suspicious; but he was at all events neutralized, and Lord Wellesley was able to deal with Tippoo alone.

Having made all his arrangements, the Governor-General directed his army to enter Mysore, and to proceed directly to Seringapatam. He justified his conduct in a proclamation simple, frank, and explicit, addressed to all the princes and people of India, showing the provocations received from Tippoo, and the fruitless efforts made to induce him to make proper reparation and satisfaction. On the 5th of March, 1799, the army under General Harris, entered the enemy's territory. The "Grand Army," as it was called, consisted (exclusive of commissioned officers) of 912 European cavalry and 4608 European infantry; of 1766 Native cavalry, and 11,000 Native infantry; 576 artillerymen, and 2726 Gun Lascars and Pioneers. General Harris, after a successful engagement by the way, in which Colonel Wellesley (afterwards the Duke of Wellington) took a prominent part, succeeded in placing himself two miles south-west of Seringapatam by the 5th of April. An army from Bombay, which had entered the Mysore territories from that side under General Stuart, and had obtained a brilliant victory over Tippoo's forces, immediately on receipt of the news of General Harris's arrival before Seringapatam, advanced and effected a junction with the Grand Army under the walls of that place. Other detachments which had been left to guard the plains were called up in support; and the full strength of the combined English armies at the commencement of the siege operations was 8704 Europeans, 26,851 Natives (Sepoys), and 2351 horses.

With the English army were 23 engineers, 3621 infantry, and 6000 cavalry of the Nizam, who were probably of some, although not much, service, and at all events proved the reality of the alliance against Tippoo. They were useful too as a further proof that the war was not a war of British aggression and conquest, but a war of two allied Indian powers against a third, who had violated a general treaty of pacification and arrangement.

By the 24th of April the approaches to the fortifications were so far advanced as to give the English the command and the possession of the enemy's advanced works, which were carried, but not without an obstinate contest, which continued through the night. The breaching batteries were without loss of time erected, and their fire began to batter in a breach on the 30th of April. By the 3rd of May the walls were so much destroyed, that the breach was reported practicable. The troops were stationed in the trenches early on the morning of the 4th, where they remained quietly until the heat of day, when the assault was suddenly given; the defenders seem to have been taken by surprise by an assault at that time of day, and were little prepared to oppose it. The sovereign, the Generals, and the army were indulging in their noon-day refreshment and repose. The assaulting force, consisting of four flank companies of Europeans, followed by four European regiments and three corps of Grenadier sepoys, one from each Presidency, and 200 of the Nizam's troops, moved at one 0'clock from the trenches, crossed the rocky bed of the Cauvery under a heavy fire, passed the glacis and ditch, ascended the breaches in the faussebraye and the rampart, and in a few minutes were in possession of the works. Resistance continued to be made from the palace of the sultan for some time, after all the firing from the works had ceased, but by half-past two the place was completely in the possession of the English. Thus fell a fortress, which from the strength of its natural position and the stupendous works by which it was surrounded, on which 6000 men had been employed for six years, might well have been deemed by its defenders impregnable.

It was soon rumored that Tippoo himself had been killed, and after much difficulty late in the evening his body, pierced by shot, was found in one of the gates under a heap of slain, who had fallen around him. His corpse was the next day recognized by his family, and interred with the honours due to his rank, in the mausoleum of his fathers. Many of his principal chiefs had also fallen in the assault. The loss of the English army from the 4th of April to the 4th of May inclusive, was of Europeans killed, 101; wounded, 622; missing, 22; of Sepoys killed, 119; wounded, 420; missing, 100. It is obvious that the brunt of the fighting had fallen on the Europeans.

In the advance the most scrupulous care had been taken, in obedience to Lord Wellesley's express injuctions, to avoid as much as possible all injury to the cultivators; and after the assault, the most effectual measures were immediately adopted to stop the confusion at first unavoidable in a city carried by assault, and to protect the inhabitants and their property. In particular every attention was paid to the families of Tippoo Sultan and to those of his chieftains, who were protected from all injury and insult.

Treasure and property to a very large extent were found in the fortress and palace. The amount of coined money, jewels, and bullion which, by a memorandum made soon after the capture, was estimated at upwards of four million of star pagodas, (nearly a million and half sterling), contrasts singularly with the poverty of the conquerors, and the extraordinary efforts by which less than half of that sum was with difficulty gathered from various quarters. All this property became at once the prize of the army.

The extent and nature of the Sultan's military preparations and resources were more strikingly shown by the 929 pieces of ordnance, half of them brass, 99,000 firelocks, carbines, &c., 22,000 musket barrels, and 424,6000 lbs. of round iron shot, and 520,000 lbs. of gunpowder, which were taken possession of. Two hundred and eighty seven guns, mounted on the works, were found, as well as buildings and machines for boring and polishing guns and muskets large arsenals, large magazines for powder, small expense magazines, armouries, foundries, and well-stored grannaries—everything in short for the defence of the place. Tippoo's private papers also were discovered; and amongst them a copy of his letter to the Executive Directory of France, and a note of the proposals to be made by his ambassadors at Paris. The letter breathed a strong and not unnatural hostility to the English, and a request for such a reinforcement of troops as, joined to his own, would enable him to attack and annihilate for ever their common enemies in Asia. The aproposals were for a force of ten or fifteen thousand French troops to be landed on the Coromandel coast, and included the restoration to Tippoo of all the provinces which in 1792 he had been compelled to cede to the British and their allies, and an equal division of all the other conquests which they should make, including the Portuguese settlements. The fall of Seringapatam and of Tippoo decided the campaign. All his sons in a few days came in and surrendered themselves to the English; the soldiers for the most part without further resistance disbanded; the forts were yielded up; and the country submitted with alacrity to their new masters, who were received with apparent cordiality.

Thus, in two months from the commencement of the campaign, the powerful kingdom of Mysore, that had been built up by Hyder Ali, and sustained with such determination and vigour by his son Tippoo, passed away like the baseless fabric of a vision. The ease with which it fell to pieces shows that it had no substantial basis to rest on. There was in fact no kingdom, no nation, no people of Mysore. It was the kingdom of Haidar, and after him became the kingdom of Tippoo; but of course the Hindoo people, the native chiefs and cultivators of the soil, could have had no love for the princes of the usurping Mohammedan dynasty or for the Mohammedan chiefs who held sway under them; nor does it appear that the princes had, either by their personal qualities or their administration, conciliated the affection of their subjects. The bearing and conduct of the Mohammedan Generals and lords would seem to have been at least as oppressive and as offensive as that of the Norman barons to their Saxon subjects, aggravated by the fierce bigotry and haughty intolerance with which the stern monotheistic followers of the Prophet regarded the idolaters around them. It has been sometimes represented, that the fall of the Mysore kingdom was mainly due to the personal incapacity and misconduct of Tippoo, who is said to have been with difficulty on the day of the assault roused to a sense of his danger, or to any efforts to meet it. In a singularly interesting and able memorandum, however, on the position and power of Tippoo, prepared before the war by Captain (afterwards Sir John) Malcolm, for the guidance of Lord Wellesley, a very different and on the whole a very favourable estimate is given of his character and ability. It appears that his intrigues were conducted with great skill and perseverance, and showed very considerable powers of political combination, and knowledge of the assailable points in the English position, of the places in their alliances which were liable to be undermined, and of the means available for such assault and undermining. He was only misled into a premature betrayal of his designs by the promise of French assistance, in which he was grievously deceived, and disappointed. During the closing scenes of his life he was at all event with his army during the siege, and he fell at last in the assault by which his capital was taken.

The extraordinary enthusiasm, with which the news of the fall of Seringapatam was received throughout British India, was probably not surpassed by that which was sixteen years later excited in England by the battle of Waterloo, and showed unmistakably the sense of the great peril from which men's minds were suddenly relieved. Addresses of congratulation poured in upon Lord Wellesley; the wisdom of his policy, the completeness off his preparations, the energy of his measures, were in all men's mouths, and were re-echoed from this country. A perusal of all the despatches and documents shows that these praises were not ill-deserved nor exaggerated. The Governor-General appears carefully to have examined the position of the country, its enemies and allies, to have accurately weighed all the difficulties and dangers on the one hand, and the means of escape and resources on the other, and after due calculation and consideration to have come to the conclusion, that a policy of energetic action was the policy alike of safety and of honour, and to have acted with promptitude and vigour upon that conclusion. His policy gave immediately the tone to all the authorities, and to the body of the civil and military sergeants of the Company throughout India. His self-reliance gave them confidence in him, and his confidence in them gave them self-reliance; but this confidence and self-reliance were wholly unmixed with rashness.

Nearly ninety years have elapsed, and the whole of the vast and populous domains which have formed the Presidency of Madras have ever since enjoyed the most profound peace. No more black clouds have hung on the hills, to burst with all the horrors of war on the Carnatic. No hostile foot has ever been set within the limits of that Government, nor has the sound of an enemy's gun disturbed the quiet of the people. The peace thus secured to their own subjects has been hard by their allies, who have been protected alike from foreign aggression and from the intestine feuds, by which for so many centuries the fair regions of India had been made one vast scene of bloodshed and devastation.

It is also satisfactory to observe in the whole of Lord Wellesley's conduct and language, throughout the events which preceded this crowning victory, the unfailing characteristic of straightforwardness. His language to all was alike simple and frank. There is not a trace of deception or duplicity to be detected by the most minute analysis; nor is there to be found in his conduct or in his language anything unworthy of an honest man or an English gentleman. There had been a great advance since the days of Clive and Hastings. In fine, there never was a war begun with more just cause, or on plainer necessity, or more unexceptionably conducted, or the prizes of which were more legitimately acquired. Tippoo, in a game of war challenged by himself, fairly lost all his dominions to his adversaries, and with the exception of his own family and a very few personal adherents and co-religionists, not a human being suffered any injury from the change of masters, or was even wounded in any feeling of patriotism or national self-love, or religion or caste. It is worthy of remark, that as the aggressions of the French on the Factory at Madras led to the first establishment of the English as a sovereign power there, and to their first territorial acquisitions, so the intervention and promises of the French led directly to the great results which followed from the capture of Seringapatam.

The Governor-General was in effect after this victory all-powerful in India. He proceeded to deal at his pleasure with the territories that had fallen into his power. He determined to restore the representative of the legitimate Hindoo sovereign whose throne had been usurped by Hyder, and assigned to him the kingdom of Mysore, which still exists under the arrangements which were then made, a kingdom of not less than 30,000 square miles. The terms of the treaty, by which this was effected, deserve detailed mention, as illustrating the nature of the alliances, which it was then and thenceforth the policy of the English to make with the native princes, who were willing to accept their protection. It was in substance as follows, viz—

1. The friends and enemies of either shall be considered as the friends and enemies of both.
2. The Company shall maintain, and the Maharajah shall receive, a military force for the defence and security of His Highness's dominions, for which he shall pay the annual sum of seven lacs of star pagodas. The disposal of the money and the arrangement for the employment of the troops are to be left entirely to the Company.
3. In case of war or preparations for war, His Highness shall contribute such further sum for the increased expense, as on an attentive consideration of the means of His Highness, the Governor-General shall deem a reasonable and just proportion to his actual net revenues.
4. In case of apprehended failure of the stipulated payments of the contributions, the Governor-General shall have power to make such regulations as he shall think fit, or to bring under the direct

management of the servants of the Company, such parts of the territories as shall appear to the Governor-General in council necessary to render the funds available in peace or war.

5. The Maharajah will abstain from interference in the affairs of any state whatever, and will not hold any communication or correspondence with any foreign state whatever, without the previous knowledge and sanction of the Company.
6. The Maharajah will not take any European foreigners into his service, and will apprehend and deliver up all Europeans found in his territories without the passports of the Company.
7. The contingent is to be employed, if required, for enforcing and maintaining the authority and government of His Highness, but not in the ordinary transactions of revenue.
8. The Maharajah promises to pay at all times the utmost attention to such advice as the Company's Government shall occasionally judge it necessary to offer to him, with a view to the economy of his finances, &c., or any other objects connected with the advancement of His Highness's interests, the happiness of his people, and the mutual welfare of both states.

The terms as such almost necessarily flow out of the relations of protecting and protected states, and the pecuniary tribute (about 250,000*l.*) rendered in exchange for military defence and protection, was certainly not immoderate.

The position of a native prince under such a treaty is pretty much what that of a feudal sovereign, duke, or count is to his suzerain paramount. So long as the paramount lord is strong enough to be dreaded, he is in effect for all military and imperial purposes, actual sovereign, and master of the resources of the dependent state. With the provision in the treaty that the superior should maintain "a military force," which of course practically means "the military force," within the territory for its protection and security, and the further provision authorizing direct interference with the management of the country in a special case, and interference by way of advice in every case, the native prince was in truth a mere vassal; and the reality of his subjection has been strikingly shown in Mysore itself, where the incapacity of the sovereign for many years made it necessary for the suzerain power to place him under tutelage, even in the internal administration of his people.

With regard to the remaining spoils of the war, they were divided between the English and the Nizam, after a vain attempt to bring the Peshwa into the same position of a subsidized and protected ally, by offering him the bribe of a considerable portion of the Mysore territory. After a short trial of the arrangement, under which the Nizam was to pay his tribute to the English, with a liability to further underfined payments in case of war, and the consequent provisions for securing the due and punctual payment, a fresh treaty was entered into, which provided for a perpetual alliance between the two powers, and a positive guarantee by the English of the rights and territories of the Nizam against any act of unprovoked hostility or aggression. It was stipulated that the English should provide eight battalions of Sepoys, (8000 firelocks), two regiments of Cavalry, with the requisite complement of Guns, European artillerymen, Lascars, Pioneers, warlike stores and ammunition, such force to be stationed in perpetuity in His Highness's territories.

For the regular payment of the whole expense of the subsidiary force, the Nizam ceded to the Company, in perpetuity, all the territories acquired by him under the Treaty of Seringapatam, as well as all those allotted to him in the recent partition of Tippoo Sultan's dominions; which territories were to be accepted by the English in full satisfaction of the pecuniary obligations of the Nizam.

The districts acquired by this treaty in absolute sovereignty by the English amounted to about 26,000 square miles; which, added to 20,000 acquired by the Treaty of Seringapatam, made an aggregate of 46,000 square miles of the territories of Tippoo Sultan, which passed under the direct rule of the English.

By these acquisitions and arrangements, the English became masters, either as sovereigns in possession or as lords paramount, of the whole of the southern part of the Peninsula.

REFERENCES

1. A crore is ten millions of rupees.
2. A lac is 100,000.

11

Acquisition of Tanjore, Carnatic and Oudh

In 1801 Lord Wellesley took steps to acquire in absolute possession, as immediate domains, the dependent territories of Tanjore and the Carnatic.

As far back as the year 1776, the Rajah of Tanjore had entered into an arrangement for placing himself under the protection of the Company, and receiving a subsidiary military force in exchange for an annual payment charged on the revenues of his country. He fell into arrears, and became deeply involved, which led to arrangements for the discharge as well of his debt to the Company as of his private debts. On his death in 1787 a dispute arose as to the right of succession, and Sir Archibald Campbell having decided in favour of Amer Sing, the latter was by the authority of the British placed on the Musnud. But Serfogee, the excluded claimant, did not acquiesce in this decision, and appealed for redress to the superior British authorities. After many years of delay and a very long investigation, a minute was made by Mr. Dundas, in which, after stating that the whole of the evidence proved that the son of the former Rajah had been unjustly and unduly deprived of his inheritance, and that it was impossible that the British Government should any longer co-operate in supporting the present usurper, he proceeded as follows:—

" . . . It must be recollected, that we are in a great degree the authors of this injustice. It was produced by our interference obtained through the misrepresentations of the person who is now reaping the benefit of it, and the rightful heir has a just claim that we should remedy that injustice which originated in our interference. If after such a lapse of time the native powers were to observe us interfering in order to carry into effect any forfeiture in our own favour, it would afford just cause of reproach, but in the present instance we would appear in the light of honourably repairing that injury which we ourselves have been the innocent instruments of committing.

"At the same time that we are interfering to do justice to the rightful heir, we ought not to forget the claims the country has to our protection against oppression, and we have a fair right to take care that the interests ascertained to us in the revenues of Tanjore be better guarded than they have been by former treaties."*

In June 1798, Lord Wellesley issued his direction to the Government of Madras to proceed to the deposition of Amer Sing and the restoration of Serfogee; assuring the former that his person should be protected, and that his private property, together with a suitable provision for his maintenance, should be secured to him so long as he should conduct himself in all respects to the satisfaction of the Government of Fort St. George. It was stipulated with Serfogee that he should assent to the appointment of a commission to inquire into the state and resources of Tanjore, and that in the meantime the Company should retain the possession of the districts, which had been assumed in consequence of the failure of Amer Sing in the payment of his debts.

It had originally been intended to assume the management of the whole country for a short time, but Lord Wellesley subsequently wrote:— "My opinion has changed

---

* Page 49, vol. v, *Wellesley Despatches*. Private Minute of Mr. Dundas, Sept. 11, 1797.

upon a further consideration. I think the assumption of the whole country, without the consent of Serfogee, even for so short a period as a year, might bear a very odious appearance in the eyes of the native powers. But if Serfogee should really be sensible of the advantages to be derived to his own interests, as well as to those of his people from entrusting the management of his country to the servants of the Company for one or two years, I think such a measure would be very beneficial to all parties. On this point, however, my desire is that the inclinations of Serfogee should dictate the arrangement, and that no other means than those of advice and persuasion should be used to induce him to propose such a measure. The proposal must come from himself in a formal manner, and must originate in his conviction of the utility of the arrangement to his permanent welfare."

This communication shows the spirit in which Lord Wellesley, in full accord with the authorities at home, dealt with the subject, and there is no reason to believe that he in any way departed from it in the ultimate arrangement which was prepared by himself, and left by him before leaving Madras in the form of a treaty, which was immediately proposed to Serfogee; nor does there seem any reason to believe that any pressure was put on the Rajah to induce him to accede to the treaty, which, by putting an end to the double government which had prevailed, was manifestly calculated to promote the prosperity of the people of Tanjore.

By that treaty, the Government of the country was vested in the Company, ample provision being made for the Rajah; the result of the inquiry having proved, that it had become indispensably necessary to establish a regular and permanent system for the better administration of the revenue of the country.

Thus the important province of Tanjore became British territory with the acquiescence of the Rajah who, munificently provided for, contritedly subsided from the position of a protected sovereign into that of a mediatized prince, to the great satisfaction of the creditors of the state, and to the incalculable advantage of the people. It is noteworthy that the registration of the titles of the landowners and the perpetual limitation of their land tax were primary articles of the treaty.

Turning now to the Carnatic, it will be recollected that the very origin of the territorial dominion of the Company in the Madras Presidency, was the contest as to the Nawabship of Arcot or the Carnatic, in which the French took one side and the English the other, and that the English candidate and faction ultimately prevailed. An alliance of the most intimate character came thus to arise between Mahomed Ali and the Company; and unfortunately for the prime he became also intimately allied with Paul Benfied and a number of other English adventurers and intriguers, including or having as accomplices many of the Company's highest officials. He was himself an intriguer of no despicable powers, but wholly unable to cope with the many accomplished masters of the arts of intrigue by whom he was surrounded, and in whose toils he was entangled. His affairs became frightfully embarrassed, and large districts of his dominions were ruined by his mortgage creditors, to whom they were assigned. In India the assignment of land revenue of a district, and the state of a country may well be conceived when under the rule of an usurious money-lender, with no object but to extract the largest amount for the satisfaction of his claims, and with no interest in the permanent welfare of the districts.

The Carnatic had been overrun and devastated by the armies of Hyder Ali, from whose power it was only rescued by the exertions of the British; and in 1787 the Company bound itself to maintain the whole military force required for the protection of the territories of the Nawab, who in return charged himself with an annual subsidy of fifteen lacs of pagodas, and it was arranged that in the event of actual war, the Company should, if deemed necessary, take the whole administration of the country into its hands.

When the great war with Tippoo Sultan took place in 1790, it was found necessary to act upon that engagement in the treaty; but after the successful termination of that arduous struggle by the Treaty of Seringapatam, the civil government was restored to the Nawab Mahomed Ali, whose territories were guaranteed by the terms of the general peace. He represented that the pecuniary obligations of the treaty of 1787 were too burthensome for his resources; and it was therefore arranged by a new treaty, in 1792, that the subsidy should be reduced from fifteen to nine lacs of star pagodas. This second treaty contained a renewal of the right of the Company, in the event of actual hostilities, to take the entire administration of the country into their hands; and was made not only with Mahomed Ali, but also with his son Omdah-ul-Omra, to whom the succession to his father's territories was thereby secured and guaranteed.

The pecuniary embarrassments of the Arcot princes became so great, that without being able to make any provision for the payment of his debts, the Nawab was only able to meet the monthly payments of the subsidy of one lacs of pagodas, as they became due, by contracting fresh debts at exorbitant rates of interest; the loans being usually accompanied by assignments of territory to the creditors, "whose vexatus management of the revenues assigned has been" (writes Lord Wellesley) "the continual cause of the most aggravated calamities to the inhabitants of the Carnatic."

The state of affairs became a source of great anxiety and much pain to the Government both in India and at home; anxiety from the apprehension, amounting almost to a certainty, that at no distant time the impoverished country would fail to yield the subsidy which then constitued a great part of the revenues of the Madras Government; and pain from the uneasy inviction, that their power alone maintained a rule by which the country was impoverished and depopulated.

In Lord Wellesley's Despatches we have evidence beyond dispute of not only the justice and moderation, but even the liberality with which the former was minded to deal with the Nawab. In a letter to the Governor of Madras he writes:—"My fixed rule was to treat him with the respect due to his rank, with the kindness due to the ancient friendship between his family and the Company, and with the delicacy demanded by his dependent situation."

When the war of 1799 broke out, Lord Wellesley took that opportunity of again addressing a letter to this price, pointing out to him that the Company were then authorized by the very terms of the treaty to take into their own hands the whole administration of his country, and exposing in very plain but very respectful terms, the ruinous consequences to himself and his country of the existing state of things, and the injurious consequences which must result to the Company. After reminding him of the liberality which had been shown in 1792, and of the position of his affairs as debtor to the Company, Lord Wellesley proposed to him an arrangement, the substance of which was:—

That a territory should be placed under the exclusive management and authority of the Company, yielding a revenue equal to the monthly payments due to the Company, which should thenceforth cease. If such territory should produce more than the amounts, the whole of the surplus to be paid to the Nawab, but if less, the loss to be borne exclusively by the Company. All the unassigned territories to be under the absolute control of the Nawab, free from any control or interference of the Company—whether in peace or war—and from all claims by them.

To these very liberal proposals, which would have relieved the country from the evils of a double government and the capacity of the creditors , and would have relieved the prince from all his difficulties and given him a much more ample revenue, he always offered one answer.

Non opossums. "My father's dying injunctions to me were never to allow the slightest deviation from the treaty of 1792, and I am bound, therefore, by the most sacred obligation to him, not even to allow a letter to be changed.

Exercise all your rights under the treaty during this war, and I will submit; I rely on British justice when the war is ended to replace me in full possession of all my rights, in strict accordance with the same treaty." So there the matter then rested.

During the war with Tippoo Sultan, however, the conduct of the Nawab was such as in Lord Clive's* judgement could only be accounted for by his having a secret understanding with the enemy. He had engaged to pay a part of the subsidy at a time when it was of the utmost importance to raise funds for General Harris's expedition; and his failure to fulfil this engagement would have probably frustrated the whole operation, but for the timely arrival of the supply of species from Bengal before mentioned. His agents and offices throughout his territory systematically and actively opposed every obstacle to the collection of the requisite supplies, and threw every difficulty in the way of the movements of the allied troops. The suspicions of his treachery arising from this otherwise inexplicable conduct, were amply justified by the documents which were found amongst Tippoo Sultan's private papers after the taking of Seringapatam.

After a careful examination of the documents, the Governor-General came to the conclusion that both Mahomed Ali and Omdah-ul-Omra the Heir Apparent, had been long in secret interaction with Tippoo Sultan, "founded on principles, and directed to objects utterly subversive of the alliance between the Nawab and the Company, and equally incompatible with the security of the British power in the Peninsula of India;" and that "these ancient allies of the Company had been found not only deficient in every active duty of the alliance, but unfaithful to its fundamental principles, and untrue to its vital spirit." It is impossible, after reading the very careful and elaborate report of Mr. Edmonstone, the Persian translator, on the various documents

* Governor of Madras.

found in the palace of Seringapatam, to avoid coming to the same conclusion. It was not unnatural that the Arcot princes should be dissatisfied with their dependent situation and the state of their affairs, and should conceive hopes of improvement from an alliance with the Company's great enemy; and there seems to have been another motive not less natural, and one not wholly blamable, for their conduct. The older Nawab especially, being in very advanced years, appears to have been moved by considerations of what he conceived to be his duty to the sacred cause of Islamism. Tippoo Sultan was considered as the great pillar of the faith in India; and it was therefore very natural that Mahomed Ali, on the verge of life, should admit the force of one of Tippoo's appeals to him:— "My hope from Almighty God, and my confidence in the Prophet is, that according to the command of God and of the Prophet, which is well known to all Mussulmans, all the faithful will exert themselves with heart and soul in maintaining and rendering permanent the religion of Mahomed. Upon your Highness, who is one of the heads of the faith, this is an absolute duty, and I am confident that your Highness will by all means constantly employ your time in performing what is obligatory on you."

Both Mahomed Ali and Omdah-ul-Omra appear indeed from the whole correspondence to have been influenced by a strong feeling of sympathy with their brother Mussulman in his contest with the infidel Government of the Company. However this may be considered morally as a palliation of their breach of faith, it could of course have no effect politically or legally in mitigation of the penalty, which was incurred by the plain violation of the treaty of alliance in its most essential terms.

Lord Wellesley therefore came to the determination that it was not only his right but his duty to proceed to the public deposition of the Nawab and the forfeiture of his sovereignty, and issued his directions to the Government of Madras accordingly. But before this could be carried into effect, the Nawab Omdah-ul-Omra was ascertained to be in a dying state, so that Lord Wellesley's determination and decision could not with proper regard to humanity be communicated to him, and he died in ignorance of what had been decreed against him. It was not, however, Lord Wellesley's intention to do otherwise than make ample provision for the Nawab suitable to his princely rank and dignity. That the Governor-General was fully justified on every ground in availing himself of the right given by the violation of the treaty to make new arrangements for the government of the Carnatic, and that it was his duty to make them such as would best secure the good government of the country and the legitimate interests of the British rule, is not open to controversy; but the manner in which he effected his object after the death of the Nawab does not appear consistent with the dignity of himself or of the Government. The right of the Nawab was wholly forfeited, and it was for the Government to give or to withhold according to its sense of right and justice, tempered by all the considerations due to the position of their former ally, and the long continuance of the relations which had existed between him and the Company; but instead of acting upon this right be proceeded in a manner, which looks too much like the ordinary course of a native Indian Court.

The Nawab died without legitimate issue, and disposed of his throne and possessions by will to his reputed and acknowledged son, Hussein Ali. It had long been expected that such a disposition would be made, and it was also known that the validity of such disposition and the fact of Hussein being the son of Omdah-ul-Omra would be questioned by Azim-ul-Doulah, the son and heir of the next brother of the deceased Nawab, and the immediate great-grandson by both his parents of the Nawab Anwar-u-deen, the founder of the family. It is difficult to imagine any principle of general Mohammedan law, by which a Mohammedan sovereign would be authorized by will to dispose of his dominions to any person whom he chose to recognize as his natural son, or that there was any such family law recognized in the Arcot royal family. Without, however, pausing to consider to whom, by the proper laws and customs applicable to the case, the possession of the Musnud belonged, it was determined at once to acknowledge Hussein Ali, if he would engage to enter into a treaty, based on the decision of the Governor-General as to the future of the country. By whatever motive impelled, Hussein Ali, with the full concurrence of his testamentary guardians, his family and friends, and after two private interviews with Lord Clive, the Governor of Madras, resolutely declined to enter into any such arrangement. Thereupon Azim-ul-Doulah, on agreeing to make the required concession, was brought forward as the legitimate successor, and installed on the Musnud by the Company's authority. By a formal treaty he immediately ceded the whole of the Carnatic dominions, in absolute sovereignty and in perpetuity, to the Company, who engaged in return to pay him one-fifth of the net revenue of the country, but never less than 12,000 star pagodas a month; and it was further stipulated, that he should in all places, on all occasions, and at all times, be treated with the respect and attention due to His Highness's rank and position as an ally of the British Government, and be furnished with a suitable guard for the protection of his person and palace.

The provisions of the treaty were under all the circumstances liberal enough; but there should have been no treaty at all. The Governor-General should have determined, on a full and impartial examination of the case with the best advice of Pundits and others, who was the rightful successor to the family dignity and estates, and have declared on that plain ground of right in favour of the person so ascertained, and should then have made for him the provision which was deemed adequate; but it was unworthy of the British name to offer to sell the succession to whichever claimant would give them their price. The whole proceedings of the British authorities, however, including even the bargaining with Hussein Ali, his refusal, and their subsequent bargain with Azim-ul-Doulah, were frankly stated in a public proclamation by which they submitted their conduct to the public opinion had judgement of the princes and people of India.

Thus ended the Nawabship of the Carnatic; its connexion with the Madras Government had throughout been discreditable to the English, and a continual source of fraud, peculation, and maladministration by officials and others under official protection; and its very termination, as if by some fatality attending it throughout, took place in a manner neither rightful, just, nor becoming. By the acquisition of the territories of the Carnatic and Tanjore, in addition to those which were obtained in the final arrangement of Tippoo Sultan's kingdom, the Presidency of Madras grew from its comparatively small dimensions into the magnificent province of 148,000 square miles, and a population of at least 35,000,000 people.

The position of affairs in the territories of the Nawab Vizier of Oude, was, if anything, still worse than in the Carnatic. Asaph-ud-Doulah, Warren Hastings' ally, died in the year 1797, and upon his death there occurred the usual Indian dispute as to succession. One Vizier Ali, claiming to be the son of the late Nawab, got together a sufficient party to enable him to seize the Musnud. Sir John Shore, the Governor-General, being satisfied that Vizier Ali had in truth no legitimate pretension to the succession, interfered on behalf of Saadat Ali, whom he ascertained to be the rightful heir, and whom he placed on the throne. By a treaty made with Saadat Ali, arrangements were entered into for the maintenance of a large British subsidiary force to be stationed in Oude. The British Government undertook to defend Oude and the new Vizier against all enemies, and it was especially stipulated that if circumstances should arise calling for a larger force, the British should furnish it, and the Vizier should defray the additional expenses thereby occasioned.

The government of Saadat Ali was very bad, and the most earnest remonstrances were addressed to him by the British Resident and the Governor-General personally, but in vain. Under British protection Oude had been maintained in the uninterrupted enjoyment of peace from without, but was rapidly and progressively declining in prosperity, population, and cultivation. There was a turbulent and mutinous army and universal discontent; and active and general support was given by Saadat Ali's subjects to an impostor who assumed the name of Vizier Ali. Sahadat Ali owned even his personal safety to the British, made frequent complaints of the state of his country to the Governor-General, requested his interference and assistance, and at length announced his deliberate determination to abdicate, on the ground, "that his mind was utterly withdrawn from the government of a people who were neither pleased with him nor he with them, and with whose evil dispositions, enmity, disobedience, and negligence he was completely disgusted."

Amongst the dangers which then threatened India, one, not the least, was the invasion of Zemaun Shah, whose avowed object was to restore in his own person the Mogul sovereignty, and amongst other pretensions in that character he had called upon the Vizier of Oude and the British as his vassals to assist him. He had reached Lahore, and the intervening Sikh chiefs and Marathas were hardly in a condition to offer effectual opposition to his advance. The military situation is necessary to take effectual steps for strengthening the British force on that frontier. Lord Wellesley determined under the provisions of the treaty to increase the subsidiary army in Oude, and called upon the Vizier to defray the expense, and to reduce and radically reform his own army, which not only exhausted the pecuniary resources of the country, but was a source of weakness and danger in a military point of view to the protecting power. As long as a turbulent and licentious native army existed in Oude, it would be always necessary to keep a large British force there to overawe them, and all military movements would be hampered if the British were liable to have their communications cut off by a disaffected body left behind. It was therefore the right and the duty of the protecting power to insist on the reduction of the native army, and the substitution for them of a sufficient and efficient British force; but this was distasteful to the Vizier, and the Governor-

General came to the conclusion, that the proposal to abdicate was a mere ruse by which the Resident and he himself were amused, so as to delay the military reforms so essential and so pressing. The Resident reported that "the Vizier instead of affording any cordial assistance for devising and carrying into execution a plan for the dismissal of the Oude battalions, had thrown every possible impediment in the way of that measure, and that he was equally desirous of impeding the progress of the additional British troops, by exposing them to difficulties in obtaining supplies of provisions." Thereupon Lord Wellesley wrote, "It is impossible for me to express in terms of sufficient force, the sentiments which this intelligence has occasioned in my mind. The conduct of your Excellency in both instances stated, but more flagrantly in the last, is of a nature so unequivocally hostile, and may prove so injurious to every interest, both of your Excellency and of the Company, that your perseverance in so dangerous a course, will leave me no other alternative than that of considering all amicable engagements between the Company and yourself to be dissolved, and of regulating my subsequent proceedings accordingly.

> "I think it necessary to entreat you not to delay for a moment, whatever further steps may be pointed out to you by the resident as necessary to effect the two urgent and indispensable objects; namely, the reform of your military establishment, and the provision of funds for the regular monthly payment of all the Company's troops in Oude. The least omission or procrastination, in either of these important points, must lead to the most serious mischief."

This remonstrance appears for a time to have produced some effect, but after the lapse of a year, the Vizier intimated that he should be probably unable to provide the necessary funds for the regular payment of the additional troops, furnished for the defence of his dominions. This in Lord Wellesley's judgement called upon him to take prompt measures for remedying the state of things in Oude. As those measures resulted in a considerable cession of territory by the Vizier, under a compulsory alteration of the existing treaty, it is necessary to state the grounds on which Lord Wellesley justified his somewhat high-handed proceeding, in his own language, in a letter addressed to the Nawab Vizier, from which the following are extracts.*

"It appears by our Excellency's statements . . . that the general resources of your dominions actually decline with a rapidity menacing the joint interests of your Excellency and of the Company in Oude with utter and speedy destruction . . . . It is evident that all my precautions must prove fruitless if the defects of the civil administration of Oude should be suffered progressively to impair the fundamental resources of the state. The continuance of the present system for a longer period will not only render your Excellency unable to discharge the subsidy on account of the additional troops; but the resources of your Excellency's country would be exhausted to such a degree as to preclude the possibility of your discharging the former subsidy . . . .

"While the Company's territories have been advancing progressively during the last ten years in prosperity, population, and opulence; your Excellency's dominions, have rapidly and progressively declined . . . . The daily increase of these evils is evident to the whole world, acknowledged by yourself, and must be progressive to the utter ruin of the resources of Oude, unless the vicious system of government be immediately abandoned . . . You have repeatedly and earnestly solicited my direct interference, and have declared it to be indispensably necessary for the purpose of effecting a complete reform in your affairs . . . .

"Having maturely considered the condition of Oude with the deliberation due to the importance of the subject, I am satisfied that no effectual security can be taken against the ruin of the country until your Excellency shall transfer to the exclusive management of the Company the civil and military

---

* See p. 429, vol. ii., Wellesley's Despatches.

government of your dominions, under such conditions as may secure the affluence and power of yourself and your illustrious family . . . . Under the Company's management your subjects would enjoy the rights of property, honest and vigorous administration of justice, and security of life. . . .

"If your excellency should be persuaded to reject these approposals, I must inform you that the funds for the payment of the subsidy must be placed beyond the hazard of failure, and I must represent to your Excellency the necessity of making a cession to the Company of such parts of your territories as shall be adequate to defray these charges."

Under the compulsion of this menacing despatch a new treaty was concluded, by which were ceded to the Company, in perpetual sovereignty, territorial possessions, the estimated land revenue of which was thirteen million and a half of Lucknow sicca rupees, in lieu of the subsidy and of all the expenses of any additional troops; the Company engaging to defend the Nawab Vizier's remaining territories against all foreign and domestic enemies. By the same treaty it was stipulated that the Vizier should maintain only the limited armed force therein specified, and an engagement was made which half a century afterwards led to most momentous results, viz.: "His Excellency engages that he will establish in his reserved dominions such a system of administration, to be carried into effect by his own officers, as shall be conducive to the prosperity of his subjects, and be calculated to secure the lives and property of the inhabitants; and his Excellency will always advise with, and act in conformity to, the counsel of the officers of the Said Company."

The territory ceded to the Company by this treaty was about 30,000 square miles, being rather more than half the then dominions of Oude, and comprehended the whole of the Lower Doab between the Ganges and the Jumna, Allahabad, and a large extent of country on the Ganges and Gogra rivers down to the frontiers of Benares.

The country left to the Vizier was still a considerable kingdom; in situation, fertility, and resources unsurpassed probably by any part of India, and protected from foreign foes and intestine war, it required nothing but ordinary good government to be a flourishing and prosperous realm.

On a dispassionate consideration at this distance of time, the important judgement of the historian must be, that the Governor-General was not actuated by any vulgar ambition of territorial aggrandizement, but acted fairly and honestly, with due regard to the faith of existing treaties, and to what was due to the people as well as to the Sovereign of Oude. If he erred at all, it was in his duty to the people of Oude, in leaving so fair and so populous a kingdom still under the power of a prince so incapable and so unworthy, and continuing still to that prince's misrule the protection of the British power. But there was no abler or better prince at hand who could give hope of a better rule; and Lord Wellesley, by inserting in the treaty the positive stipulations for the disbanding of almost the whole of the disorderly battalions, and for a better administration of the civil Government, might reasonably have hoped for the removal of most of the evils by which the country had been desolated.

12

Sir Charles Metcalfe, 1785–1846

Charles Metcalfe was the son of Major Metcalfe who had made a fortune in India during the early days of the Company's rule. He had returned to England, and became a director of the East India Company, and was afterwards created a baronet. Charles was born in Calcutta, but was sent to England to be educated at Eton. His tastes at school ran in a literary direction rather than towards athletics. The ordinary school curriculum of Latin and Greek failed to satisfy his ambition, and as there were many spare hours in the Eton of those days, he utilized them by studying modern languages, and acquired sufficient proficiency in French and Italian to be able to read books in those languages.

In the early days of British rule in India, men went out to India young. Metcalfe was no exception to this rule. He was only fifteen when his father obtained a writership in Bengal for him. He did not like leaving Eton, but he acceded to his father's wish, and duly proceeded to India, and arrived in that country early in 1801, being then only sixteen. The Marquis Wellesley, who was Governor-General at the time, realized the dangers and temptations surrounding the youngsters who were being sent out to India fresh from the wholesome discipline of school into an atmosphere so entirely different, and into a society whose tone was not always of the highest at this period of Anglo-Indian history. It was on their behalf, therefore, that he conceived the plan of a residential college, with the view of giving them a good start in their new careers. 'The college was to be,' he wrote, 'a place where the writers on their first arrival in India, should be subjected for a period of two or three years to rules and discipline and where the languages and laws of the country might be studied, and habits of activity regularity, and decency might be for med, instead of those of sloth, indolence, low debauchery, and vulgarity, which were too apt to grow on those young men who have been sent at an early age into the interior of the country, and have laid the foundition of their life and manners among the coarse vices and indulgence of those countries.' The Marquis was a man of high ideals and his influence was potent for good on those young civilians who had the good fortune to come within the sphere of that influence, and so many of whom afterwards became distinguished public servants. The college had a short career, as the directors did not sanction its up-keep: short as that career was, some distinguished names appeared on its rolls, and first amongst these was that of Charles Metcalfe. The conception of the Marquis Wellesley had given the directors a hint: they also began to realize that there was much 'to seek' in the education of young civilians, and Haileybury College was the outcome of their deliberations. As the hot weather came on, young Metacalfe, like many a man destined to achieve fame in India, before and after him, began to grow weary of the country, and he wrote to his father begging to be allowed to return home and to be put into any place, however small, in some public office. His mother, fortunately for Metcalfe, appears to have been a woman of no ordinary common sense, and it is recorded that 'her only reply to his letter was the despatch of a box of pills, she realized that he was suffering from a temporary depression of spirits, with the pills she also gave him some excellent advice': 'You will probably laugh,' she wrote to him, 'at my sending you the pills, but I think you are bilious, and they will be of great service: you study too much: you should dissipate a little. On account of your health you should relax. Ride on horseback. When intense thinking is joined with the want of exercise, the consequences must be bad.' Similarly it is recorded that his father, who knew what the Indian climate was, wrote and told him of his own experiences, 'how one morning in a fit of bile, he waited upon his commanding officer with an intention of resigning the service, and returning to England, but that, fortunately for him, the conversation at breakfast took a pleasant turn, and a hearty fit of laughter got the better of his blue devils, and he returned to his quarters with a determination to persevere.' Want of occupation had doubtless had much to do with this temporary depression: it had all passed off before the end of the year when the first summons came to him to enter the arena of active employment. The Marquis, who was a good judge of character, had noted the latent capacity of the youngster, and gave him the appointment of assistant to the Resident at the court of Scindhia.

The Governor-General had recently left Calcutta for a tour up country, and Metcalfe obtained permission, after proceeding some distance on his way, to join his camp, and accompany it as far as Lucknow. He had doubtless, in his boyhood, dreamt, as many another boys had done, of the romance and splendour of 'the gorgeous East', and it is recorded that in the court of the King of Oudh at Lucknow, he found that 'the reality even exceeded the romance of his dreams, everything recalled to his imagination the *Arabian Night*'. He had not yet had time to see behind the scenes. He did not remain long at the court of Scindhia: he resigned his post there as he was unable to hit it off with his chief, the Resident, who, from the sobriquet he had earned of 'King Collins', must have been what in Indian parlance is known as 'a bit of a Bahadur'. Given an hereditary tendency this way, a long career in the East, unbroken by an occasional wholesome visit to the old country, will tend to intensify such a domineering disposition: this wholesome break in the continuity of a life under Oriental conditions, was not always possible at this period of British rule in India. Metcalfe left Scindia's court, and returned to Calcutta again.

In returning to Calcutta, Metcalfe was fortunate enough to get a place, in what was styled 'Lord Wellesley's Office', among a number of other young civilians: he was thus brought directly within the sphere of influence of that distinguished man: and the experience he thus gained was to stand him in good stead. He was engaged in this pleasant duty for some two years. Apart from his recognition of his young assistant's abilities, the Governor-General had another reason for being willing to advance his interests: Metcalfe's father was one of the few Directors who steadily supported his policy. This may or may not have weighed with him, but even the greatest of men are only human after all: anyhow, Metcalfe found himself, at the age of nineteen, appointed to the congenial post of political assistant to Lord Lake, who was in command of the military operations against the Marathas in that portion of the country lying between the Jumna and the Ganges.

It illustrates the disturbed state of the country at the time to find it recorded that on his way up country to join his appointment, young Metcalfe was attacked, robbed, and badly wounded by a party of armed Dakaits, or highway robbers. Some time elapsed, till nursed back to health, before he could join the British camp. Lord Lake had no great desire to have men about him, while on active service, who wielded the pen: he thought they were out of place in the field. It was a dictum of his, as has been recorded, that men of the sword 'should mind their fighting and not their writing', similarly he held that men of the pen 'should mind their writing and not their fighting'. There was some excuse for him: the Great Duke had not then written his despatches, nor was the poet born who had thus sung of 'the quill-driving Clerk:

> I maintain my friend of Plassey proved a warrior every whit
>
> Worth your Alexanders, Caesars, Marlboroughs, and what said Pitt?
>
> Frederick the fierce himself.

Anyhow, his opinion being what they were, it was not surprising that Lord Lake did not welcome very cordially the arrival in his camp of the young civilian: but Metcalfe was soon to show him that he could wield the sword with the best of his soldiers. And the story of how he did this is thus told: 'An opportunity soon came. The army was before the strong fortress of Deeg. The storming party was told off, and the non-combatant clerk volunteered to accompany it. He was one of the first to enter the breach. This excited the admiration of the old general, who made most honourable mention of him in his despatch, and ever afterwards throughout the campaign spoke of him as his "little stormer".' Indeed, his gallantry on this occasion was never forgotten: at the great banquet that was given to him on the eve of his leaving India for good the toast that was drunk with the greatest enthusiasm was 'Charles Metcalfe, the soldier of Deeg'. Towards the end of the campaign, Metcalfe was sent on a special mission to Holkar to convey assurances of British friendship and goodwill. It is recorded that 'he accomplished this task with temper and tact': and it required an exercise of such qualities, for the great Pathan leader, Amir Khan, was at the meeting, and was somewhat inclined to be insolent to the youthful English diplomatist: Metcalfe, however, practically ignored him, and confined his conversation to Holkar.

Metcalfe's next appointment was that of assistant to the Resident at Delhi, a Colonel Seton. He was a man of a different type from 'King Collins', and carried the courtesy and politeness that is said to have distinguished him rather to excess: indeed his bearing towards the old Mogul Emperor, Shah Alam, approached to obsequiousness; but doubtless the blindness and general helplessness of the aged monarch appealed to his sense of chivalry. In 1808, the then Governor-General of India, Lord Minto, resolved to send missions to the various princes on the frontiers of India with the view of checkmating the anticipated hostile aggression of the Rusian and French sovereigns, who had, only in the previous year, formed an alliance together at Tilsit: and it was suspected that an invasion of India was amongst their plans. A poet has given expression to these not unnatural fears—

> The life-time long alliance Russia swore
> At Tilsit, for the English Realm's undoing

Metcalfe was selected to proceed to the court of the Sikh Maharaja, Ranjit Singh. Considering that he was only twenty-three at the time, it says much for the reputation he had already gained with the Government that he should have been so selected: as events proved, his selection was fully justified.

At the first meeting between the young envoy and Ranjit Singh, Courtesies only were exchanged. It is interesting to note as going to show how in many respects conditions are much the some now as they were then, that chairs were borrowed from the English camp to enable Ranjit Singh and his Sardars to do honour to their visitors by adopting the European custom of sitting on chairs: the old and more comfortable attitude of reclining on the Gadi, the pillowed couch, is still in force among the Indian potentates when receiving visitors from among their own countrymen. The Maharaja made one notable pronouncement at this first meeting. A courtier having remarked that the British Government was known for its good faith, the Maharaja replied that 'the word of the British Government included everything'. The great ambition of the Sikh Ruler at this time was to be recognized as the sovereign ruler over the whole Sikh population on both sides of the Sutlej. This was always in his view whenever he was pressed to make a Treaty of alliance. The British Government could naturally not grant this: it would have entailed their desertion of the cause of the great Sikh houses on either side of the Sutlej, to whom they stood in the light of protectors. Under such circumstances negotiations were naturally protracted: but Metcalfe never lost patience, though the suspicious bearing of the Sikh ruler on all occasions might very well have led a less patient man to do so. This patience eventually won the day. Metcalfe had occasion one day to tell the Maharaja very plainly that the Governor-General would never dream of sacrificing the chiefs on the either side of the Sutlej to his ambition. The effect of this frank declaration on Ranjit Singh has been thus recorded: 'Ranjit left the room, descended to the courtyard below, mounted a horse, and began caracolling about what the young English envoy described as "surprising levity". But it was not levity. He was striving to subdue his strong feelings, and was gaining time to consider the answer he was to give the British envoy. After a while he returned to another room, and took counsel with his ministers, who, when they rejoined Metcalfe, told him that the Raja would consent to all the demands of the British Government.' At this point, however, and just as success seemed to have been achieved, negotiations were very nearly being broken off altogether: the Raja wished to withdraw his words almost as soon as he had uttered them; and only the firmness of the young envoy prevented this. Had they been broken off at this stage, nothing could have prevented war, as the Raja would have liked nothing better than a throw with the British. At last, early in 1809, an incident occurred that finally decided Ranjit Singh to sign the desired Treaty of Alliance. The Maharaja had been wanting to test the qualities of British soldiers. And one day in February, it is recorded, he had the opportunity of doing so: 'Metcalfe's escort of British Sepoys came into collision at Amritsar, with a party of Akalis, Sikh fanatics, half soldiers and half saints. There was a sharp conflict between them: but after a little while, the steady discipline of the little band of trained soldiers prevailed, and the Sikhs broke and fled. This appears to have made a great impression on Ranjit's mind. He saw clearly that the English, who could make such good soldiers of men not naturally warlike, were a people not to be despised'. The Treaty that was at last concluded was faithfully observed by Ranjit Singh to the day of his death, some thirty years later. The manner in which the young envoy had conducted the negotiations proved that he had in him the making of a statesman, and from that time his career was assured. He was personally thanked by Lord Minto, on behalf of the Government, in most flattering terms; what the great Sikh Maharaja himself thought of the young Englishman has been recorded in his own words: 'If their beardless young men are so wise, what must their old men be!'

Metcalfe's next appointment as Resident at the court of Scindhia was not a congenial one, and he only held it for about a year. Lord Minto then conferred upon him one of the most important appointments in his gift—that of Resident of Delhi: he did so in these complimentary terms: 'I shall, with or without young consent, name you to the Residency of Delhi. I cannot find a better man in the list of the Company's servants, and hope therefore for your indulgence on this occasion'. Metcalfe felt very much at this time the separation from all home ties which a long residence in India entails. In a letter he wrote to an aunt to dissuade her from sending her son out to India he thus gave expression to this feeling: 'I cannot say that I approve of the plan of sending children out to India for all their lives. There is no other service in which a man does not see his friends sometimes. Here it is perpetual banishment. I lead a vexatious and joyless life, and it is only the hope of home at last that keeps me alive and merry.'

Tempora mutantur et nos mutamur in illis:

India need no longer be the land of exile that it has sometimes been called: let a man only make up his mind to make it the country of his adoption during the years he is called upon to serve, and he need never fear that he will feel his life to be one of 'perpetual banishment'. The Englishman in India now has not only plenty of opportunities for leave home and for keeping up his connexion with the life of the rest of his family at home, which opportunities, if he is wise, he will avail himself to the full of: but he also has abundant opportunities for relaxation in the congenial company of his countrymen. In Metcalfe's time, however, such amenities did not exist, and many men indeed remained in India for the whole of their service, as did Metcalfe himself, who never took a single day's leave out of India during his thirty-eight years service; others only took leave after a quarter of a century's continuous service at least, as did Thomas Munro. Metcalfe was still at Delhi when the Marquis of Hastings came out to succeed Lord Minto as Governor-General of India.

The arrival of the Marquis of Hastings was the signal for a more active and vigorous policy being pursued towards the Native States. The policy of non-interference that had been inaugurated by the immediate successors of the Marquis Wellesley had not proved a success. The Marathas and the Pindaris had become increasingly aggressive, and it had become necessary to bring matters to a final issue, which should decide once for all the question of supremacy. The Governor-General wished to have a man about him who knew something of these people, and he therefore appointed Metcalfe to the office of Political Secretary. Before he could be spared from Delhi he had to settle certain matters that required very careful handling to succeed in bringing the Pathan chief, Amir Khan, whom he had once met at Indore, to terms: he also succeeded in bringing the great chiefs of Rajputana into friendly alliance with the Government. He was not called upon to take any part in the military operations, as his friend Malcolm was. He had first met Malcolm some eight years before in Lord Lake's camp, and he always looked back upon his conversations with him as having had a great influence in shaping his own career: the feature that had specially struck him in Malcolm's character was his enthusiasm; and he always used to say that any success he gained in after life was due to Malcolm having succeeded in infecting him with his own enthusiasm. It was with some regret that Metcalfe finally left Delhi to join his new appointment at the head quarters of the Government. He could, without undue boastfulness, claim that his administration of the Delhi territory had been a success. He himself has recorded how 'swords and other implements of intestine warfare to which the people were prone, were turned into ploughshares, not figuratively alone but literally also: villagers being made to give up their arms which were returned to them in the shape of implements of agriculture.'

Metcalfe did not feel altogether at home in his new sphere of work as Political Secretary: though his social position was a high one, he felt that he was doing only ministerial work. It is recorded that his old friend Sir John Malcolm, tried to console him and wrote to him as follows: 'Had I been near you, the King of Delhi should have been dissuaded from becoming an executive officer, and resigning power to jostle for influence. But you acted from high motives, and should not be dissatisfied with yourself.' However, he was not destined to be long without active political employment. On the important appointment of Resident at the court of the Nizam falling vacant, it was offered to him, and he at once accepted. The Governor-General wrote him a very cordial letter on his appointment, assuring him of his best wishes for his welfare.

On arriving at Haidarabad, he found that his predecessor had somewhat misled him in letting it be supposed that he had an easy task before him. A sympathetic letter he received from Sir John Malcolm may be regarded as a measure of the difficulties that really confronted him, and which were to try to the utmost even his marvellous patience and endurance. The letter was thus worded:—

'Every step that you take to ameliorate the condition of the country will be misrepresented by fellows who have objects as incompatible with public virtue and good government, as darkness is with light. You have to fight the good fight and to stand with the resolute and calm feelings such a cause must inspire, against all species of attacks that artful and sordid men can make, or that weak and prejudiced men can support. I am quite confident in your ultimate triumph, though I expect that you will have great vexation and annoyance.' The Government of the Nizam had become heavily involved in debt, and in order to get means to carry on the Government at all, the Nizam's ministers had to have recourse to many oppressive measures; it was to be Metcalfe's mission to devise means to check this injustice and oppression whereby the very life of the people was being squeezed out of them. One proposal he made that he thought might help in bringing this desirable result about was, that the country should be divided into districts, and English assistants placed in charge: it was no part of his plan that they should supersede the regular officials of the Nizam, who were still to be held responsible for the collection of the revenue, and the general administration: they were to be there only for supervision and general control, ask a check upon injustice or breach of faith: and when their work was done, they could be removed without the ordinary machinery of Government being put out of gear. It was a statesman-like idea, and worthy of the mind that conceived it. But he saw plainly that no real reform could be effected so long as the country was in the bonds of debt: these must be removed and the finance placed on a sounder footing. This then was the great problem before him; and it was not made any lighter for him by the fact that the debts, under which the State was burdened, were due to a great English Banking Company, with which a number of influential men were very closely connected. Metcalfe had to encounter very great opposition to the proposals he put forward for meeting the situation: one suggestion he made that a loan should be raised to be guaranteed by the Government, for the purpose of paying off the debts to the bank, was rejected. The struggle was a long one and in the course of it he was destined, as Malcolm had foreseen, to make many enemies, and temporarily even to estrange many friends. Among those who were thus for a time estranged was the Governor-General himself: but eventually he triumphed, and it was recognized, and by none more readily than by the Governor-General, that he had been actuated by no feelings of hostility against the firm, but only by a sincere wish to do what was right. His triumph, however, had been won at the cost of his health. He fell seriously ill, and was obliged to go to Calcutta to procure that medical aid he was sorely in need of.

After a stay of a few months in Calcutta, he returned to his post at Haidarabad. His troubles were now over, and his life was a tranquil one. He was ever 'on hospitable thoughts intent', and his house was open to all. There were times, however, when he longed for a little more privacy to enable him to prosecute his literary studies: such a country-house would have suited him to retire occasionally to, as Elphinstone built for himself outside Nagpur. He wrote a humorous letter on the subject to a friend: 'I live at the Residency, it will be a public-house, and as long as the billiard-table stands, the Residency will be a tavern. I wish that I could introduce a nest of white ants secretly, without any one's keening thereof, if the said ants would devour the said table, and cause it to disappear.' His happy disposition was very largely the outcome of a deep religious sense: he once gave expression to this feeling in one of his letters: 'I live in a state of frequent and incessant gratitude to God for the favours and mercies which I have experienced throughout my life.'

The attention of the new Governor-General, Lord Amherst, had been called to the unrest that prevailed on the North-West confines of British territory. Bhurtpore was one of the places affected by this unrest. The old Raja had recently died, and a cousin had usurped the Gadi. The fortress had long had the reputation of being impregnable. Sir John Kaye had said thus of it: 'For more than twenty years it had seemed to snort defiance at the victorious Feringhi.' An expedition was decided on with the object of restoring the boy-prince, the rightful heir, to the throne. Metcalfe had been transferred from Haidarabad to Delhi to deal with the crisis: he had been instructed to see what diplomacy would do. Diplomacy failed, and so war was declared. Metcalfe was now placed in political control of the expedition that was despatched against the fortress. As history has recorded Bhurtpore fell, and with its fall was removed for ever the reproach that the British would never be able to capture it. There was said to be a tradition among the people that Bhurtpore would never be captured till the Lord of the Crocodiles came up against it.

When therefore Lord Combermere, or as he would be called in Oriental parlance, Kumbhir Mir, 'Prince of Crocodiles,' came against it, they recognized a fulfilment of the prophecy. The story 'se non e vero molto e ben trovato.' Metcalfe did not remain long at the Residency of Delhi. In 1827, he was offered and accepted a seat in the Supreme Council. His elder brother having recently died, he had succeeded to the baronetcy, and was now Sir Charles Metcalfe.

The Governor-General's council consisted in those days of the Governor-General himself, the commander-in-chief, and two covenanted civilians. Metcalfe had anticipated a certain amount of leisure in his new office, and Malcolm had written to him:— 'If you are my "beau ideal" of a good Coucillor, you content yourself with reading what comes before you, and writing a full minute now and then when the subject merits it: and do not fret yourself and perplex others by making much of small matters. Supposing this to be the case you must have leisure, and if I find you have, I must now and then intrude upon it.' He found, however, that he had even less leisure than formerly. After trying for some time, but without success, to make a systematic distribution of his time, he wrote to a friend: 'I now go pell-mell at all in the ring.' Apart from his official duties, there were the social claims upon his time: he still kept up his old habit of hospitality on the grand scale. But he would never allow his hours of seclussion as he called his hours of work from breakfast to dinner, of his kindly and genial nature that he broke this rule in favour of some of his friends' children, 'who,' he wrote, 'would trot up frequently to my loft in the third story, where I have my sitting-room, and library, and bedroom, and insist on my showing them my pictures, being privileged by infancy to supersede all affairs of every kind.' Ordinarily, Metcalfe's term of office would have expired when he had completed five years' tenure. This time arrived in 1832, when Lord William Bentinck was Governor-General. Lord William Bentinck had found in him a colleague after his own heart, and he wrote to the Board of Directors strongly recommending his retention in office, or at any rate, his being appointed to a post that would keep him near. The terms of the despatch ran thus:— 'Sir Charles Metcalfe will be a great loss to me. He quite ranks with Sir Thomas Munro, Sir John Malcolm, and Mr. Elphinstone: if it be intended, and the necessity cannot admit of a doubt, to form a second Local Government in Bengal, he undoubtedly ought to be at the head. I strongly recommend him, while he has always maintained perfect independence of character and conduct, he has been to me a most zealous supporter and friendly colleague.' As the result of this strong recommendation, Metcalfe's period of office in the Supreme Council was extended to 1834.

On the creation of the new Government of Agra, Metcalfe was appointed its first Governor, and at the same time he was nominated Provisional Governor-General of India to succeed on the death, or the resignation of Lord William Bentinck, in the event of an interregnum in the Government. He had only just taken up his new office, when the news reached him of the intended departure of Lord William Bentinck from India. He had to return to Calcutta at once. On handing over the reins of Government to the man who had been deputed temporarily to hold them, Lord William Bentinck spoke of him in the following complimentary terms:— 'My connexion with Sir Charles Metcalfe in Council during more than six years ought to make me the best of witnesses, unless indeed friendship should have blinded me and conquered my detestation of flattery, which I trust is not the case. I therefore unhesitatingly declare that, whether in public or in private life, I never met with the individual, whose integrity, liberality of sentiment, and delicacy of mind excited in a greater degree my respect and admiration. The State never had a more able or upright councillor, nor any Governor-General a more valuable and independent assistant and friend. Suffice it to express my sincere impression that among all the statesmen, who, since my first connexion with India, have best served their country, and have most exalted its reputation and interests in the East, Sir Arthur Wellesley, Elphinstone, Munro, and Malcolm, equal rank and equal honour ought to be given to Sir charles Metcalfe.'

There were many who thought that Metcalfe would have received the substantive appointment of Governor-General of India: and this was said to have been the wish of the Directors. But the ministry of the day ruled that it was inadvisable for any servant of the Company to be appointed to the highest office of the Indian Government. As it was, a new precedent had been established in giving Indian Governorships to officers of the services, civil and military, who had worked their way up from the lowest grades, and it was only the distinguished merits of the men who were so honoured that had influenced Government in making that new departure. But beyond this the Government did not feel disposed to go. It was afterwards the good fortune of the first Lord Lawrence to show that there was no rule without an exception, and he was the first civilian to rise from the lowest grades in the Civil Service to the highest post in the gift of the Crown, the Vice-Royalty of India.

The chief feature of Metcalfe's brief administration was the liberation of the Indian Press. Though there had been little actual restriction on freedom of speech, still, as long as there existed a law which placed restrictions on the liberty of the Press, complete freedom of speech could not be said to exist. Indeed, Elphinstone, when Governor of Bombay, had felt it incumbent on him to deport an editor for transgressing the limits of what he considered reasonable criticism. The only restriction that was afterwards imposed was a censorship, even this was finally done away with at a later date. Deportation has again had to be resorted to in these latter days, but only as a temporary measure, and not of an editor, but of a public agitator; the time being one of unrest and excitement, putting the safety of the State in peril, the circumstances demanded this action. When the dangerous excitement passed, Government exerted its prerogative of mercy and withdrew the punishment. The words which Metcalfe wrote in justification of his measure for the complete emancipation of the Press mark the liberal-minded Statesman:— 'If the argument of those who are opposed to this measure be that the spread of knowledge may eventually be fatal to our rule in India, I close with them on that point, and maintain that, whatever may be the consequences it is our duty to communicate the benefits of knowledge. If India could be preserved as a part of the British Empire only by keeping its inhabitants in a state of ignorance, our domination would be a curse to the country and ought to cease. But I see more ground for just apprehension in ignorance itself. I look to the increase of knowledge with a hope that it may strengthen our Empire, that it may remove prejudices, soften asperities, and substitute a rational conviction of the benefits of our Government: that it may unite the people and their rulers in sympathy, and that the differences that separate them may be gradually lessened and ultimately anihilated. Whatever, however, be the will of Almighty Providence respecting the future Government of India, it is clearly our duty as long as the charge be confided to our hands, to execute the trust to the best of our ability for the good of the people.' And who is there, who is capable of reading history alright, who shall deny that such a high ideal has ever inspired the rulers of India? A question that has often occurred to the writer of this sketch is how it has come about that men, who, from his own observation, were themselves distinguished, during their India service, for high ideals and devotion to duty, can, on their return to England, fall to give their countrymen, who are still serving in India, and under far harder conditions than they themselves were ever called upon to serve, credit for similar qualities; and why a member of the Indian Civil Service, who has returned to England, should be styled 'A high-minded Englishman', while one who is still serving his country in India should be dubbed 'An unsympathetic bureaucrat'? The answer will not be found in prejudice alone nor in disappointed ambition alone: it may possibly be found in an Orientation of the reason and imagination. On resigning his high office into the hands of Lord Auckland, in the spring of 1836, Sir Charles Metcalfe was appointed a Grand Commander of the Bath: and for a second time he received the reversion of the Governor-Generalship.

He had now spent thirty-six years in India without having left the country for a single day, and his thoughts began, not unnaturally to turn to retirement from the public service. But he could not yet be spared: and Lord Auckland expressed his wish that he should return and take up his old post at Agra. The original idea of making Agra into a Presidency with a Governor as its ruler had been given up, and it had been converted into a Lieutenant-Governorship. Metcalfe resumed his work with all his old enthusiasm: but he did not remain long in the Province. In 1838, he finally resolved to sever his connexion with India. One of the moving causes of his intention to resign, has been said to have been a report that had reached him from private sources that some of the Directors of the Company had passed strictures on his measures for the emancipation of the Press. Certain correspondence had passed between himself and the Directors on the subject. And it is said that he was not over pleased with the reply he received. He seems to have been one of those public men, and they are not a few, who, possessing 'the mind conscious to itself of rectitude', are extremely sensitive on the score of their official reputation, and regard what less sensitive men treat only as legitimate criticism from their superiors in office that comes all in a day's work, as a stain on their escutcheon. The historian, in recording the incident, has thus written: 'The one flaw in an otherwise perfect character was over sensitiveness; and a wise man has remarked "the longer I live, the more convinced I am that over-sensitiveness is a fault in a public man". In Metcalfe's case this over-sensitiveness may have been an infirmity, but it was the infirmity of a noble mind, and it detracts nothing from the general admiration to which he was entitled. It arose out of what one, who knew him well, described as his very quick and delicate and noble sense of public character.' And the historian significantly adds:— 'The very fact of a public servant in India feeling sensitive on the score of his official reputation, and eager to repel all assaults upon it, was becoming a new thing in Indian official life, and marks better than anything else the great frontier line between the old and the new race of public servants in India.' And from that time to the present day this honourable feeling has continued to be the distinguishing mark of all holding high office in India: and the Indian Services, Civil and Military, have come to be recognized by all as 'the highest-minded services in the world.'

When the time came for Metcalfe to leave India for good, all the different communities in Calcutta vied with each other in manifesting their esteem and admiration of a great public servant. Few men have left India better beloved than he was, and this was largely due to his having chosen, says the historian, 'the Christian precept "Do as you would be done by", as the motto not only of his private, but also of his public life.' He was now fifty-three, and after his thirty-eight years of unbroken service, he did not anticipate further re-employment by the State. But his country still needed him. He had made his mark in England's greatest dependency in the Old World: he was yet to make it in her greatest Colony in the New World. The after-career of the great administrators of India, when once they have passed from the scene, does not, as a rule, fall within the scope of these sketches, but the case of Sir Charles Metcalfe is an exceptional one, and no picture of him would be complete without some account of that after-career. He is reported once to have said: 'I have risen in the East, and must set in the West': and it is that setting that has to be dealt with in the concluding portion of this sketch, but it can only be so dealt with briefly.

Metcalfe had been contemplating a Parliamentary career, but when the offer came to him of the Governorship of Jamaica, he at once accepted it. On hearing of his appointment, his old chief, the Marquis Wellesley, congratulated him in these memorable words:— 'It is a matter of cordial joy and affectionate pride to me to witness the elevation of a personage whose great talents and virtues have been cultivated under my anxious care and directed by my hand to the public service in India. No appointment has ever received an equal share of applause. You were once pleased to tell me that you were educated in my school, and that it was the school of virtue, integrity, and honour. That school has produced much good fruit for the service of India.' Metcalfe's task in Jamaica was no light one, it was a period of transition: there was still a great gulf between the different classes of the community: on the one side were the negroes who had only recently been emancipated from slavery, on the other the Europeans, who had but recently been the masters and owners of these slaves. Though he was not entirely successful in reconciling all classes to his policy, he did succeed in narrowing this gulf, and in reconciling to a very large extent the Colony to the Mother-country. The principles on which he acted have been given in his own words: 'On my taking charge of the Government, the course which I laid down for myself was to conciliate all parties, and by the aid of all parties to promote the happiness and welfare of Jamaica:' and it would have been strange, indeed, if a man with his past record, 'who,' as the historian has written, 'loved all men, all races, and all classes,' had not been able to achieve a very fair measure of success in his efforts in that direction.

He returned to England in 1842. It was at this period of his career that he had to undergo an operation for cancer in the cheek, a disease that had first manifested itself as far back as 1937. The operation gave him temporary relief; and he was again settling down to a life of retired leisure, when his next call came to serve his country: this time in the shape of an offer of the important post of Governor-General of Canada. His sense of duty to his country again led him to accept the appointment.

The high office that he had now undertaken was to tax all his powers. He was destined to be in continual conflict with one party or another that tried to get all power into their own hands. He did not consider it consonant with his duty to his sovereign that her representative should be regarded as a nonentity in the Government: but his characteristic qualities, and especially his marvellous patience, never deserted him. A political writer of the day thus described one scene at which he was himself present. 'I am speaking now of what I saw myself and could not have believed without seeing. It was not merely quiet endurance, but a constant good humoured cheerfulness and lightness of heart in the midst of trouble enough to provoke a saint or make a strong man ill. To those, who, like me, have seen three Governors of Canada literally worried to death, this was a glorious spectacle.' This display of patience was all the more wonderful, as all this time Metcalfe was suffering intensely from his deadly malady: he had already lost one eye, and his work had to be done in a darkened room; and whenever he drove abroad he had to be carefully protected from all dust and glare. An eminent surgeon had been sent out by the Queen's Government to see what he could do, but he had found he could do nothing, and had returned to England. Metcalfe had recently been given to honour of a peer of the realm, and he was now Lord Metcalfe: this had been some consolation to him in his sufferings: he still held on to the post of duty with undiminished courage and resolution: and only when he felt his sufferings were impairing his efficiency, did he suggest to the English Ministry that he should be allowed to retire: he left the final decision, however, with his own ministers in Canada, whom he called together to discuss the matter with them at his country-house. The historian has thus recorded the incident: 'It was a scene never to be forgotten by any who were present on this memorable occasion in the Governor-General's sheltered room. Some were dissolved in tear; all were agitated by a strong emotion of sorrow and sympathy, mingled with a sort of wondering admiration of the heroic constancy of their chief. He told them that if they desired his continuance at the head of the Government, he would willingly abide by their decision: but that the Queen had graciously signified her willingness that he should be relieved and that he doubted much whether the adequate performance of his duties had not almost ceased to be a physical possibility. It need not be said what was their decision. They besought him to depart, and he consented. A nobler spectacle than that of this agonized man resolutely offering to die at his post, the world has seen only once before.' The present generation has had an example of similar fortitude and devotion to duty under almost similar circumstances. The late Sir Denzil Ibbetson, when Lieutenant-Governor of the Punjab, had been recommended to proceed to England to undergo an operation for a similar malady at a time when there was every prospect of such an operation proving successful. A crisis suddenly occurred in the country, and he refused to leave his post till it was over. The malady had by this time obtained a grip, and the possibility of a successful operation became exceedingly doubtful. He proceeded to England, and produce would have counselled his remaining there. He returned to India with the sentence of death upon him. The circumstances under which he decided to return have been thus recorded in *The Times*: 'There had been base insinuations against him of timidity in the least reputable section of the vernacular Press, when illness compelled him to come home, and it is quite possible that his resignation before the expiry of his leave would have been wilfully misrepresented as an indication that he had lost the confidence of his official chiefs. So he returned to Lahore, and in spite of grave physical infirmity laboured for a few months longer with fortitude and zeal, making the impress of his strong personality felt on all branches of the administration. From the same sense of duty, he resigned his charge when no longer able to fulfil its obligations efficiently; and he came home to certain early death, calm and courageous to the last.' It was a noble end to a noble career, and the writer of this sketch may congratulate himself that he served for a time under such a man, and is himself one of those who have felt the impress of his strong, and at the same time kindly, personality.

Lord Metcalfe returned to England only to die, and within a few months after leaving Canada, he passed away peacefully. His biographer relates that 'the last sounds which reached him were the sweet strains of his sister's harp, and his last words were "How sweet those sounds are". Forty-Five of the sixty-one years of his life had been spent in strenuous public service "in foreign lands and under hostile skies", and during the whole of that time he had scarcely known either home or rest.'

To Lord Macaulay was entrusted the task of composing an inscription on a tablet that was erected to his memory, by his friends, in his old parish church: it is an inscription worthy of the man whose merits it immortalizes, and of the man who composed its noble language.

Near this stone is laid
Charles Theophilus, First and Last Lord Metcalfe,
a Statesman tried in many high posts, and different conjuctures,
and found equal to all.
The three greatest Dependencies of the British Crown
were successively entrusted to his care.
In India his fortitude, his wisdom, his probity and his moderation
are held in honourable remembrance
by men of many races, languages, and religions.
In Jamaica, still convulsed by a social revolution,
he calmed the evil passions
which long suffering had engendered in one class,
and long domination in another.
In Canada, not yet recovered from the calamities of civil war,
he reconciled contending factions
to each other and to the Mother Country.
Public esteem was the just reward of his public virtue,
but those only who enjoyed the privilege of his friendship
could appreciate the whole worth of his gentle and noble nature.
Costly monuments in Asiatic and American cities attest the gratitude
of Nations which he ruled;
this stable records the sorrow and the pride
with which his memory is cherished by private affection.
He was born the 30th day of January, 1785.
He died the 5th day of September, 1846.

13

Sir John Malcolm, 1769-1833

John Malcolm was born in Scotland, and it is of interest to note that the Great Duke, who was destined to become one of his greatest friends, was born in the same month and the same year, and almost on the same day. He was an active-minded boy and full of innocent mischief while at school; and it is recorded that, whenever anything mischievous out of the common occurred, the head master used to say, 'Ah! Jock's at the bottom of it.' In after years, when Malcolm had become a distinguished man, he sent his old schoolmaster a copy of his *History of Persia,* with 'Jock's at the bottom of it', written on the title-page.

In order to qualify for a cadetship in the East India Company's service, which he was anxious to get, he had to appear before the Board of Directors at the early age of twelve. This was the usual procedure in those days, just as in these, candidates for a cadetship in the Royal Navy have to appear before a special Board of Naval Officers. This system of inspection of candidates has many advantages. Personality may begin to stamp itself on the features at an early age: a boy wears no mask and his face is often an index to his character. A judge of character, therefore, may often in this way get some idea of a boy's pregnant capacity, and the boy, for his part, has some chance of showing some side of himself which reveals latent characteristics that may appeal to his judges. Thus John Malcolm's bearing made a very favourable impression on the Board. One of the members of the Board put this question to him: 'My little man, what would you do, if you were to meet Haidar Ali?' 'Do', replied the boy, nothing daunted, 'I would take out my sword, and cut off his head.' The Directors were delighted and at once passed him as a cadet. He was too young to be sent out to India at once, and so was sent to school for another year or so. He was only fourteen when he eventually proceeded to India. In the following year, fifteen was fixed as the minimum age for entrance into the Company's military service.

When he first arrived in India war was in progress, not only between the English and the French, but also between the English and Tipu Sultan, the Ruler of Mysore. He was too young to be sent on active service. The war with the French ceased soon after his arrival: and the war with Tipu was brought to a conclusion the year after. An exchange of prisoners had been arranged for, and Malcolm, young as he was, was entrusted with the mission. An amusing story is related relative to this; 'The British officer, a Major Dallas, who was deputed to escort the prisoners out of Tipu's territories, and to hand them over to the British detachment sent to the frontier, seeing a slight rosy healthy-looking English boy astride on a rough pony, with some English troops, asked him for his commanding officer. "I am the commanding officer," said the boy, drawing himself up in the saddle. The Major smiled: the boy was John Malcolm.' He was only fifteen at the time: he and the Major became life-long friends. Like many other youngsters on first arriving in India, John Malcolm was not long in getting into debt: in these early days there was some excuse for this, as pay was so small. In Bengal there was an expression in common use to illustrate the extent to which some young civilians used to become involved: it used to be said of such a one, 'He has turned his lakh.' John Malcolm, fortunately for himself, did not get very heavily involved, and having once got in, he determined to get out again, and eventually he managed to do so, though as he said he had to stint and starve himself. A story has been told to illustrate the hardships he suffered while thus extricating himself: 'An old native woman in the regimental bazaar, taking compassion upon his youth, implored him to receive supplies from her, to be paid for at his convenience. He was for ever grateful for this act of kindness and humanity, and in after years he settled a pension on her for the rest of her life.

On war again breaking out with Tipu, an opportunity came to Malcolm of seeing active service. His regiment was ordered to co-operate with the troops of the Nizam of Haidarabad. This proved to be the turning-point in his career. His biographer recorded how his meeting with some celebrated political officers in the Nizam's camp caused a new ambition to stir within him. He made up his mind to become a great political man. He was now a man of twenty-one, and was noted as a crack shot, and a gymnast: he was always so active and fond of sports that the sobriquet 'Boy Malcolm', given him in his youth, stuck to him till late in life, even after he had become a distinguished public servant. Up to this time had been regarded as 'a careless, good-humoured fellow, illiterate, but with pregnant ability.' And, considering that he had entered on the active business of life at an age when most boys are at school, it was no reproach to him to be styled so: but he was soon to remove the stigma of illiteracy, and his pregnant ability was soon to manifest itself to the world in the field of thought, as it had already begun to do in the field of action. He no longer confined his attention to physical exercises, but began seriously to devote himself to study. He took steps to acquire the native languages, and especially a knowledge of the courtly Persian, acquaintance with which is to this day a passport to influence at many an Oriental court. It was, indeed, his speaking acquaintance with Persian that made the visits of the diplomatist, Earl Dufferin, so welcome to Indian princes. Malcolm also applied himself to the study of Indian history. The philosopher, Bacon, has remarked in one of his essays on worldly wisdom: 'Reading maketh a full man; conference a ready man; and writing an exact man.' Much conference with the world of books had made of Malcolm a full man:

much writing had made him an exact man: reading and writing even went hand in hand with him, and he even wrote with a ready pen. He would record on paper his meditations on the principles on which the great Indian Empire has been ever administered, by the observance of which it was founded and on which alone it can be maintained; and his observations have ever been regarded as most sound. His biographer gives an account of Malcolm's exceeding keenness to obtain a political appcintment, and of his great disappointment when he one day only missed getting such an appointment by being only half an hour too late in his application: 'He went back to his tent, flung himself down on his couch, and gave way to a flood of tears. But he lived, as many a man before and since has lived, to see in his first crushing miscarriage the crowning mercy of his life. The officer who carried off the prize so coveted by him was murdered on his first appearance at the native court to which he had been accredited. This made a deep impression on Malcolm's mind, and was ever after gratefully remembered. He often spoke of it in later days as an illustration of the little that man knows of what is realy for his good, and he taught others, as he himself had learnt, "never to repine at the accidents and mischances of life, but to see in all the hand of an all-merciful Providence, working benignly for our good."

His opportunity arrived at last: he was appointed Persian interpreter to a detachment of the British army serving with the Nizam at Seringapatam. He wrote that Lord Cornwallis had appointed him 'because he considered him the officer with that corps better qualified for the station.' At this crisis in his career his health unfortunately failed, and he had to seek health again in England. He returned to India as military secretary to the Commander-in-Chief of the Madras Army, and he retained this office under General Clarke's successor ,General Harris, who was also for a time Governor of Madras. He was holding the appointment of Town-Major of Madras when an opportunity presented itself to him which he was not slow to avail himself of. The new governor-General, Lord Mornington, afterwards the Marquis Wellesley, touched at

Madras on his way to take up his appointment in Calcutta. John Malcolm was introduced to him: in the course of his historical studies, Malcolm had drafted certain reports on British relations with the Native States, and especially with the State of Haidarabad: he sent these to the Governor-General. His reward was an appointment as assistant to the Resident at the court of the Nizam. He had now obtained what he had long coveted, definite employment in the political department. He was, more over, fortunate in receiving a mission, the successful issue to which was to prove his capacity. A strong body of troops in the Nizam's service was officered by Frenchmen, who had French revolutionary colours, and wore French revolutionary symbols on their uniforms. This corps was to be disbanded, and it was Malcolm's business to effect this. The story is thus told: 'The Sepoys at first refused to listen to him and threatened to treat him as they had their own officers: at this juncture some of the Sepoys who had been in the Company's service recognized him, and remembering the kindnesses they had received from him when he was their company officer, went to his rescue: they lifted him up above the crowd and bore him on their heads to a lace of safety, out of the reach of the exasperated mob of mutinous Sepoys.' Eventually the corps was disbanded, and without bloodshed. Malcolm was summoned to Calcutta, and took with him the colours of the disbanded regiment. From the date of Malcolm's interview with the Governor-General in Calcutta, his future was assured. The Marquis Wellesley, like the great Pitt knew a man when he saw him, and as the historian remarks; 'He saw in Malcolm a man to be trusted and employed.'

The time had now come for the final struggle for supremacy in Southern India between the British and the Mysore Power. Tipu Sultan was offered peace, but on English terms. The negotiations failed, and there was no alternative but war. The Governor-General, when once he had decided what was the right thing to do, was not the man to delay, and he proceeded in person to Madras to expedite matters. He took Malcolm with him as his political assistant, giving him, at the same time, the appointment of military commander over the troops of the Nizam that were to co-operate with the British in the military operations against Tipu. Malcolm's first duty was to quell a dangerous mutiny among these troops, and this he did to the admiration of the Nizam's officers: at the same time he attracted the attention of Sir Arthur Wellesley, who was in command of the British troops attached to the Nizam's contingent; this proved the commencement of that friendship between the two distinguished men that lasted till Malcolm's death. General Harris was in supreme command of the operations, which in the end were completely successful, though there was a time on the eve of the final assault on the great fortress when matters looked very serious for the British. The story is thus told by the historian: 'The storming party had been told off, and the hour for their advance had nearly arrived, when Malcolm entered the tent of the Commander-in-Chief. The General was sitting alone very gravely pondering the important work before him, and the great interests at stake. "Why, my Lord, so thoughtful," cried Malcolm, congratulating him, by anticipation, on the peerage within his reach. The lightness of his tone was not pleasing to the over-burdened General, who answered sternly, 'Malcolm, this is no time for compliments. We have serious work in hand: don't you see that the European sentry over my tent is so weak from want of food and exhaustion, that a Sepoy could push him down. We must take this fort, or perish in the attempt." There was similar anxiety in Tipu's camp; only a short time before, finding he had been out generalled by the British, he had summoned his principal officers, and had exclaimed, "We have arrived at our last stage: what now are we to do? What is your determination?" The officers had replied, "We will all die with you." And it was a fight to a finish. Seringapatam fell, and with it fell its chief: "with his fall ended the great Muhammadan usurpation of Southern India." John Malcolm was joint-secretary, with Thomas Munro, of the Commission appointed by the Marquis Wellesley for the partition of the Mysore territories.

Malcolm had been able to give his chief fresh evidence of his capacity. He was now to be employed on a mission requiring the exercise of more tactful and delicate diplomacy than he had hitherto been called upon to display. The Governor-General, having in view the necessity of checking the intrigues of the Ruler of Afghanistan, Zaman Shah, and of checkmating the suspected designs of France on India, resolved on the despatch of a mission to Persia, and to place John Malcolm at the head of it. The mission left India for the Persian Gulf in 1799. After a visit to Muscat, Malcolm landed at Bushire, and proceeded to Teheran. Englishmen were not so well known in the East in those days as they are now, and it was a good thing for the prestige of England that the young Englishmen who represented at the courts of Eastern sovereigns were men whose personality was in every way calculated to make a good impression. The historian has recorded the impression Malcolm's personal appearance made on the court of the Shah: 'His fine stature, his commanding presence, and the mixture of good-humour and of resolute prowess with which he conducted all his negotiations, compelled them to form a high estimate of the English people. He was in their eyes a Rustam, or hero of the first magnitude.' Similarly, it has been recorded, young Metcalfe compelled the admiration of the great Sikh Maharaja, Ranjit Singh. The Governor-General considered Malcolm's conduct of the negotiations to have been eminently praiseworthy; and on his return to India he was summoned to Calcutta for an interview, and was most cordially received. The Marquis promised him the next high appointment in the political service that he had at his disposal. His letters home at this period had kept his family acquainted with the variety of his work, and his father wrote to him in reply: 'The account of your employment is like fairy tales to us; your filial effusions brought tears of joy to the eyes of your parents. A good head will gain you the esteem and applause of the world, but a good heart alone gives happiness. It is a continual feast.'

Malcolm had been temporarily appointed private secretary to the Governor-General, and he accompanied him on a tour up-country in that capacity. Upon their reaching Allahabad, the Governor-General received the serious news that the envoy of the Persian court had been shot in the course of an affray in the streets of Bombay. Malcolm was sent on a special mission to put matters straight with the Persian court. The work took him about six weeks: he succeeded so well in his mission by the letters of explanation he wrote from Bombay to the Shah, and by his liberal expenditure of money, that is was said afterwards in Persia that 'the English might kill a dozen ambassadors if he would always pay for them at the same rate.

On his return from Bombay he was appointed Resident of Mysore. He did not take up the appointment at once: he paid a short visit to Madras, and then proceeded to join the camp of Sir Arthur Wellesley, who was engaged in military operations against the Marathas, and he was able to be of some assistance to Wellesley in restoring the Peshwa, Baji Rao, to the throne of Puna. He had the misfortune to be absent when the great victory of Assaye was won: he had been obliged to run down to Bombay, to pick up after a serious illness. A visit to Bombay, in order to get a breath of sea-air, was at this time regarded as a panacea for all the ills that English flesh is heir to in the East.

The next political work Malcolm was engaged on was the negotiation of a Treaty with the young Daulat Rao Scindhia. Oriental Darbars are usually very solemn ceremonials indeed. The Darbar, which was held to receive Malcolm, appears to have been at one stage a lively scene enough, from the description that has been given of it: 'A hailstorm suddenly came on and hailstones were brought in and presented in all quarters, and all began to cat, or rather to drink them. For ten minutes the scene more resembled a school at the moment when the boys have got to play than an Eastern Darbar'. In one of the best novels of travel ever written, *Eothen,* a statement is made that the character that appeals most to the Oriental is that of the frank and hearty sailor-man, however bluff he may be. There is much truth in this, and it is similarly true that the character that least appeals to them is that of the man who is always studiously polite in his dealings with them. Orientals have ever a keen perception of character and they can quickly detect the false ring that often accompanies an attitude of studied politeness. The one character attracts: the other repels. Malcolm's frank and hearty geniality, which he displayed on all occasions, soon completely captivated the imagination of the young Maharaja. He invited Malcolm to go tiger-shooting with him, and on another occasion he invited him, and this perhaps was the greatest mark of favour he could show, to play Holi with him. The incident has been thus recorded in Malcolm's own words: 'I am to deliver the Treaty to-day and afterward to play Holi, for which I have prepared an old coat and an old hat. Scindia is furnished with an engine of great power, by which he can play upon a fellow at fifty yards' distance. He has, besides, a magazine of syringes, so I expect to be well squirted.' There are two sides to the celebration of the festival known as 'The Holi Festival'. On its more boisterous side it consists in throwing red powder and squirting water in which red powder has been dissolved at everybody within reach: and with the more ignorant masses of the population it is often accompanied with much unrestrained licence and revelling; under this aspect it approaches to the Roman Saturnalia. This is the side that is most often seen, especially by Englishmen, and it is this side of it that meets with not altogether undeserved reproach. But there is another side that only reveals itself to those who take the trouble to know something about the intimate life of the people, and who are honoured by their confidence. Under this aspect it is marked by the exchange of very pleasant civilities and courtesies. An Englishman who is fortunate enough to be so honoured may congratulate himself that he has to some extent won the goodwill of his Indian friends. The Treaty which Malcolm had been sent to negotiate was at last signed and despatched to Calcutta. Malcolm was a little doubtful as to how it would be received by the Governor-General; but he was not a man to be afraid of responsibility: his views on this subject have been thus recorded: 'A man who flees from responsibility in public affairs is like a soldier who quits the rank inaction: he is certain of ignominy and does not escape danger.' The Governor general, after a certain amount of correspondence, eventually wrote his full approval.

Like most Englishmen who have risen to any eminence in India, Malcolm had always kept up his home ties. He experienced about this time the greatest loss that a man can experience: his father died, and it seemed to him, as, indeed, a similar bereavement has seemed to others similarly situated, as if his chief stimulus to exertion had been removed: the sudden cessation of a regular correspondence and interchange of sympathy seems to have temporarily a paralysing effect upon the mind: and most men, living a life of distant exile in the East, have at some period or other of that life experienced this feeling. Filial affection was deeply engraved in Malcolm's heart, and it is characteristic of him that he at once placed all his resources at the disposal of his mother and sisters. This domestic trouble, and a return of his old malady, compelled him again to go to the sea-coast to recruit his health: this time he went to Vizagapatam on the East Coast.

On regaining his usual health, and with it his buoyancy of spirits, he proceeded to rejoin his appointment at Mysore. On the way he stayed at Madras to bid farewell to Sir Arthur Wellesley, who was now leaving India for good. He had just settled down, and was engaged on his *History of Persia,* when he received summons to Calcutta, where he found that he was again wanted to go on a special mission to the court of Scindia. Complications had arisen owing to Scindia having become reconciled to Holkar, who was still in arms against the British, and having moved his troops up to support Holkar. It was to be Malcolm's delicate mission to detach Scindia from his new alliance and to get the Maratha Brahma, who had been his evil counsellor, dismissed. His instructions were that if negotiations failed, and Scindia committed any hostile act, he was to be at once attacked. Malcolm had to proceed at the honest time of the year to Upper India to join the camp of Lord Lake, who was operating against Holkar. What a journey in the hottest season of the year meant in the days when the present amenities of travel did not exist, may be judged by a visit to any old cemetery in the interior of India: in one such, perhaps the oldest of its kind, which the author of this sketch well remembers being visited by the late Sir W. W. Hunter, when searching for materials for his interesting pictures of life and work in India, it is no uncommon thing to see an inscription engraved on the headstone of a grave to this effect: 'Died on a palki journey during the month of May.' Even now men are often struck down by heat apoplexy when travelling at the height of the hot weather. On reaching Lord Lake's camp, Malcolm found the army temporarily halted perforce on account of the fierce scorching winds, then prevalent. Meanwhile his old chief, the Marquis Wellesley, had been succeeded by Lord Cornwallis, who had come out as Governor-General for a second term of office with instructions to reverse the policy of his predecessor. Lord Lake received orders to bring the operations against Holkar to as speedy a close as possible. Lord Lake decided that Holkar's various aggressive acts required reprisals on his part, and the army continued its advance. Holkar retreated and crossed the Sutlej. It looked at one time as if the Sepoys of the British army would not cross this river. The incident has been thus told: 'There were signs of wavering, and the leading companies at dawn on the banks, when Malcolm rode upto them, spoke in his brave hearty manner a few cheering words to them reminding them that the holy shrine of Amritsar was in advance, and asking them if they would shrink from such a pilgrimage. And the story runs that such was the magic effect of these words, that the Sepoys started upto a man, crossed the river, and soon, followed, by their comrades, were in full march into the Punjab,' Holkar submitted, and sent his envoys to treat for peace, A Treaty "as made with him and a new one with

Scindia. Amongst others who sent envoys at the same time were certain Sikh chiefs. A characteristic story is told of an incident that occurred one day when Malcolm was giving an audience in his tent to some of their envoys: 'Two of his friends suddenly burst into the tent with the news that there were two large tigers in the neighbourhood. Malcolm at the moment had been in some perilexity what reply to give to the envoys, so the interruption was not unwelcome. Starting up and seizing his ever-ready gun he cried out to the astonished Sikhs, "Bagh! Bagh!" (a tiger! a tiger!), and ordering his elephant to be brought round rushed out of the tent. Joining his friends, he shot the tigers, returned with the spoil, and replacing the gun in the corner of his tent, he resumed his seat, and took up the thread of the conversation as if nothing had happened. The envoys in the meanwhile had been declaring that the English gentleman was mad. But there was method in such madness. He had done more than shoot the tigers. He had gained time. He returned with his mind fully made up on an important point which required consideration. And the envoys received a different and a wiser answer than would have been given if the tiger-hut had not formed an episode in the day's Council.' The task of disbanding the Irregular Levies proved a more onerous task than that of Treaty-making; and though not altogether pleased with the new policy of non-interference in the affairs of Native States so recently inaugurated, he worked loyally in carrying it out, and remained in Upper India as long as any thing remained to be done.

On the conclusion of his mission Malcolm returned to Calcutta; and after a short stay there he proceeded to Madras on his way to Mysore. While in Madras he was again taken ill. His popularity was so great that he was never left for long alone in his sickness; he was still in the prime of life, but he did not lack 'that which should accompany old age, as honour love, obedience, troops of friends'; and he speaks of his sick-room being turned into a chamber levee. Soon after he returned to Mysore he married, and then definitely gave up the intention he had of retiring from the service; he had already had twenty-four years of service, but he was still a comparatively young man, and was destined not to finally sever his connexion with the country till he had completed in all forty-seven years' service.

Persian affairs had again come to the front. The Sovereigns of Russia and France had but recently formed an alliance; and they were suspected by the British Government of designs against the possessions of the East India Company. The despatch of an ambassador to the court of Persia had been determined on, Malcolm's friends in England, and among them Sir Arthur Wellesley, had not been successful in getting him nominated to that office. Sir Harford Jones, who was appointed, had, however, taken what Lord Minto, now Governor-General, had thought such an unconscionable time upon the way, that he determined to send a special mission, with Malcolm at its head, from Calcutta. The French already had a magnificent mission at Teheran, and it was thought expedient that England should be represented in an equally magnificent manner. In making his arrangements' therefore, Malcolm had practically a free hand. He left Bombay 1st April morning in 1808, just as the King's ambassador was in close proximity to that port. Sir Harford Jones received instructions from Lord Minto to remain in Bombay. Meanwhile, Malcolm duly arrived in Persia. The messenger he had sent on with despatches to the Shah was not allowed to proceed beyond Shiraj: the Persian authorities there ordered him to negotiate with the Prince-Governor of the Province. This was all due to the intrigues of the French, whose influence was all-powerful at Teheran. Malcolm regarded it as a direct insult to England, to be met only by his withdrawal from Persian soil, and he determined to return to India to consult with Lord Minto. This he did, leaving a representative at Bushir, who was ordered 'to hold on as best as he could.'

He was very cordially received by the Governor-General, and, as a result of his conferences with him, he was directed to return to the Persian Gulf and establish himself with a small force on an island in the Gulf, from which he could threaten the Persian seaboard. The wording of the instructions he received from Lord Minto was a measure of the confidence reposed in him: 'Your duties are not to be defined. All I can say is you are placed in a situation where you are as likely to go wrong from prudence as from the want of it.' This again gave him a free hand, and was just such a roving commission as suited his temperament. He had only just left Calcutta, and was still in the river, when he was recalled by Lord Minto, who had received the news that Sir Harford Jones had given them the slip and had set sail suddenly for Persia. Meanwhile, Malcolm had to remain in Calcutta in more or less enforced inactivity. An amusing incident that occurred during this time is thus recorded in his own words: 'One day Lord Minto caught me employing myself with John Elliot and other boys in trying how long we could keep up two cricket-balls. He says he must send me on a mission to some very young monarch, for that I shall never have the gravity of an ambassador for a prince turned of twelve. He however, added the well-known and admirable story of Henry IV of France, who, when caught on all fours carrying one of his children, by the Spanish envoy, looked up, and said, "Is your Excellency married?" "I am, and have a family," was the reply. "Well then," said the Monarch, "I am satisfied, and shall take another turn round the room." And off he galloped, with his little son flogging and spurring him, on his back.' At last the Council of the Governor-General came to the decision to practically ignore the King's ambassador; and once again Malcolm started for Bombay: he had just completed his arrangements there when he received fresh orders from the Governor-General to suspend his operations. Sir Harford Jones had got the start of them, and had already left Bushire for Teheran, when Lord Minto's despatches ordering him to return reached that port. There was therefore no help for it; Lord Minto did not wish to complicate matters by a hostile expedition while the King of England was negotiating, through his ambassador, with the King of Persia. This seemed to be the end of all hope of Malcolm's conducting a second mission to Persia; but, as it turned out, it was only a postponement.

On the receipt of his orders to suspend operations in Bombay, Malcolm decided to return to his charge in Mysore. On the way there he was detained in the Madras Persidency, upon the invitation of the Governor of Madras, to assist him in the delicate and difficult task of restoring discipline amongst the European officers of the Madras army. He had most difficulty with the European regiment as Masulipatam, for in this case there was the additional danger of the men of the regiment following the lead of their officers and becoming insubordinate in their turn. The story of how he helped to bring the officers back to their allegiance is thus told: "He met the officers, talked the matter over freely and candidly with them, admitting as much as he safely could, and afterwards joined them at mess." After dinner, a young officer, flushed with wine, proposed as a toast "Our Common Cause"; with characteristic readiness of address, Malcolm rose and said, "Aye! the Common Cause of our country." The amendment was received and drunk with enthusiasm, and soon afterwards his own health was toasted with universal applause. This policy succeeded at last in gaining time until the difficulties gradually disappeared, and discipline was eventually restored. Malcolm's special characteristics were never shown to better advantage than on this occasion, much criticized as his conduct was at the time. He believed thoroughly in the innate goodness of human nature, and that it only required the exercise of a little common sense combined with tact and temper to bring it out.

There is some soul of goodness in things evil represented to him not a mere poetic fancy, but a living and ever-present truth.

Meanwhile news of Sir Harford Jones's progress in Persia had reached Lord Minto at Calcutta: it seemed to him, to say the least, undignified, and not consonant with the traditions of the country whose representative he was. He decided that the situation demanded an ambassador of a different type, and one who would maintain those traditions with the dignity that befitted them. He looked to Malcolm to do this, and he worded his invitation to him in these flattering terms: 'I entreat you to go and lift us to our own height, and to the station that belongs to us once more.' He summoned Malcolm to meet him at Madras, and arranged with him the final details for the business in hand. Malcolm eventually sailed for the Persian Gulf early in 1810, nearly two years after his first start. Things were done more deliberately in those 'spacious times of Anglo-Indian History. On his arrival at Bushire, he again sent his messenger in advance with the letter of which he was the bearer to the Shah; while waiting for an answer, he finished the *Political History of India,* that he was engaged on, and then began to enjoy his unwanted leisure in his congenial spots of hunting, shooting and riding: he had learnt one secret of retaining buoyancy of spirits at a more or less advanced age by enjoying the companionship of youth, and he was always attended on his excursions by his numerous staff of young officers.

At last he received orders to advance. The Persian officials on the route showed themselves eager for English gold and English gifts. The King's ambassador who had preceded him had been distributing largesse with a lavish hand. To the Oriental mind such lavishness is only considered an imitation of Oriental ways, and any such imitation brings with it only contempt: it brings no respect. This attitude of the Oriental mind is well illustrated in the history of Lord Macartney's mission to China. It is recorded that 'the English mission had taken no presents with them expressly for the purpose of presentation: indeed, Lord Macartney was hard put to it to eke out the few valuables she had taken with him, when he was asked for presents for the court'. The English mission, moreover, declined to perform all the elaborate and obsequious ceremonial customary at the court of Pekin. The Dutch mission that followed were laden with presents, and outdid even Chinese officials in their servility and obsequiousness: and yet the English mission, though in the enigmatical Oriental way they received polite hints that their room was preferable to their company, were at any rate treated with respect: the Dutch mission, on the other hand, were treated with contumely and contempt. On this occasion the lavish presents of Sir Harford Jones were regarded by Persian officials in the light of bribes, and so Malcolm found it. They were as ready to bribe, moreover, as to be bribed themselves. The story is told how, 'whilst Malcolm was at Shiraz, it was intimated to him by the minister that a costly present of jewels had been prepared as gift to his wife. Checking his first feeling of indignation, Malcolm replied, "Tell your master that when I was at Mysore, the minister there would gladly have heaped costly presents upon us; but instead of this, on my persuasion, he made a fine new road that was much wanted and dedicated it to Mrs. Malcolm. Such are the presents I like." It was a wise policy on the part of the Government of India to interdict its officials from receiving presents from the people. Fruit and flowers may alone be accepted. The most acceptable gift that the author of this sketch used to receive from a Hindu gentleman who used to visit him ceremoniously at all great festivals, was a single flower plucked out of his own garden: it showed real genuineness of feeling without display. Malcolm succeeded, but not without some trouble, in getting the King's ambassador to work with him. He was well received by the Shah, who instituted for his special honour the decoration of the Lion and the Sun: he expressed a wish also to retain Malcolm as his military adviser. Though the actual results of the mission were not great—indeed, one writer has recorded that 'the creation of a new Order, and the introduction of potatoes, was the sole result of this long and costly expedition'—still, the part that Malcolm had taken in it had only enhanced his great reputation.

On his return from Persia, Malcolm remained for some time in Bombay, previous to taking furlough to England. On arriving in England he felt half inclined to remain there for good: but he was only forty-eight, and he felt that he still had many years of active and vigorous life before him, and he finally made up his mind that, if the opportunity presented itself, he would return to India. On his way home he had the misfortune to lose his mother. And one of the first things he did after his return to England, was to visit the graves of his parents in Scotland. His visit has been thus recorded: 'Visited the graves of my parents, and heard the noblest praise of them from the aged, the infirm, and the poor that they had aided and supported; and to whom the aid and support of the family are still given.' This last sentence was characteristic: one of Malcolm's most marked traits was his open handed generosity. His chief occupation during this period of leisure was the completion of his *History of Persia,* which he was at length to publish: it was at once most favourably received in England, and when, at a late period, he visited France, it was as the Historian of Persia that he was welcomed. He was called upon to give evidence before a committee of the House of Commons at the time when the Company's charter was about to be renewed. He would have liked nothing better than active military employment under his old friend, Sir Arthur Wellesley, now the Duke of Wellington, but the Peninsular War was near it's end, and when the Duke visited England for a spell, in 1814, he advised Malcolm to enter Parliament, if he could, as one chance of bringing himself into notice, and so of obtaining the high public employment he was in search of. He had been knighted some time before and he received the still greater distinction, mainly, it is believed, through the influence of the Duke, of a Knight-Commandership, of the Bath. After the entry of the Allies into Paris, on the morrow of the battle of Waterloo, he saw the great Duke again, in Paris, and enjoyed many conversations with him. One such is recorded: the conversation had turned on the Duke's great victory: 'People ask me', said Welling to, 'for an account of the action. I tell them it was hard pounding on both sides, and we pounded the hardest.' Before Malcolm returned to India, in 1816, he received yet another high distinction. The University of Oxford conferred upon him the honorary degree of Doctor of Civil Law.

The Marquis of Hastings was no Governor-General of India. He had certain operations in view against the free-booting levies of the Pindaris, who were so closely bound up with the Marathas, being, it was generally supposed, largely subsidized if not actively supported by the Maratha Princes of Central India, that it was thought possible that the operations against them would involve the British in war with the Marathas. And so eventually indeed it proved. Malcolm was known to know more about the Central India States than any man in India at the time. The Governor-General summoned him to Calcutta, and entrusted him with a twofold mission: he was to be Brigadier-General in Command of the most advanced force, and at the same time the Governor-General's agent in supreme control of all political work. The remark he made on the occasion has been recorded, and is eminently characteristic: 'What is really delightful, from the Governor-General down to the lowest black, or white, red or brown, clothed or naked, all appear happy at my advancement.' In his capacity as political officer, he visited the residencies of Mysore, Haidarabad, Pune, and Nagpur. His journeys were generally made on horse back or by Palki. He gave some excellent advice to the Peshwa, Baji Rao, at Pune, which that prince promised to follow, but history has recorded that, when the hour of trial came, he failed to keep his promise. Active operations against the Pindaris having commenced, his political duties had to give way to military exigencies. He took command of his own division of the army, and proceeded to join the main body of the army of the Deccan. News soon arrived in the camp of the revolt of the Peshwa, and of the Bhonsla, and of the march southward of the army of Holkar. Malcolm had first tried what diplomacy could do with the envoys from Indore, but as this had failed, hostilities could not be averted. The result was the defeat of Holkar's army at Mahidpur. The battle was mainly won by Malcolm's division, spurred on, as they were, to enthusiasm by Malcolm's own example, who rarely displayed his military qualities of fearlessness and courage to better advantage than on this occasion. An anecdote is told in illustration of this: 'The officers of his staff were often alarmed for his safety, but he had no thought for himself: on one occasion he was so far in front, having gone forward to rectify some error in the advancing line, that he was in danger of being shot by his own men. His native aide de camp rode up to one of his officers, and said, "Look at the General! He is in front of our men who are firing: for God's sake bring him back." The officer rode forward to bring his chief, back, but he only returned when he had done his work. Sir John Kaye has said of Malcolm that 'he was one of those soldier-statesmen of the first class, whose vocation it was to pass rapidly from the command of an army to the negotiation of a Treaty, and to be equally at home in camp and in council.' Military operations having come to a close, Malcolm now resumed his political duties. He concluded a Treaty with the Maratha envoys from Indore, and spent some time with the young Maharaja. He has recorded his experiences at the court: 'All the chiefs of Holkar are in good humour. The boy himself is at present delighted with a small elephant, which he had lost and I recovered and sent back to him, which dances like a dancing-girl, and a little Pegu pony of which I made him a present, and which ambles at a great rate. I went out to hunt with him the other day, and we, had great fun. The little fellow, though only eleven, rides beautifully. He expressed grief at my going away, as he discovered that I was very fond of play and hunting.' He had far greater difficulty with the Peshwa; but he succeeded at last by dint of great tact and judgement in effecting what the British government desired, his complete and unconditional submission to the British terms. He was to become for ever a pensioner of the British Government. The terms which Malcolm offered were exceedingly liberal, and included the handsome provision for life of an annuity of £80,000. This liberal provision was much criticized at the time; and the Governor-General himself, though he wisely accepted the arrangements made by his agent, thought that they erred on the side of liberality. It is of interest to note that the adopted son of the Peshwa, known to all time in Anglo-Indian records as 'The infamous Nana Sahib', made it the basis of his vindictive hate of the British Government of his time that this annuity was not continued to him on his adoptive father's death.

Perhaps the greatest of all Malcolm's achievements in India, and that for which he won undying fame, was his pacification and settlement of a country that had long been given upto anarchy and confusion. He hither to had opportunities of showing his capacity as a statesman and as a soldier: he was now to shine forth as an administrator. Malwa was the Province entrusted to him to reduce to order and prosperity. It has been recorded that the three secrets of his successful administration were 'trusting to time, keeping people in a good humour, and accessibility to all'. He once wrote to a friend: 'The fault I find with the younger politicians is that they are too impatient of abuses, and too eager for reform I do not think they know as well as we old ones what a valuable gentleman Time is: how much better work is done when it does itself than when done by the best of us.' Of his accessibility it is recorded, 'He had a word for every one, high and low'; he once wrote to a friend: "I wish I had you here for a week, to show you my Nawabs, Rajas, Bhil Chiefs, Patels, and Ryots. My room is a thoroughfare from morning to night. No Munshis, Diwans, Dubashes, or even Chobdars, but 'Char darwaze khole', all four doors open, that the inhabitants of these countries may learn what our principles are at the fountain-head." The subordinate officials about his tents were never allowed to block access to the presence of the Sahib Bahadur, as they so well know how to do. Cicero, in one of his famous letters to the Governors of Roman Provinces, had counselled similar principles of conduct. No one who does not know his India well, and the ways of subordinate officials, can realize the extent to which they can open or bar the way at their pleasure to the presence of the Hakim, or at any rate accelerate, or retard, access: the only 'Open Sesame' known to them is the magic watchword 'Bakshish'. The historian has recorded that 'when Bishop Heber travelled through Central India, he found everywhere indications of the affectionate remembrance in which Malcolm and his god deeds were held by the people of the country. The name of Malcolm on an amulet was regarded as a charm to protect the wearer of it from the powers of evil.' Malcolm himself also has recorded how" a custom prevailed among the Bhil ladies of tying a string upon the right arm of their children, whilst the priest pronounced the name of Malcolm three times, as sovereign cure for a fever'. The author of this short sketch can also testify to the esteem and honour in which the name of Malcolm is still held in Central India. He received a visit one day from an old Muhammadan gentleman, who brought with him a package: he proceeded to unroll the numerous foldings of cloth in which Indians ever wrap their most cherished treasures, and brought to light a document bearing the signature 'John Malcolm': it set forth the services rendered by the grandfather of its possessor in coming to the aid of the British at the time of the Pindari operations with a contingent of 2,000 horsemen. When his work of pacification and settlement was over Malcolm determined to proceed on furlough to England: this time he thought he was really leaving India for good.

He felt Bombay towards the end of 1821, amid universal demonstrations of respect. On his way home, he travelled through Egypt, and was most hospitably entertained by its then ruler, Mehemet Ali. Literary work occupied a good deal of his leisure time while he was at home, but his temperament demanded a life of action. The Duke of Wellington at his request tried to get him the Governorship of Madras, but was not successful, and he again recommended Malcolm to give up all thought of further employment in India, and to enter Parliament. At last, however, came the offer of the Governorship of Bombay; and he at once accepted it. Mr. George Canning was at the time Prime Minister of England, and it was to his recognition of Malcolm's great services in India that he owed his elevation to a Governorship.

Malcolm took up his office at the end of 1827 and he remained in office for some three years: these were years of comparative tranquillity in India, and Malcolm's duties assumed more of a routine nature than had hitherto been the case. He still retained his old characteristic of accessibility to all. He has described the system he adopted whereby all might have easy access to his presence: 'I hold a public breakfast at Government House for six days in the week, to which every one can come that likes. It is a social levee, without formality or distinction. I am down half an hour before breakfast, and stay as long after it. Every human being who desires it, from writer to judge, from cadet to general, has his turn at the Governor. At half-past ten I am in my own room, have no visitors, and am entirely given up to business.' Malcolm had just made up his mind to leave India for good, when he received the offer of the newly created Lieutenant-Governorship of Agra, from Lord William Bentinck. In declining the offer, he informed the governor General of his wish to return to England; he was sixty-two years of age, and had been connected with India in one capacity or another for forty-seven years: his hopes were now centred on entering Parliament where, he told Lord William Bentinck, he still hoped to work for his country and for India. He left India finally at the end of 1830.

He died three years after his return home. A monumental statue by the celebrated sculptor, Chantrey, was erected to his memory in Westminister Abbey. At that great banquet that was given him on the eve of his departure from England to take up his office as Governor of Bombay, the Prime Minister of England, Mr. Canning, used these eloquent words, which, while intended at the time specially to apply to Sir John Malcolm were also meant to include the long roll of distinguished men who have done conspicuous public service for their country in India: 'There can not be found in the history of Europe the existence of any monarchy, which within a given time has produced so many men of the first talents in civil and military life, as India has first trained for herself, and then given to their native country.' Similarly, the Duke of Wellington said: 'It is now thirty years since I formed an intimate friendship with Sir John Malcolm. During that eventful period there has been no operation of consequence, no diplomatic measure, in which my friend has not borne a conspicuous part. Alike distinguished by courage and by talent, the history of his life during this period would be the history of the glory of his country in India.'

With these words from two men so qualified to speak, this sketch concludes.

14

Mountstuart Elphinstone, 1779-1859

Elphinstone is chiefly famous for his work in Western India: to this day his memory is revered in Bombay by Englishmen and Indians alike for his nobility of character, his justice, and his encouragement of education. Besides being a diplomatist and an administrator, he was an historian, and his *History of India* has won for whim a permanent place in literature. He was practically the maker of South-West India, and as such he takes rank as a Ruler of India. A sketch of his career is practically a sketch of the overthrow of Maratha supremacy, and of the introduction of British rule in the Deccan.

He was one of the many distinguished men who helped to carry out the policy designed by the master mind of the great Marquis Wellesley, and among his contemporaries were such men as Metcalfe, Malcolm, and Munro. One striking characteristic of this period of British-Indian history is the extremely youthful age at which so many of the men who were afterwards so famous in the annals of British India were launched into active careers in India. Thus Malcolm obtained his cadetship at the age of twelve, and landed at Madras before he was fourteen. Metcalfe was a writer in Calcutta at the age of fifteen. Elphinstone was only fifteen when he left home, and Munro was eighteen. It was an age of adventure fitted to stimulate the energies of the young, and youth proved no bar to their rapid advancement and promotion. Instances are not wanting in the history of Eastern nations of practically young boys being invested with responsibility and power: thus Babar was only twelve when he became King of Ferghana, and Akbar became Emperor of India at the age of eighteen.

Another characteristic that marks this generation of Anglo-Indian officials was the union of bodily activity with great intellectual accomplishments: they lived an open-air life, and were equally at home in the camp, the hunting field, and the Darbar, and owing to the greater leisure they possessed they had greater facilities for study, perhaps, than their successors: considering that they had been thus launched into public life when most boys are still at school, and considering, moreover, that the stock of learning they started with could not, under the circumstances, have been large, it rebounded all the more to their credit that they should have become the scholars that most of them did become. The record of Elphinstone's reading during one of his long journeys, when he was only twenty-one, would have done credit to that 'Prince of Readers, Lord Macaluay'. He generally travelled with two camel-loads of books, so arranged that he could readily lay his hands on any volume he wanted. His love of study did not prevent his being at the same time distinguished for his soldierly qualities. The great Duke himself, who saw him under fire at Argaum and at Assaye, remarked that he had mistaken his vocation, and ought to have been a soldier. He was also an administrator of no mean an order, and his bearing at the native courts he was accredited to, proved him to be possessed of rare diplomatic powers. In him were all combined: 'The courtier's, soldier's scholar's eye, tongue, sword.' He became Governor of Bombay at the early age of thirty-nine, and more than once, after his retirement, he refused the high office of Governor-General of India.

Elphinstone came of distinguished ancestry: his father, who had fought under Wolf in Canada, and his uncles had all done conspicuous public service. His brothers also held high office. Examples of devotion in their country's service were not wanting, therefore, had he required such to stimulate his own devotion. As a boy, his ambition had been to enter the Army, but he was content to accept a writership on the Bengal Establishment. He had to leave for India direct from his school in London, and was thus unable, to his own great sorrow, to bid farewell to his mother and sisters in their home in Scotland.

Sir John Shore was Governor-General when he landed in India in 1796, after a voyage from England of eight months. His first appointment was to Benares, which was the frontier station of Bengal to the North-West at this period. His quiet career here was suddenly interrupted by the rising against the English which was organized by the deposed sovereign of Oudh, the Nawab Wazir Ali, who was living at Benares at the time, under the surveillance of the British authorities. The Resident, Mr. Cherry, was murdered, and elphinstone himself had to flee for his life. This affair led to his receiving his first diplomatic mission, which was to find out how far certain natives of high rank at Benares were implicated in the plot. It was at Benares, under the influence of his chief, Mr. Davis, a noted Sanskrit scholar, that Elphinstone seems to have acquired that taste for reading that became his most congenial occupation in his leisure hours.

Having received an offer of the post of assistant-secretary to the Resident at Pune, Elphinstone hesitated about accepting the appointment until he had consulted Mr. Davis on the subject. Mr. Davis's only reply was a quotation from the great World-Poet Shakespeare": 'What pleasure, Sir, we find in life to lock it from action and adventure?' This quotation, which Elphinstone said ever after range in his ears, decided the matter: he accepted the appointment. He travelled to his new station with another young civilian, in a very leisurely manner, and by a long détour. The journey took them the better part of a year. In passing through Orissa, which was then Maratha territory, they could not help noticing the change in the demeanour of the people from what it was in British territory: they were not actually rude, but they showed no respect. They would crowd round the encampment in the evening, and watch the young Englishmen going through their exercises, which consisted of throwing the spear, sword exercise, and firing at a mark with pistols. A curious incident that occurred at Puri, when they were close to the Temple of Jagannath, 'Lord of the World,' impressed their imagination; they met a Faqir, who called the young men to him and said, 'Listen, when will you take this country? This country needs you. The Hindus here are villains, but you are true men, when will you take this country?' We answered, 'Never.' He replied, 'Yes, you will certainly take it.' Within a short two years indeed the British did take the country, and the strange prophecy of the Faqir was fulfilled. At Seringapatam, they were the guests of Colonel Arthus Wellesley. They spent three months at the court of Haidarabad, then, as now, the most magnificent court in India. The Resident was Major Kirkpatrick: he had married the Persian minister's daughter, and Elphinstone describes him as an Orientalized Englishman. 'His manners were affected, and his conversation most affected; he wore mustachise, and dyed his fingers with henna, but in other respects he resembled an Englishman. In the presence of the Nizam, he behaved like a native of the country, and with great propriety.'

On arriving at his destination, Elphinstone was presented to the Peshwa. In a comparison of the meanness of the Peshwa's court, as compared with the magnificence of the Nizam's court, he remarked that none of the Maratha chiefs were even like native gentlemen. He had not yet learnt that this so-called meanness was really a characteristic of the simplicity that is so marked a feature of the true Maratha gentleman, especially in his dress and personal habits. The Maratha temperament, moreover, differs essentially from that of the Muhammadan: he loves power, it is true, but he cares not for the trappings of power or display.

About a year after Elphinstone's arrival at his post, the second Maratha War broke out. The Marathas were the only Native Power that had steadily refused to recognize the

British Government as the paramount Power in India. When, therefore, the Peshwa of Pune, Baji Rao, signed the Treaty of Bassein with the British, by which he agreed to have no diplomatic relations with other Powers, except through them, the other Maratha princes considered this tantamount to a recognition of British supremacy: this they refused to accept, and hence the war: apart from this, they had long determined to try conclusions again with the British. The campaign, once started, was soon on in three different parts of the country: in Hindustan, under Lord Lake; in the Deccan, under Sir Arthur Wellesley; and in Orissa. Owing to the illness of Sir John Malcolm, Elphinstone was deputed to attend Sir Arthur Wellesley in a more or less undefined capacity as his confidential secretary: he acted chiefly as interpreter, an office which he was very well capable of holding, owing to his great linguistic attainments: he was a good Mahratti, Persian, and Hindustani scholar. He was also the head of the intelligence department: he does not seem, however, to have been very hard worked. The soldiering life, especially with so distinguished an exponent of the art of war as Sir Arthur Wellesley, was thoroughly to his taste. What he especially enjoyed was 'the combination of society, study, business, action, and adventure'. Amongst the booty taken at Ahmadnagar had been an Arabic Prayer-Book, and Elphinstone records how Sir Arthur Wellesley restored it to its owner, a very famous Dervish, who had predicted the fall of the Fortress-City. Earl Roberts, it may be noted, displayed a similar reverence for the religious feelings of those he was fighting against, when he ordered the restoration to their owners of all sacred books captured in the course of the Boer War. Elphinstone rode by the General's side throughout the day of the battle of Assaye: he and another member of the staff were the only two who were not touched, though they seemed to have had some very narrow escapes. Sir Arthur Wellesley displayed his usual coolness of bearing, and Elphinstone noted how at one critical moment of the battle, he had galloped close up to the enemy's line by mistake: three horses of the party were knocked over:

upon some one remarking, 'Sir, that is the enemy's line', the General replied, 'Is it? Ha, dame, so it is,' and turned his horse. At the battle of Argaum, in Berar, Elphinstone again rode by the General's side, and took part in the great cavalry charge. He has thus recorded his experiences: "The balls knocked up the dust under our horses' feet, I had no narrow escapes this time, and I felt quite unconcerned, never winced, nor cared how the shot came about the worst time. And all the while I was at pains to see how the people looked, and every gentleman seemed at ease as much as if he were riding a-hunting". One of the most realistic descriptions of a cavalry charge in literature occurs in that most realistic of M. Zola's novels, *La Débâcle;* it is almost possible to hear the thunder of the horses' hoofs as they charge madly across the plain. Elphinstone picked up a wounded Hindustani soldier on the field of battle next morning; the man became his servant, and remained in his service till he finally left India, a period of more than twenty-five years. Elphinstone's graphic description of the storming of a fort in which he took part is of special interest, as being the description of a man who, a soldier at heart, was also a philosopher and an historian: "Our advance was silent, deliberate, and even solemn. When we went on to the breach, I thought I was going to a great danger; but my mind was so made up to it that I did not care for anything, the party going to the storm put me in mind of the eighth and ninth verses of the third book of the Iliad of Homer:— 'Forward advanced the Greeks, in silence breathing threats, each passionately eager to outdo each other.' And after one gets over the breach, one is too busy and animated to think of anything but how to get on."

This campaign had been Elphinstone's opportunity: he had proved his worth, and the road to rapid promotion was not made comparatively easy for him. A word from Sir Arthur Wellesley to his brother, the Marquis, and Elphinstone received the important appointment of Resident at the court of the Bhonsla, which carried with it a salary of three thousand rupees a month. He was only twenty-four at the times. It was no easy task that he had thus entered upon, and he knew it from the first. He realized that another struggle with the Marathas was impending, and that all that could be done was to postpone the evil day. One of his duties was to get intelligence as to what was going on at the Raja's court: he knew that there were intrigues, but it was not in his nature to meet intrigue with intrigue, and anything like what is significantly called espionage was abhorrent to him. The difficulty was to get the intelligence he wanted, and at the same time to avoid anything like secret methods in obtaining it. The conclusion he finally came to is given in his own words: "I must never forget to be always and absolutely open; if I try cunning management, I act contrary to my own character, and that of my nation, and perhaps fail after all. My diplomatic motto ought to be:—'Fair and above-board in all my dealings, avoiding all dissimulation and deceit.' Characteristically, he illustrates his remarks with a classical quotation: 'He is as inimical to me as are the Gates of Hades, who hides one thing in his thoughts, and utters another.' The success of Elphinstone's diplomacy was especially gratifying to the Marquis Wellesley, one of the features of whose system of training his young civilians was their early initiation into the arts of diplomacy, and he complimented him upon it.

Certain incidents that occurred at court in Elphinstone's time go to show that the Raja himself was of a less truculent disposition than the men about him, who had been giving Elphinstone so much trouble by their war proclivities. He has thus recorded two such incidents: "A servant on one occasion washed the Raja's hands with scalding water, the courtiers were all for putting the man to death: the Raja, however, forgave him. On another occasion, when the Raja wanted water, he found the lotah, that is the brass vessel in common use, filled with ghee: again the courtiers called out to have the man who had brought it killed at once; and one of them, indeed, was on the point of killing him; but the Raja said, 'Let him go: it is easy to kill a man, but not so easy to make another.'" And yet these very men, who were ready enough to kill in order to satisfy a whim, were not prepared to do so to satisfy the ends of justice: Elphinstone had asked the minister to execute some men who had really deserved death as robbers and murderers, and the minister had replied: 'He knew the English put people to death for such offences, but his Highness shuddered at the name of execution.' But to the Western imagination the workings of the Oriental mind ever appear inconsistent and illogical. Elphinstone describes the answer as 'a mirror of slavish ideas and Hindustani manners.'

Elphinstone had a fairly tranquil time at Nagpur, varied occasionally by alarms from the Pindaris. He himself had a narrow escape on one of his marches: some of his tent equipage and followers were carried off, while straggling in the rear. The pindaris travelled with incredible swiftness; beaten off at one place; they would appear somewhere else sixty miles off the same day: they thus succeeded in ravaging wide tracts of territory within a very short space of time. The native sports of hawking and coursing afforded him a means of relaxation during this period, together with an occasional beat for pig and for tigers; but reading formed his principal relaxation; with Prospero he could say:—

"My Library
Is Dukedom large enough."

In order to enjoy his favourite pursuit undisturbed he build himself a bungalow some little distance out of Nagpur, and called it 'Falconer's Hall'. In one of his Minutes on Education, issued when he was Governor of Bombay, he had recorded his opinion of classical poetry as a valuable factor in education, in these terms: 'Other compositions may fall into disuse and oblivion as knowledge increases with people, but not so their poetry: the standard works maintain their reputation undiminished in every age: they form the models of composition, and the fountains of classical language, and the writers of the rudest ages are those who contribute the most of the posterity.' Classical poetry formed his favourite reading in this retreat, but he found himself compelled to give up reading Persian poetry, as it gave him, he said, 'the blue devils.' Had he known Sanskrit, he would have found in the grand and sonorous cadence of the language of its poetry something to stimulate his imagination, and to contribute to his peace of mind quite as much as did Greek poetry, to which he was obliged to return, when he found Persian poetry having a depressing effect upon his mind.

After some four years spent in Nagpur, Elphinstone took furlough in India for a year. On his way to Calcutta, he passed through Chhota Nagpur, then a forest-clad and almost unexplored hill country: he visited and had much conversation with the Chief of Udaipur in that country on sport, and especially on the Gond methods of killing tigers. The chiefs of this part of the country have not altered much in this respect; they are still as great sportsmen as ever, and their sons are initiated into the 'Sport of Kings' at a very early age. He was still young, as his remarks on his enjoyment of the gay doings in the capital evidence: 'Such lots of women, and laughing and philandering, that I was in Heaven'.

Soon after his return to Nagpur 'Elphinstone received orders to join the court of Scindia. The Maharaja was at the time moving about the country with a enormous camp, somewhat after the manner of the Mogul Emperors, whose camps were almost like towns on the march. He was only about two months with Scindia, when he was ordered to Delhi to take charge of an embassy that was to proceed to the court of the Amir of Afghanistan.

At Delhi he met Metcalfe, who was starting on a similar mission to the court of Ranjit Singh at Lahore. The danger that seemed to threaten the British position in India at this period was an invasion of India by Napoleon Bonaparte, who was now at the height of his power, and was known to have designs on India: he is said even to have chosen his route. It was to guard against this danger that Lord Minto resolved to establish friendly relations with the several Powers holding the keys of the North-Western Frontiers, as they then were. Besides the missions of Metcalfe and Elphinstone, another under Malcolm was despatched to Persia: as well as missions on a smaller scale to Sindh and Baluchistan. Elphinstone's mission was on a magnificent scale: he had a staff of thirteen selected British officers. He found the Amir, Shah Shuja, at Peshawar, and soon discovered that his position was by no means so secure as had been thought: and, indeed, within a few weeks of his signing a Treaty between himself and the British, he had been driven from his throne, and had become an exile in Punjab. He still, however, kept up the show of royal magnificence, and much of the ceremonial tradition with the court of the Amirs of Afghanistan. Elphinstone gives an amusing picture of the ancient ceremonial: "The ambassador to be introduced is brought into court by two officers, who hold him firmly by the arms: on coming in sight of the king, who appears at a high window, the ambassador is made to run forward for a certain distance, when he stops for a moment and prays for the king. He is then made to run forward again, and prays once more, and after another run the king calls out 'Khillat', a dress, which is followed by the Turkish word, 'Getshin,' begone, from an officer of State, and the unfortunate ambassador is made to run out of the court, and sees no more of the king, unless summoned to a private audience." Needless to say, Elphinstone did not conform to this ancient etiquette; he was received with courtesy and dignity. He has recorded his impressions of the Shah: 'It will scarcely be believed of an Eastern monarch how much he had the manners of a gentlemen, or how well he preserved his dignity, while he seemed only anxious to please.' Elphinstone did not see more than the borders of Afghanistan, but he acquired a good deal of information through his usual practice of mixing and conversing with all classes of people: he was especially charmed with the conversation of two Afghan gentlemen he met, one of whom astonished him with his knowledge of European history and politics, and the other by his taste for mathematics and his acquisition of Sanskrit, which he was learning solely in order to discover the treasures of Hindu learning. He was also pleased with the civility he and his party received from the country people, who constantly pressed them to partake of hospitality and would take no refusal. In the light of the various expeditions that have been forced on the British Government by the raids of the border tribes round and about Peshwar on to British territory in these later days, it is interesting to record the remark of an Afghan chief to Elphinstone on the characteristics of the people generally: 'We are content with discord, we are content with alarms, we are content with blood; but we will never be content with a master.' The British Government has ever shown great patience in dealing with these border tribes, but cannot be content with discord, or alarms, or bloodshed in its own territories, and expeditions against them have from time to time been inevitable. A proverb current among these people, which was recently quoted by *The Times,* proves that they are the first to acknowledge the justice of this: 'The patience of the British Government is as long as a summer day, but its arm is as long as a winter night.' The mission was eventually broken up at Delhi, and Elphinstone was ordered to Calcutta, where he presented his report.

Elphinstone was next appointed Resident at the court of Pune, an appointment which he took up without much enthusiasm; and he looked forward to retirement at the end of it. He had already shown that he was a diplomatist, he was now to show that he could be an administrator as well, and one of the first rank. On his voyage from Calcutta to Bombay by sea, he had Henry Martyn, the great missionary, as one of his fellow travellers. He thus describes him: 'He is an excellent scholar, and one of the mildest, cheerfullest, and pleasantest men I ever saw, who, though extremely religious, talks on all subjects, sacred and profane, and laughs and makes others laugh as heartily as he could do if he were an infidel.'

One of his first acts in his new appointment was to intervene on behalf of the class of Jaghirdars, the hereditary nobles of the Southern Maratha country, who had received their grants of rent-free lands from the Mogul Emperors: the claim of the Peshwa to their military service was acknowledged, but they were guaranteed against further exactions by a pledge of security from the British Government. The Chief of Kolhapur was at the same time recognized as an independent sovereign in return for his surrender of a fort and harbour in the Konkan, which had long been a nest of pirates. On one of his marches he came across an extraordinary scene: 'A manservant of a Maratha gentleman, in performance of a vow for a child, was rolling along the road from Pune to Pandarpur: he had been a month at it, and had become so expert that he went on smoothly and without pausing, and kept rolling evenly along the middle of the road over stones and everything; he travelled at the rate of eight miles a day'. Those who have lived much in the country districts of India are not unacquainted with similar instances of religious zeal: pilgrims walking backwards from one shrine to another, measuring their length at every step along the road, may thus not uncommonly be met with. He published his *History of Kabul* during this period of his career, a work which cost him immense labour, and which still remains the standard authority on Afghanistan. He led a very simple life, and his diet was spared almost to austerity: while his lunch consisted of a few sandwiches and figs, and a glass of water, he often dined off a few potatoes, and a glass or two of claret; he never neglected either his long ride in the morning and his gymnastic exercises twice a day, or his private reading in the afternoons; public business occupied his mornings.

With the appointment of Lord Moira, afterwards the Marquis of Hastings, to the head of affairs, a more vigorous policy in connexion with the Native States was inaugurated. The Governor-General determined to crush the great predatory hordes of Pindaris that were the primary cause of the suffering and anarchy prevailing over a very large portion of the Deccan, they were largely encouraged and supported by the Maratha princes; and there were not wanting signs that these princes themselves were becoming restless, and anxious to try conclusions again with the British. Elphinstone had organized an intelligence department of his own, and knew all that was going on, even to the colour of the javelin carried by the news-writers whom he found were being utilized to convey correspondence between the several Maratha courts from the headquarters at Pune. Each court had its distinctive colour painted on the javelins carried by its messengers: it was a sort of livery and was recognized as such by the officials of the several princes; similar javelins were used by the bankers of the different cities in the Native States, but they were for the most part painted in one colour. The system of news-writers is a very ancient one in the East, and to this day there is not a family of any eminence in Indians that has no service of its own. Elphinstone describes the precautions that he found it necessary to observe in connexion with all official correspondence at this critical time: 'All correspondence had to be written on the smallest slips of paper rolled up and conveyed in quills, like Birhis.' The usual form in which tobacco is smoked in Central India is a kind of tobacco-leafed cigarette, called a Birhi.

The crisis arrived at last in connexion with a man named Trimbakji Danglia, one of the favourites of Baji Rao: he had been a menial servant whom Baji Rao had raised to the rank of a minister. This man had barbarously murdered an envoy from the Baroda State who was travelling under a safe - conduct from the British Government. Elphinstone demanded his surrender, and the Peshwa had only acceded to the demand after Elphinstone had moved up a strong body of troops. Trimbakji was imprisoned in a fort, and a European guard placed in charge. He managed to escape, and a romantic story is attached to the manner of his escape. A Maratha groom took service with an officer of the garrison, and while daily walking his master's horse up and down under the windows of the fort, used to recite a chant: the English sentry of course could not understand the tenor of it: the prisoner learnt from it that arrangements were in progress for his escape. When all was ready, a hole was dug through the wall, and Trimbakji escaped, and took refuge among the mountains of the Western Ghats. A Maratha ballad, which is still sung by wandering bards who may be met with all over the Deccan, tells, with picturesque additions, the romantic story. Trimbakji was subsequently recaptured, but only after the close of the war, of which he was a primary cause, and was again imprisoned: this time at the Chunar Fort on the Ganges. Some years afterwards he was visited by Bishop Heber, who has thus versified the chant of the Maratha groom:—

Behind the bush the bowmen hide,
The horse beneath the tree:
Where shall I find a Knight will ride
The jungle paths with me?
There are five and fifty coursers there,
And four and fifty men:
When the fifty-fifth shall mount his steed,
The Deccan thrives again.

With Trimbakji's escape, in the autumn of 1816, the crisis again became acute. Elphinstone was informed that the Peshwa was collecting forces at a Temple of Mahadeo, the National Deity of the Marathas, somewhere in the hills, and he also received the still more disquieting information that a General rising was in contemplation. While addressing remonstrances to the Peshwa, Elphinstone went on with his military preparations, as he felt that at any moment disturbances might break out: indeed, they very nearly did break out on the very night of the day on which the Peshwa had apparently submitted to Elphinstone's demands. He was playing cards when an officer reported that Pune was full of armed men and that the Peshwa was in full Darbar discussing with his nobles the question of immediate war. For a moment the idea was conceived of attacking the city at once from the British cantonments: but fortunately his usual coolness did not forsake Elphinstone: he decided to wait for the morning. The Peshwa, it transpired, could not summon up courage to give the signal for attack, and so the danger passed, but temporarily only. Elphinstone, however, realized that the time for action had arrived, and he resolved to issue his ultimatum, without waiting for a reply to the despatches he had sent to Calcutta on the situation. His personal courage at this crisis may be illustrated from the fact that he visited the Peshwa in person the night before he issued his ultimatum, knowing full well the risk he was running in doing so. But he could not help liking Baji Rao, with all his faults, and he has thus recorded his feelings on the occasion: 'I thought it possible that in these extremities he might seize me for a hostage, and carry me off to Singarh, but he seemed not to have the most distant thought that way: with all his crimes and all his perfidy, I shall be sorry if Baji Rao throws away his sovereignty'. The Peshwa accepted the ultimatum, and agreed to surrender three important forts, as securities for the capture of Trimbakji within a month. Meanwhile the expected despatched from the Governor-General arrived: these imposed still harder terms. A new Treaty was to be signed, the Peshwa was to renounce all claim to the titular headship of the Maratha Confederacy, and to acknowledge his entire dependence upon the British Government: he was further required to surrender territory for the maintenance of the subsidiary force, and to acknowledge on the face of the Treaty his belief in Trimbakji's guilt. These humiliating conditions, however, were to be insisted on only in the event of the Peshwa taking no active measures for the arrest of Trimbakji. The Peshwa would do nothing in this direction, and so Elphinstone had no alternative but to force the Treaty upon him. The Peshwa signed it, but both parties to it were fully aware that only the military superiority of the British would secure its fulfilment, and that the military superiority would very shortly be put to the test. It was to be shown once for all who were to be the supreme power in India, the Marathas, or the British.

The war that ensued is known in history as the third Maratha War. It was the great Pindari Hunt, as Elphinstone called it, which had been organized by the Marquis of Hastings for the final suppression of these predatory hordes, that eventually brought the British into collision with the Marathas. And the war owes its real importance to the part played in it by the Peshwa, the Raja of Nagpur, and Holkar of Indore. Malcolm had been specially deputed by the Governor-General to visit these princes, that he might have the opportunity of consulting the Residents at their courts, and of reassuring the minds of the princes. He thus visited the court of the Peshwa, and he seems to have placed more confidence in his protestations of fidelity than Elphinstone had done: he even went so far as to reverse much of the latter's policy. Elphinstone, though he doubted the wisdom of Malcolm's acts, loyally supported him, as he knew he was acting under superior orders. Events proved that Elphinstone was right, and Malcolm wrong in his estimate of the Peshwa's character. Within two months of Malcolm's departure from Pune the crisis arrived. The Peshwa began ostentatiously to prepare for war, and Elphinstone was obliged to order back to Pune the British forces which had been sent away by Malcolm; he had the cantonments removed to the high ground overlooking the city of Pune. With his usual courage, he remained at the Residency, though he was well aware of the plot formed by some of the Peshwa's followers for his assassination. The Peshwa then openly demanded the withdrawal of the British troops; Elphinstone sent him a spacific message, saying that he was still anxious for peace, but that, if the Maratha forces advanced, he would attack them. The Peshwa's reply was to move his troops out in the direction of the new cantonments: this of course meant war. Elphinstone had barely time to escape from the Residency simply 'with the clothes on his back' before the whole of it was in a blaze. All his personal effects, including his valuable library, were burnt. The battle that ensued, known as the battle of Kirki, resulted in the dispersal of the Maratha army. The Peshwa fled from his capital, which he was never destined to see again. Desultory fighting still went on for some five months. One incident occurred during this period which Elphinstone has described as 'a strong incitement never to despair': this was the heroic stand made by a small body of Sepoys under a few British officers at a place called Koregaum, against the whole Maratha army. The incident is thus described: 'The detachment had been marching all night when it found itself face to face with the enemy; Baji Rao himself with his sardars sat on a hill two miles off to watch the battle; it lasted throughout the whole day and part of the next night; and just as the situation seemed most desperate, the Maratha army drew off, alarmed at the approach of a British General with the main body of the British Army.' The Peshwa finally surrendered to Malcolm. Elphinstone had meanwhile been protecting the city of Pune from the vengeance of his own Sepoys, thus, as he remarked, 'maintaining our general reputation and conciliating friends.' At the close of the campaign Elphinstone issued a proclamation to the people of the Deccan, in which he recited the story of the perfidy of the Peshwa, which had compelled the British to drive him from his throne, and he stated that a portion of his territory would be reserved for the Raja of Satara. Mr. Canning, in moving a vote of thanks to the Marquis of Hastings and the Army, after the conclusion of the war, paid a special tribute to Elphinstone's services: 'On that, and not on that occasion only, but on many others in the course of this singular campaign, Mr. Elphinstone displayed talents and resources which would have rendered him no mean General in a country where Generals are of no mean excellence and reputation.'

Elphinstone was appointed Commissioner of the Deccan early in 1818; and pending the complete restoration of civil authority he had the pleasing task of formally restoring the young Raja of Satara to the throne of Shivaji. The Marquis of Hastings had left it to Elphinstone whether to give a sovereignty or simply a jaghir, or grant of rent-free lands; Elphinstone had chosen to make a king. He did not regret his choice; the young prince had many good qualities which attracted Elphinstone, and he formed a good opinion both of his business capacity and of his character in these early days. The young prince, moreover, showed himself eager to requite the good will shown him. Elphinstone gives a pleasing picture of his daily routine: 'He had invited me to visit him in his private office; he produced his civil and criminal register, and his minute of revenue demands, collections, and balances for the last quarter, and began explaining the state of his country as eagerly as a young collector; he always sits in his court of justice, and conducts his business with the utmost regularity; he has his country in excellent order, and everything, to his roads and aquaducts, in a style that would do credit to a European. The furniture in his private sitting-room is extremely simple; it contains a single table covered with green velvet, at which the descendant of Shivaji sits and writes letters, as well as a journal of his transactions, with his own hand. He gave me at parting the celebrated Bagh Nakh, or tiger's claws, with which Shivaji had slain Afzul Khan.' His conduct in the hunting-field one day especially struck Elphinstone, who thus records it: 'A young gentleman just in front of me had a bad fall, and lay for dead. When I got off, I found a horseman dismounted and supporting his head, and, to my surprise, it was the Raja who had let his horses go and run to his assistance.'

In his settlement of the new country, Elphinstone thought it his first duty to preserve as much as possible of the existing system of administration as the best for the circumstances, and for the time, though not ideally the best. He knew that British Courts of Law and Regulations would ultimately have to be introduced, but he was desirous of postponing their introduction, and of developing in the meantime all that could be discovered of good in the native institutions. He used to tell a story to illustrate the dread which British Courts of Law and Regulations used to inspire in the early days of the introduction of British rule in a newly acquired Province, and before the people had grown familiarized with British justice and impartiality: "When the North-West was first annexed, the inhabitants of a newly occupied village were encountered in full flight: asked if Lord Lake was coming, they replied, 'No, the Adalat is coming'. "The Adalat was the British Tribunal, now represented by the Civil Courts. The task that Elphinstone had before him was the two fold one of conciliation and inquiry. Like his two great contemporaries, Munro and Malcolm, the leading principles of his administration were sympathy and a general recognition of native prejudices and native aspirations. He always kept before himself the duty of investigating thoroughly the indigenous institutions, and the importance of introducing as few changes as possible.

Much tact was necessary on Elphinstone's part in dealing with the different classes in the country, to enable him to arrive at a satisfactory settlement. He had already shown that he had no intention of disregarding Maratha sentiment so far as the way had been prepared by the cessation of organized opposition on the part of the people; at the same time he knew that he could not expect the contented acquiescence of all in the new state of affairs. The cultivators had indeed accepted the position with their usual phlegm, but there were plenty of men, who had been officials under the old regime, who were ready to use their influence against active contentment on their part. Elphinstone did his best to relieve this class from the excessive demands they had been accustomed to, and especially to do away with that engine of exaction, the farming system. There was not much difficulty experienced with the more important class of the landed proprietors, the greater Jaghirdars: Elphinstone had at an earlier period interested himself in establishing their status on a satisfactory footing; he had, however, to bring special tact to bear upon one member of this class, whom he described as a man 'possessing a narrow and crooked understanding, a litigious spirit, and a capricious temper'; it says much for Elphinstone's concillatory powers that his talk with him completely restored his good homour, and made him apparently cordially satisfied. The case of the lesser Jagirdars, however, caused him much thought and anxiety; he wished, as far as he could, to preserve their status as an upper class intermediate between the cultivators and the officials, and to prevent their decay, though he saw that in most cases this was inevitable. He succeeded in obtaining many privileges for this class, which they specially valued: one of these was their exemption from the ordinary procedure of the Civil Courts, and making them subject in criminal matters to the jurisdiction of the collector, in his capacity as political agent, after previous reference to the commissioner. The most difficult class of all whom Elphinstone had to deal with were the Maratha Brahmans. From having been the recognized depositories of learning they had become practically mendicants, living on the bounty of the Peshwa, who used to distribute amongst them £50,000 a year. In a country where mendicancy is recognized as one of the honourable professions, this had not diminished their old influence in the country. Elphinstone described them as being generally discontented and only restrained by fear from being treasonable; of course there were exceptions, and Elphinstone was able to say: 'There are among them many instances of decent and respectable lives and although they are generally subtle and insincere, I have met with some upon whom I could depend for sound and candid opinions.' Conspicuous generosity marked Elphinstone's treatment of this class: he publicly proclaimed that they would be allowed quiet possession of their lands and pecuniary allowances, and he distributed liberal alms amongst them. And yet it was from this class that the only serious attempt came to over throw British rule. Elphinstone discovered that they had formed a plot to massacre all Europeans, to seize all hill forts and to get possession of the person of the young Raja of Satara. He showed them then that he could be as righteously stern as he had been conspicuously generous: he had the leading conspirators blown from guns. Of this mode of execution Elphinstone said: 'It contained two valuable elements of capital punishment: it is painless to the criminal and terrible to the beholder.' The then Governor of Bombay suggested that Elphinstone should get an indemnity for his act from the Supreme Government; to this his characteristic reply was: 'If I have done wrong, I deserve to be punished: If I have done right, I do not require an indemnity.'

In this inquiries into police matters, he was very favourably impressed with the indigenous system of village watch and ward. Much responsibility attached to the office of village watchman: he required to be a man of much acuteness of character, with keen powers of inquisitiveness and observation, for one of this duties was to know the character of every man in this village. In the department of criminal justice, Elphinstone found a state of things prevailing which he could only describe as beggarly description: there was no recognized code of law, and no prescribed form of trial; all the revenue officers had judicial powers; punishments were left more or less to the caprice of the officials, with the natural result that 'some were too dreadful to be inflicted, and others were too trifling to be deterrent'. Elphinstone took care to introduce his reforms with scrupulous regard, as far as possible, to native sentiment and prejudices. With the exception of capital punishment, all criminal jurisdiction was vested in the collector; Elphinstone also made several suggestions on the subject of imprisonment, many of which formed a model for future action. In the department of civil justice, Elphinstone found no regular judicial officers, except in the great towns, where an official styled 'President of Equity', tried cases in the name of the Peshwa. The old primitive system of the Panchayat, or 'Council of Five Members', was, however, in full force in all the country districts. He recognized the respect for the authority of this Council as one of the fundamental principles that held Hindu society together; he mentions an old proverb in illustration of this: 'Panchayat men Parameshwar,' 'The Lord is in the Council of Five.' Its special advantage to him lay in the consideration that the interest of the people was enlisted in ascertaining and protecting their own rights, while litigiousness was not encouraged. He did his best therefore to preserve this old institution while ridding it of some of its objectionable features; he arranged that an appeal should lie to the collector from a decision of the Council, but only in a case of gross corruption or injustice: the object of this appeal being rather to watch over the purity of the court than to amend its decisions.

After he had held office as Commissioner of the Deccan for rather more than a year, Elphinstone received the higher appointment of Governor of Bombay. This appointment was the tribute which the British Government paid to be exceptional ability he had displayed during his career in India; a similar tribute was paid to Munro, who became Governor of Madras, and to Malcolm, who succeeded Elphinstone in this Governorship of Bombay. The new Province that Elphinstone had been administering was, moreover, about to be incorporated in the Presidency of Bombay, and it was considered desirable to have the benefit of his experience while the incorporation was taking effect, and a new and larger Presidency being created. Elphinstone bade farewell to the Deccan in these terms: 'I feel a short of respect, as well as attachment, for this fine picturesque country, which I am leaving for the flat and crowded roads of Bombay, and I cannot but think with affectionate regret of the romantic scenes and manly sports of the Deccan'. He characteristically concluded with a classical quotation from the Idylls of Theocritus:–

Oh! farewell to wolves, and jackals, and bears,
Ye denizens wild of the jungles and hills,
In brake, and in grove, in the forests' deep shade
A herdsman and huntsman, no more shall I roam.
Oh! Ye springs and ye rivers! A long farewell.

Bishop Heber, that acute observer of men and things, has left on record his impressions of Elphinstone as Governor of Bombay: 'No Government in India pays so much attention to schools and public institutions for education; in none are the taxes lighter, and in the administration of justice to the natives in their own languages, in the establishment of Panchayats, in the degree in which he employs the natives in official situations, and the countenance and familiarity he extends to all the natives of rank who approach him, he seems to have reduced to practice almost all the reforms which had struck me as most required in the system of government in those Provinces of our Eastern Empire which had been previously visited. All other public men had their enemies and their friends, but of Mr. Elphinstone everybody spoke highly.' During his eight years' rule he visited every part of his large charge twice. The British districts gave him but little trouble. During his tours in the Native States he did his best to minimize some of the inevitable hardships incidental to the inauguration of a reign of law and order, succeeding a more or less free and independent regime under which every man did what was right in his own eyes. He was glad to find, however, that on the whole the introduction of the British Courts of Justice was not unpopular with the people generally. To make them more popular, he had Guzerati substituted for Persian in the courts of the extreme west of his Province, were Guzerati was the vernacular of the people, and by removing the Civil Court from Bombay to Surat he rendered it easier for the people to settle their civil disputes.

Press criticism could be as embarrassing to a Ruler in those days as in these, but Government had its own way of dealing with any editor who over-stepped the limits of what was considered legitimate criticism. The Press was not the free and independent agent it now is; and Elphinstone found it necessary to deport the editor of a local paper in consequence of his strictures on the judges of the High Court. Prestige has always gone for much in the East; and the maintenance of British prestige, and especially the prestige of British Courts of Justice, was almost a matter of life and death in those early days of the establishment of British rule; and Elphinstone considered his action fully justified by these considerations.

One subject that Elphinstone had always had a heart was the preparation of a complete digest of Hindu Civil Law, based partly upon the written books and partly upon existing customs. It proved a task beyond even his great powers and knowledge; and none knew the real difficulties better than himself, as a letter he wrote to a celebrated jurist shows: 'The written law was that of the Hindus, always vague and unknown to the bulk of the people, often absurd, and still oftener entirely discussed. The unwritten law was composed of the maxims that occur to people of common sense in a country not remarkably enlightened, modified by Hindu law and Hindu opinion, and constantly influenced by the direct lawful interference of the prince, who was the fountain of all law, and by the weight of rank, and wealth, and interest. Besides, what we call Hindu law applies to the Brahmans only; each caste has separate laws and customs of its own, and even these vary according to the part of the country in which the different portions of a caste are settled.' The task was entrusted to a committee, and it must have appeared from the very outset a hopeless one. Notwithstanding, immense labour was expended on the work, and a vast mass of information collected and embodied in reports; a Sanskrit work on inheritance was, moreover, translated; eventually, however, the scheme in its entirely was dropped when Elphinstone left Bombay.

Elphinstone was a great advocate for the admission of Indians to high office, and he looked forward to the time when Indians would be found eligible for the Council of the Governor-General. Though his schemes did not come to fruition during his tenure of office, still under the liberal policy that has actuated successive Rulers of India, most of them did before his death: the path of distinction has been gradually opened, until at the present day Indians are found in the highest offices, and drawing salaries far greater than Elphinstone ever dreamed of; and not only are they found in the Council of the Governor-General, but in that of the Secretary of State for India in England itself, and immediately under the aegis of the British Parliament.

In Elphinstone's time education was the great difficulty: he wrote several minutes on the subject, and most of the schemes he propounded have been put into operation since his day. He has been called the founder of that system of instruction not in the Vernacular and in English that has given the Bombay Presidency the high place it holds among the other Provinces of the Indian Empire. He saw clearly that in education lay the best hope of ameliorating the condition of the people of India, both materially and morally. The problem that has taxed the minds of all Rulers of India, how best to promote morality and to find the teaching of morality a place in any scheme of general education for the people, also presented itself to his mind; and he looked at the subject from the point of view of a philosopher. While realizing that morality must finally rest upon the sanctions of religion, he also realized how impossible it was for a British Government to be otherwise than neutral in the sphere of religion. His own idea of how the problem might possibly be solved is given in an extract from one of his Minutes on Education : 'It would be better to call the prejudices of the Hindus to our aid in reforming them and to control their vices by the ties of religion, which are stronger than those of law. By maintaining and purifying their present tenets, at the same time that we enlighten their understanding, we shall bring them nearer to that standard of perfection at which all concur in desiring that they should arrive.' He suggested the printing and cheap distributing of Hindu tales inculcating sound morals, and also religious books tending more directly to the same end. It will be seen that he had Hindus only in his mind; the reason is not far to seek. Mohammedans, who have a recognized Canon of Scripture, have always cared for the education of their children in the religious tenets of their father. Hindus, who have no such recognized Canon, have not been in times past so careful in this direction. It is of interest, therefore, to note that in more recent years there has been a decided movement amongst them for having their sons at school taught the faith of their fathers. Textbooks, such as Elphinstone recommended, have been prepared, some on orthodox lines, others on theosophical lines, and are in use in not a few schools in different parts of India. At the same time, it must not be forgotten that reality has always been taught indirectly in Hindu families. The traditions and tales interspersed in their greater epics, the Mahabharata and Ramayana, with which the minds and imaginations of children are stirred from their infancy, all inculcate a high ethical standard, and practically form the basis of their moral education.

After an unbroken service of thirty years, Elphinstone felt that his work was done : in 1826, therefore, he resigned office. Of the addresses that poured in, as usual with a departing Governor, the one that Elphinstone most valued was the Indian address announcing the foundation of the Elphinstone Institution in his honour. This address concluded with these words: 'Having beheld with admiration for so long a period the affable and encouraging manners, the freedom from prejudice, the consideration at all times evinced for the interests and welfare of the people of this country, the regard shown to their ancient customs and laws, the constant endeavours to extend amongst them the inestimable advantages of intellectual and moral improvement, the commanding abilities applied to ensure permanent amelioratio in the condition of all classes, and to promote their prosperity on the soundest principles, by which your private and public conduct has been so pre-eminently distinguished, we are led to consider the influence of the British Government as the most important and desirable blessing which the superior being could have bestowed upon our native land.'

With this recognition of the benign rule of the British Government, due to a highly-gifted and exceptional man having made himself the personal embodiment of that benign rule, this sketch now concludes.

15

Last Days in India (1803-1805)

Before the campaign recorded in the last chapter had been finished, the great Marques had quit India. Whilst he had been engaged in employing all his energies to defeat the formidable Maratha confederacy which threatened the very existence of British authority in India, the Court of Directors, true to their petty traditions, had been worrying him in a manner which would have induced any one less conscientious to resign his high office in disgust. The war with the Marathas, a war which we have seen was forced upon the Marquess by Scindhia, had touched the money-grabbing instincts of the members of that honourable Court. When the news reached England that the war had broken out, India stocks, which had been at 215, fell to 160. This fall was naturally attributed to the policy of Lord Wellesley. It was impossible for a Governor-General to commit a greater crime. There arose, then, against the man who was securing permanent security for British interests in India an exceeding great and bitter cry. The proprietors of India stock urged on the directors, and these, nothing loth, used every devour to heap insult after insult on their energetic servant in India. He was rebuked for legislating when away from his Council. Cases, describing individual instances of the exercise of his patronage when so absent, and therefore unaided by the concurrent advice, and unsupported by the sanction, of all its members, were sent for the opinion of lawyers in Lincoln's

Inn, and the opinion so obtained, always, from the manner in which the case was drawn, friendly to the Court, was at once converted into a condemnatory resolution, and sent out to the Governor-General.*

The clamour became so violent that even the Board of Control seemed to yield to it, and the action of Lord Wellesley in complying with the urgent request of the Peshwa to extend to him British protection—an act which conduced as much, at least, as any act of his reign to the ensuring of the stability of British interests in India—was gently but decidely codemned.

> "The eagerness," wrote Lord Castlereagh, President of the Board, dealing with this question, "with which we appeared to press our connection upon all leading States in succession, might naturally lead them to apprehend that we meant more than we avowed that our object was ultimately to be masters rather than allies, and that, having obtained either possession of or absolute influence over every State, except the Marathas, with whom we had been in connection, our object was to

---

* 'It would be amusing, if it were not so provocative of contempt for the petty and puerile policy of the Court of Directors, to read the reasons upon which they and the lawyers they consulted based their condemnation of the conduct of the Marquess Wellesley. When, in 1803, war with the Marathas seemed imminent, the Governor-General had delegated to Lieutenant-General Stuart, and Major-General Wellesley, the powers necessary for dealing with the enemy, without the necessity of making further reference to him; that is, he authorised them to act as circumstances on the spot might require. The reader will recollect that the Governor-General was in Bengal, kept there by orders repeatedly insisted upon: the Generals were in Western India; that there were no telegraphs; no horse-posts; and that communications took at least a fortnight. Yet, the Directors and their sapient legal advisers recorded that, in 850 delegating his powers, the Governor-General had exceeded his authority, that to enable him to delegate his powers in the way he had done, even to act himself when absent from his council, the confirming authority of an Act of Parliament was required.

obtain a similar influence over their councils. Under whatever estimate of our views it may have been formed, the fact is indisputable that a general repugnance to the British connection on the terms proposed, universally prevailed amongst the great Maratha powers. It was avoided by all as long as they had any choice. It was only embraced by the Peshwa when an exile from his dominions; and the jealousy of it was such as to have since led Holkar and Scindhia to forget their animosities, and to league with the Rajah of Berar against the Company and the Peshwa. How long the Peshwa will continue being faithful to engagements which were contracted from necessity and not from choice, in opposition to the other Maratha States, is yet to be seen. The practical question to be considered is, whether an alliance formed under such circumstances can rest upon any other foundation than more force; and if not, whether the means by which it was to be upheld are not destructive of its professed advantages. The Marathas have never in any instance commenced hostilities against us; so far then as past experience goes, there seems to be no special ground to apprehend future danger from them. The French officers in Scindhia's army are just objects of jealousy, and their mixing themselves in the affairs of native powers must be watched, and be matter of alarm in proportion to the degree in which it takes place, and as those States are near to, or remote from, our possessions; but this alone cannot render the alliance prudent, nor is this danger at present of a magnitude to call for the adoption of a system otherwise of dubious policy. As far as the Maratha interests are concerned, what motive can they have in acquiescing in the ostensible head of their empire being placed in our hands? Whatever we may hold out to reconcile the Peshwa to the alliance, and however we may profess to respect his independence in the management of his own affairs, we cannot deny that in fact as well as in appearance, whilst a British Army is at Puna, he can be considered in no other light than as politically dependent on us. The same motives which before opposed Scindhia and Holkar to each other now oppose them both to us, and the Rajah of Berar joins the confederacy. Nor is it to be expected that independent States, predatory and warlike, can wish to make us the arbiter of their destiny. To aim at a permanent connection with the Maratha powers, must be, to say the least of it, extremely hazardous. It must be difficult and expensive to establish, not less difficult and expensive to retain. Such a result we disavow as our object, as in principle and policy against the laws of the land; and we should avoid therefore a course of measures, the tendency of which leads naturally to that result. It may be said, if the treaty had not been pushed with the Peshwa while at Bassein, he might have refused it afterwards; but it is doubtful whether a treaty so obtained is a benefit, or whether it might not have been better to let Holkar and Scindhia fight it out before proposing any permanent connection. The advantages of such a connection, had always been overrated. By keeping an army of observation on the frontier, and not mixing with Maratha politics, except upon sure grounds, if we gained no more than securing our own territory, as well as that of our ally, the Nizam, from insult, we escaped war, whilst the Maratha princes wasted their strength."

The historical student of the present day who shall read these platitudes, based upon half-truths and imperfect knowledge, will rejoice that it was to the Marquess Wellesley, and not to Lord Castlereagh, that the destines of the British empire in India were entrusted. Whilst the former reasoned as a *doctrinaire*, the latter acted as a wise and far-seeing statesman. Yet the Home Government, uncertain of the issue, far from assuring him of their support, began to take into consideration whether, by his treaty with the Peshwa, the treaty thereafter proudly referred to as the Treaty of Basein, the Governor-General had not exceeded his powers, and what instructions should be sent to him to curb his future action. The result of these considerations was that instructions were sent to Lord Wellesley to cancel the Treaty of Bassein, and forbidding him to make war with Scindhia or with Holkar. Fortunately, these instructions reached Lord Wellesley at a time when it had become impossible to execute them. They reached him after he had waged war with Scindhia and the Bhonsla, and had forced both to sue for peace; at the very moment, in fact, when he had actually signed that treaty with Scindhia which brought him very nearly within the category of protected princes. The electric telegraph did not, happily, exist in those days, or the folly of the Home Government would have placed British interests in India in a situation of very great peril.

The Governor-General was not less subjected, however, to annoyances which chafed his proud spirit. In the fourth chapter, reference has been made to the Secretary to the Madras Government, Mr. Webbe, as a gentleman who had at the outset opposed Lord Mornington's policy. But Mr. Webbe was a very able man, and not wedded to his own opinions because they were his opinions, he had gradually recognised the wisdom of the policy which he had formerly opposed. When Lord Clive came to Madras as Governor he had found in the experience, the knowledge, and the ready resource of Mr. Webbe, a support upon which he could count in any emergency. The ability and rectitude of that gentleman had also won for him the esteem and good opinion of Lord Wellesley. Yet, notwithstanding that Mr. Webbe possessed the confidence of the Governor under whom he was immediately serving, and of the Governor-General of India, the Court of Directors, in the exercise of their power, directed that he should be removed from his office. In vain did Lord Clive remonstrate. Vainly did Lord Wellesley inform the Prime Minister that the removal of Mr. Webbe would be a severe blow to the Government. The Court of Directors wanted the appointment for one of their *proteqes* and persisted in their order. Rather than carry it out, Lord Clive resigned his office in disgust. Lord Wellesley could not repress his indignation at the nefarious transaction. He informed Mr. Pitt, in the letter just referred to, that the direct appointment from home to the most confidential office under the Governor "comprised every degree of personal indignity that could be offered to Lord Clive and himself, and the result had been to drive that honest, diligent, prudent, and able public servant from India."

Among other rebuffs that were administered to him was one connected with the proposed erection of a house or palace for the Governor-General in the park of Barrackpur. Lord Wellesley had taken over, on his appointment as Captain-General, the residence theretofore allotted to the Commander-in-Chief. That residence was neither large enough nor commodious enough for the lodgment of the Governor-General of India and his suite. Yet it was desirable that one engaged in the arduous duty of governing India should possess a place in the country to which he could occasionally retire for rest and recreation. No locality appeared to the Marquess to be so well suited for such a purpose as the park at Barrackpur. It is the only piece of enclosed ground in India that bears any resemblance to an English park. No sound from the outer world reaches the palatial residence. The majestic Hugli flows calmly on one side, its surface gay with craft of varied shapes. On the other were magnificent trees, undulating grounds, and a fine garden. Successive Governors-General have found there a place of real solace after the cares of Calcutta. The wife of one of the noblest of them, the courageous and high-minded Lady Canning, loved it so much that, when she died in India, her remains were transferred to the spot in the garden of the park on which, when living, she delighted to sit and gaze at the river flowing beneath her. In this park Lord Wellesley designed to build a residence worthy of the representative of England's power in the East. He had the plans made and the estimates prepared. The builders were about to commence their work, when the Court of Directors, delighted to thwart him, forbade him to proceed. The work, in the style in which it was intended, was therefore abandoned.

The reader can well imagine how the great Marquess had been cheered and delighted by the success of his generals in the war against Scindhia; how he had followed their course of victory without a check with swelling hear and beaming eye. He was essentially a soldier, and the campaigns, both in the north-west and south-west, had been conducted on plans, the general ideas of which are to be found in his letters. In the victories which followed he saw not only the justification of his policy, but the impossibility of disturbing it; and, in that impossibility, the consolidation of the British power in India. Before his time the great danger to that power had lain in an union between the Maratha powers. How real that danger had been any one who studies the life of Madhaji Scindhia will at once recognise. There was no guarantee that a second Madhaji—a man with foresight as keen, with a will as resolute—might not again come to the front. It was the iron will of the Marquess Wellesley which, as was proved after his departure from India, prevented the reintroduction into the Government policy of the principles of Sir John Shore. A Maratha empire united, pitted against a British India governed on those principles, would at least have had a great chance. But the Marquess Wellesley had rendered such a combination impossible. He had neutralised the Peshwa, smitten to the ground Scindhia and the Bhonsla, despite the factious orders of the Court of Directors, then fortunately on the bottom of the ocean, to leave them alone; and he rejoiced, as only a king of men can rejoice, that action so necessary to the safety of the great trust committed to him had been accomplished before it had been possible for mediocrity to prevent it. He felt that he had, in very deed, deserved well of his country.

Nor, whilst rejoicing at the success of plans which were his very own, did he complain when misfortune followed the attempted execution of a project which failed mainly because his recommendations with respect to the carrying out of it had been neglected, although he knew that he alone would have to pay the penalty of such misfortune. When it became necessary for Lake to defend the allies of England against the assault of Holkar, and that General intimated his intention of detaching a force, under Colonel Monson, to Jaipur, Lord Wellesley urgently pressed upon him the advisability of sending with it a due proportion of European troops. But the hot weather had set in, Lake did not care to expose his Europeans, and he would not. Monson, I have always held, owed his misfortune to not continuing his advance on Holkar's position at Rampura (on the Chambal). He changed his advance into a retreat because he, a man who had no experience of native troops, did not care to run the risk of a further advance with native troops only. The misfortune that followed was due, then, to the neglect by General Lake of Lord Wellesley's advice. But, instead of whining at the disaster, of casting the blame on others, Lord Wellesley met in the way natural to his noble nature:—

> "I received this morning," he wrote to Lake (Sept. 11th, 1804), "your letter of Sept. 2nd. Grievous and disastrous as the events are, the extent of the calamity does not exceed my expectation; from the first hour of Colonel Monson's retreat, I have always augured the ruin of that detachment, and if any part of it be saved I count it so much gain. I trust that the greater part of it has arrived at Agra, but I fear that my poor friend Monson is gone. Whatever may have been his face, or whatever the result of his misfortunes to my own fame, I will endeavour to shield his character from obloquy, not will I attempt the mean purpose of sacrificing his reputation to save mine. His former services and his zeal entitle him to indulgence; and, however I may lament and suffer for his errors, I will not reproach his memory if he be lost, or his character if he survives. Your letter manifests your usual judgement and spirit. We must endeavour rather to retrieve than to blame what is past and under your auspices I entertain no doubt of success. Time, however, is the main consideration. Every hour that shall be left to this plunderer will be marked by some calamity; we must expect a great defection of the allies, and even

confusion in our own territories, unless we can attack Holkar's main force immediately with decisive success. I trust that you will be enabled to assemble your army in sufficient time to prevent further mischief; I highly applaud your determination to leave nothing to fortune, and rather to risk the internal tranquillity of the province for a season, than to hazard any contest on unequal grounds with the enemy. Holkar defeated, all alarm and danger will instantly vanish. When I look at the date of this letter I cannot entertain a shadow of apprehension for the result of this war. This is the anniversary of the battle of Delhi,—a victory gained under circumstances infinitely more unfavourable than the present. Your triumphs of last year proceeded chiefly from your vigorous system of attack. In every war the native States will always gain courage in proportion as we shall allow them to attack us; and I know that you will always bear this in mind, especially against such a power as Holkar. If we cannot reduce him, we have lost our ascendancy in India. You will perceive that the only effect produced on my mind by this misfortune is an anxious solicitude to afford you every aid in remedying its consequences with every degree of despatch."

The men of the present generation who shall read this noble letter will at once understand how proud the good men and true of his day were to serve under such a chief. Recollect that Lord Wellesley knew that Monson's disaster would be his death-warrant with the Court of Directors. That disaster had happended mainly because his advice had been neglected. How truly royal, under such circumstances, is his demeanour. For Monson only consideration and sympathy; for himself a determination to assume the entire responsibility, whilst urging Lake to lose no time in retrieving the disaster. Then, how delicate his advice to Lake. The earnest wish of his heart is that Lake shall advance with all the dash of the war against Holkar, and annihilate his enemy. He thinks, in his heart, that Lake has not done well to leave

Monson so far without support. But he is careful not to say so. He does not utter a word which can grate on the feelings of that gallant soldier. On the contrary, he invokes the glories he had gained in the last war by prompt action; indicates the danger of allowing the enemy to gather head and to attack; and thus insinuates rather than directs the course to be pursued. How Lake responded to this call, how he sprang upon Holkar and annihilated him, I have already told. He, at least, appreciated the generous nature of his large-minded Captain-General.

Six weeks later a solace to the wound caused by Monson's disaster was vouchsafed to the Governor-General by the receipt of the manner in which his victorious campaign against the two Maratha chiefs had been received in Parliament. He had the satisfaction of reading that in the House of Lords the brilliant success which had been achieved was attributed to the vigorous and comprehensive system of measures pursued by the Marquess Wellesley for bringing the various armies with promptitude and effect into the field. In the commons, Lord Castlereagh, without committing himself to the policy of the war, passed a glowing eulogium on the splendid conduct of all concerned in it, and the vote of thanks was unanimous. Even the Court of Directors, though they declined to pronounce an opinion on the political questions involved in the campaign, passed a resolution that:—

> "Taking into consideration the despatches relative to the late brilliant successes in the war with the Maratha chiefs, their thanks be given to the Marquess Wellesley for the zeal, vigour, activity, and ability displayed in preparing the armies of the several Presidencies to take the field, to which might be attributed, in a great measure, the rapid and brilliant successes which had crowned the British arms in the East Indies."

The Court of Proprietors, hitherto so bitter against him, recorded their approval in identical terms.

It can easily be understood, especially by those who have had experience of India, why votes of thanks unaccompanied by expressions of approval of policy, gave no satisfaction to Lord Wellesley. The actual expression of thanks was he knew well, his due, and could not be withheld without a public scandal. But there was one sentence in the preamble to the resolution which seemed to him to compromise his position in India. In that preamble the Court had declined to express an opinion as to the origin and justice of the war. Lord Wellesley felt that he could not publish in the *Calcutta Gazette* the vote of thanks without at the same time publishing the preamble. "The determination," he wrote to the Court, some months later, when explaining why, when he published in the *Gazette* the resolution conveying the thanks of the Court to other officers therein named, he had withheld all mention of himself:—

> "expressed to withhold all judgement upon the original justice, necessity, and policy of the war, could not have been published in India by a formal act of the Government without conveying an universal impression of doubt and ambiguity respecting the stability of every arrangement connected with the progress and success of our arms. The permanency of all treaties of peace, partition, subsidy and alliance must have been exposed to hazard by such a public declaration, proceeding from the high authority of your Honourable Court and the Court of Proprietors: and announced by your Government in India to all your subjects, dependents, and allies. It could not be supposed that either your Honourable Court or the Court of Proprietors would try the justice of our cause by the success of our arms; the prosperous result of the war, therefore, could not have removed the doubts of its justice arising from the reservations expressed in your resolution; and the irresistible inference in the minds of all Native States would have been that your Honourable Court and the Court of Proprietors might ultimately censure the whole transaction; while the general fame of your equity and

magnanimity would have precluded any supposition that in condemning the justice of our cause, you would retain the fruits of your success, or enjoy the benefits of the peace, while you repudiated the necessity and policy of the war. If the origin and policy of the war shall ultimately be condemned, and the treaties of peace, subsidy, and alliance, shall finally be abrogated by the commands of your Honourable Court, those commands will be issued in such terms, and accompanied by such arrangements, as shall render the execution of your orders an additional bulwark to the public safety, and a fresh security to the public faith. During whatever interval of time your Honourable Court may be consistent with the welfare of the Honourable Company in India, nor with the respect due to your high authority, that one of your servants, for the gratification of personal ambition, by the ostentatious display of the honours which you had been pleased to confer upon him, should pursue a course which might embarrass the free and deliberate exercise of your wisdom and justice in a matter of the utmost importance to the national interests and honour; or that, by a premature and unseasonable publication of your favourable acceptance of his services, the same servant should risk the main object of those services, and endanger the immediate security of a great political system of arrangement which it might possibly be your future pleasure to confirm."

As a specimen of finished irony this letter is not to be surpassed. The writing of it releived the mind of the injured and offended Proconsul. He showed plainly to the honourable masters who had been unable alike to appreciate him, or the real interests of the country they had invited him to administer, how little he was affected by their praise or their dispraise. His mind was wholly absorbed by a desire that the India which he had received from them weak, threatened, so terrified that it dared not make preparations for war lest it should provoke war, only one amongst three rivals for empire, should be transferred from his hands to those of his successor strong, compact, predominant. ready for any action and for any emergency. He was proudly conscious that, despite the innumerable obstacles cast in his way by masters incapable of appreciating him or the condition of affairs in India. He had accomplished that end; and he was, therefore, utterly indifferent as to whether such masters should dole out to him praise or blame. He, at least, had faith in the verdict of posterity.

How Lake had avenged the retreat of Monson I have told in the previous chapter. But his repulse at Bhartpur had again roused hopes in the breast of Scindhia, who, asked by Mr. Jenkins, the British Resident at his Court, to explain his preparations, proceeded to the length of seizing the person of that minister and plundering his property. Although he apologised for this insult by casting the blame on others, he still continued his preparations, and, but for an opportune meeting with Holkar, and the disclosure at that meeting of the divergent views entertained by the two chieftains, would probably have proceeded to hostilities. Convinced at that meeting that Holkar was impossible as an ally, he made his submission, dismissed his warlike minister, and adopted a peaceful programme. But in the meanwhile, events were occurring in England which were to relieve him and the native princes of India of the watchful glance which had noted and had baffled all their intrigues. The news of Monson's retreat, which reached England early in 1805, gave the Court of Directors the opportunity for which they had been longing. Up to that time, although they had hated Lord Wellesley they had bowed the knee to his success. Defeat exaggerated as to its possible consequences, as all defeats are exaggereated, gave them the chance of indulging in their personal feelings. The second Ministry of Mr. Pitt was weak at home, and was too burdened with the responsibilities of the war with Napoleon, to be able to pay much attention to India. The opportunity, then, was not to be foregone. Lord Cornwallis, who had already held the high office of Governor-General, and who, it was known, condemned the policy of the Maratha wars, was asked if he would go out to succeed Lord Wellesley. The old man, not so accustomed to victory as Wellesley, at first declined. Much entreaty, however, procured in the end a reluctant consent, and he set out. He landed in Calcutta July 30th, 1805.

The manner in which Lord Wellesley heard of the appointment of a successor was worthy of the Court he had served so well. They did not, in the first instance, communicate personally with him.

> "In May, 1805," writes Mr. Torrens, in his interesting biography of the Marquess Wellesley,* "two letters were received in Calcutta by the overland route, announcing the re-appointment of Lord Cornwallis to the Governor-Generalship of India. One of these letters was received by Mr. J. Alexander, the other by Mr. Tucker. Both gentlemen determined to keep their information to themselves; but a rumour was soon in circulation to the effect that overland letters had been received in Calcutta, and Lord Wellesley sent for Mr. Tucker. After some conversation, the Governor-General exclaimed: 'I hear you have received letters from England.' Mr. Tucker assented, and Lord Wellesley asked, 'Do they contain any news of importance?' 'The appointment of Lord Cornwallis,' was the reply. The accomplished actor was too much master of himself to indicate by look or gesture any opinion of the choice which had been made. But he had abundant information from confidential sources of the reasons which had led to it, and he well knew that it implied the reversal, in many essential particulars, if not the general renunciation, of his comprehensive policy."

Monson's retreat had injured British prestige in India only to an extent which the victories of Lord Lake, the following year, were able to repair. The effect of the same retreat in England was to cause the reversal of a policy which had been successful in all its bearings: which had ensured

---

* *The Marquess Wellesley, Architect of Empire: an Historic Portrait.* Chatto & Windus., 1880.

predominance to England and security to protected princes: which had, therefore, been merciful in its action, ensuring to the weak protection against the strong. All this was now to be reversed. The protected princes of Rajputana were to be delivered to the tender mercies of freebooters like Amir Khan, and robbers like the Pandaris. The rule of murder and plunder was to succeed the era of peace and prosperity; and another war, waged by a Governor-General approaching more nearly to the Wellesley type, was required to restore Central India, after an interregnum of twelve years, to the state in which he had left it.

The great Marquess has been avenged. Even the India Office had paid a tribute to his memory, full of appreciative justice. The historian of that august body, Mr. Thornton, concludes the record of the events of the brilliant rule of the Marquess Wellesley, with the following eloquent summary, to which the posterity who have witnessed in India the effects of his administration, will, I am confident, enthusiastically subscribe.

"The unrivalled brilliancy of the Marquess Wellesley's administration has perhaps tended to obscure the rare qualities which led to its success. The first of those qualities was his extraordinary sagacity. He saw the true position of the British Government in India—a vision withheld not only from his predecessors, but from his contemporaries. It is common to say of the great minds whose genius stands out in bold relief amid universal tameness, that they are beyond their age; and if ever this were true of living man, it is of the Marquess Wellesley. His mind was not led captive by words—it was not to be trammelled by conventional opinions. He neither gave credence to the prevailing cant of his time on the subject of India, nor affected to give credence to it; and this leads to the notice of another striking point in his character—the manly boldness with which he avowed and maintained opinions not lightly formed, and which he therefore felt were not lightly to be abandoned. The vigour with which he carried into action the great plans which his genius suggested is scarcely less remarkable than his sagacity. When resolved to strike a blow at Maisur, he was met by difficulties which ordinary minds would have deemed insuperable. He determined that they should be overcome, and they were overcome. The same determination of purpose—the same unshrinking energy—are manifested in his transactions with Arkat, with Oudh, with the Peshwa, and indeed in all the principal acts of his government. Like all truly great men, he was not the slave of circumstances—he made circumstances promote his purposes.

'Eminent talents are a blessing or a curse alike to their possessor and to the world, according to the use made of them. Those of the Marquess Wellesley were invariably directed to the highest and best ends—the promotion of peace, of the interests of the two coúntries with which he was connected, with one by birth, and with the other by office—and to the happiness of mankind. He laid in India the foundations of peace and of increasing prosperity, and if the superstructure was not completed in accordance with the original design, the crime rests on the head of others.

"In describing the characters of great men, the speak of human infirmity, which is to be found in all, should not be passed over. The Marquess Wellesley was ambitious; but his ambition sought gratification not in mere personal aggrandisement, but in connecting his own fame with that of the land to which he belonged, and of the Government which he administered—in the diffusion of sound and liberal knowledge, and the extension of the means of happiness among millions of men who knew not his person, and some of them scarcely his name. That name is, however, stamped for ever on their history. The British Government in India may pass away; its duration, as far as human means are concerned, will depend on the degree in which the policy of the Marquess Wellesley is maintained or abandoned—but whatever its fate, or the length of its existence, the name and memory of the greatest statesman by whom it was ever administered are imperishable."

I make no apology for the length of this extract. It conveys, in terms as true as they are precise, the verdict of history regarding the Indian administration of the Marquess Wellesley. He who recorded that verdict was not a personal follower of the great Proconsul. He was, on the contrary, an official in the service of that India Office, which had been the bitterest opponent of the Marquess Wellesley during the last four years of his administration, commissioned by that office to write such a history of the British administration of India as they could place in the hands of their covenanted civil servants when they started for that country. To each civil servant a copy of Thornton's History was invariably given on his appointment. The book may therefore be regarded as stamped with the approval of the India Office. It is for this reason that I have preferred that the estimate of Lord Wellesley's administration, an estimate in which I entirely concur, should be drawn from a source not unduly prejudiced in his favour, for it is the source whence proceeded the most persistent hostility to him during his tenure of the chief authority in India.

Index

C

D

E

F

G

H

I

❑❑❑